Reforming the European Commission

Many international and supranational organisations have lately been busy modernising their internal administration. But nowhere has management change received a similar amount of attention than in the case of the European Commission. Although the perception prevails that the Commission has been loosing out in recent years, this vivid interest, academic as well as public, in the so-called Kinnock reform suggests that this organisation still remains "at the heart of the Union". The proposition of this book thus is simple. If it remains true that the Commission is an essential part within the (admittedly complex) equation of EU policy-making, changes of the administration basis of this actor are likely to have broader implications. Consequently, this book poses three crucial questions about the recent administrative reform of the European Commission: why was such a comprehensive reform possible, what are its specific implications for the Commission as an organisation and what is the likely impact for the policy process.

In short, this book puts the organisational base of EU policy-making centre stage. In the quest for answers the authors of the subsequent chapters take distinct perspectives, use various research strategies and methods, and attempt to solve diverse empirical puzzles. But all attempt to add to our understanding of this organisational base, and how to systematically study it.

This book was published as a special issue of the *Journal of European Public Policy*.

Michael W. Bauer is Assistant Professor for Comparative Public Policy and Administration at the Department of Politics and Management, University of Konstanz, Germany.

Journal of European Public Policy Series

Series Editor: Jeremy Richardson is a Professor at Nuffield College, Oxford University

This series seeks to bring together some of the finest edited works on European Public Policy. Reprinting from Special Issues of the 'Journal of European Public Policy,' the focus is on using a wide range of social sciences approaches, both qualitative and quantitative, to gain a comprehensive and definitive understanding of Public Policy in Europe.

Reforming the European Commission

Edited by Michael W. Bauer

Routledge
Taylor & Francis Group

LONDON AND NEW YORK

First published 2009 by Routledge

2 Park Square, Milton Park, Abingdon, Oxon OX14 4RN
711 Third Avenue, New York, NY 10017, USA

Routledge is an imprint of the Taylor & Francis Group, an informa business

First issued in paperback 2016

Copyright © 2009 Edited by Michael W. Bauer

Typeset in Times by Value Chain, India

British Library Cataloguing in Publication Data
A catalogue record for this book is available from the British Library

ISBN 13: 978-0-415-46629-5 (hbk)
ISBN 13: 978-1-138-98485-1 (pbk)

Contents

Preface

When the organizational basis of politics changes, do policies then also change, and if so, how? The chapters in this book (a special issue of the *Journal of European Public Policy*) raise this question, focusing on recent administrative reforms in the European Commission. Scholars have started thinking and writing about organizational change in the Commission, and about the recent changes in the position and functions of the Commission in European Union (EU) policymaking in the context of task expansion and various enlargements. However, we do not yet understand how organizational change affects supranational policy dynamics. Only by sharpening our analytical concepts, and by improving our theoretical understanding of how organizational alterations are expected to impinge on policy outputs, will the study of internal organizational change generate signi.cant insights meaningful to virtually all students of EU politics. The presumption is that alterations in the organizational basis of a political actor encroach on this actor's capacities and may eventually also affect policy outcomes. This book starts to show how and draws lessons for further empirical analysis and theory development from the recent most contested and, by all standards, most comprehensive organizational change ever to affect the European Commission, namely the Kinnock reform.

This book would not have been possible without the help and engagement of many people. I am particularly indebted to Tim Balint, Michael Barzelay, Nathalie Behnke, Anna-Lena Beilschmidt, Dominik Bernauer, Julian Bernauer, Simon Bulmer, Michelle Cini, Udo Dietrichs, Michael Dobbins, Christina Eder, Morten Egeberg, Antonis Ellinas, Stefan Grohs, Elise Hadman, Stephan Heichel, Barbara Heisserer, Liesbet Hooghe, Hussein Kassim, Christoph Knill, Roger Levy, John Peterson, Diana Pitschel, Jeremy Richardson, Ansgar Schäfer, Emmanuelle Schön-Quinlivan, Gerald Schneider, Ezra Suleiman, Semin Suvarierol, Ulf Svertrup, Philipp Studinger, Andrew Thompson, Dorota Tomalak, Jale Tosun, Jarle Trondal, Stine

Waibel, Natascha Warta, Anchrit Wille, Alexander Wohlwender and Gabriele Zander.

I am also most grateful to the Fritz-Thyssen-Stiftung Foundation, the Zentrum für den wissenschaftlichen Nachwuchs der Universität Konstanz, and the Ausschuss für Forschungsförderung der Universität Konstanz for their valuable suppport.

Michael W. Bauer, Konstanz

Introduction: Organizational change, management reform and EU policy-making

Michael W. Bauer

Many international and supranational public organizations have recently been busy modernizing their internal administration (Bauer and Knill 2007). Yet nowhere has management or administrative change received a similar degree of attention as in the case of the European Commission.[1] Although the perception prevails that the Commission has been losing out compared to the Council and European Parliament in terms of political clout in recent years, this avid interest, academic as well as public, in the Kinnock reform[2] suggests that the European Commission still remains at the heart of the Union (Nugent 1997). It is thus only natural to take a closer look at the recent administrative reforms within the European Commission. If it remains true that the Commission is an essential part within the (admittedly complex) equation of European Union (EU) policy-making, changes in the organizational basis of this key actor are likely to have broader implications (Bauer 2006; Trondal 2007). Consequently, three crucial questions have to be asked about the recent administrative reform of the European Commission: why was such a comprehensive reform possible, what are its speci"c implications for the Commission as an organization, and what is the likely impact of organizational change for the EU policy process? In short, studying the reform of the European Commission means putting the organizational base of EU policy-making centre stage (Egeberg 1999; Olsen 2006). In the following article I will attempt to develop the case for the importance of studying organizational change in order to enhance our understanding of the EU policy-making process. I therefore must address conceptual matters as well as the historical and theoretical context of *reforming the European Commission.*

2. THE 'LOW' POLITICS OF EU POLICY-MAKING

As regards the conceptualization of organizational change a narrow de"nition is adopted. To de"ne an analytical starting point, the focus lies at the internal administrative or managerial basis of the Commission as an international public bureaucracy. This means that close attention will be paid to the internal rules and procedures as regards internal resource management, horizontal and vertical co-ordination, planning, monitoring, control as well as personnel related matters like recruitment, promotion, transparency, professional ethics, and so forth. In Brussels and Strasbourg these issues have come to "gure under the label of governance in the European Commission .³ The working hypothesis is *that such formal and informal organization of administrative interactions and daily routines structure and condition the capacities and subsequently the impact of the Commission as an actor in EU policy-making.* Admittedly, this is a narrow de"nition. A broader view of organizational in this context would perhaps also include issues such as alterations with respect to the Commission s of"cial relationships with other institutions, substantial policy competences, number or formal powers of Commissioners or of the Commission President himself and the like (Spence 2000). However, for the purpose of the present research endeavour these kinds of changes are perceived more as *institutional* than *organizational,* since they refer to the speci"c web of inter-organizational relationships and they usually require comprehensive treaty revisions to be changed. To make the differentiation clearer, one may think of the classical distinction between high and low politics. Sticking to this metaphor used in the early days of theorizing about the process of European integration (Hoffmann 1966), *organizational change* in this volume can be subsumed into the category of low politics and *institutional change* would fall into the category of high politics of (inter-)organizational engineering. It is obvious that occasionally such institutional and organizational features relate to or may even condition each other and where necessary also the institutional component has to be included in the organizational analyses (Peterson 2008). However, analysing the occurrence and the implications of the recent organizational changes within the European Commission administration remains the principal objective of the subsequent investigations.

3. HISTORICAL CONTEXT

To understand the present state of internal management and to identify the challenges ahead, a glance at the history of administrative change in the European Commission   also as a topic of academic research   appears indispensable. While in the early 1990s one could still claim that there was a surprising dearth of academic and other study of the European Commission (Edwards and Spence 1994: 1; Christiansen 1997), today the Commission is perhaps the most intensely researched international bureaucracy. There is no shortage of "rst-rate textbooks and hundreds of more speci"c monographs and journal articles (for overviews, see Cini 1996; Nugent 1997, 2001; Spence and Edwards 2006). But only recently and still very sparsely has more attention been paid to the internal organizational life of this crucial actor (Hooghe 2001; Bauer 2001; Trondal 2007; Suvarierol 2007). This new interest[4] in the European Commission as a public administration has been ampli"ed by the shock waves produced by the resignation of the Santer Commission under allegations of fraud and internal mismanagement in 1999. The Santer crisis and subsequent fears that an organizational image of an inef"cient, inept and mismanaged bureaucracy may stick in the public perception, and further limit the Commission s political room for manoeuvre, paved the way for the Kinnock reform (Peterson 1999, 2004; Metcalfe 2000). It also boosted academic interest in the organizational foundations of the European Commission. The result is a growing number of works on what used to be despised as the nitty-gritty of supranational bureaucracy (cf. Kratochwil and Ruggie 1986; Barnett and Finnemore 2004; Benner et al. 2007). There is a broad consensus that Neil Kinnock s administrative reform was a product of the political attempt to quickly restore trust in and the credibility of the Commission. But from a comparative public administration perspective this is hardly astonishing. Administrative reform is rarely an objective in itself but usually a highly politicized exercise (Pollitt and Bouckaert 2004; Peters 2001). Nevertheless, reform effects, positive or negative, apparent or real, have impacts, albeit rarely (only) those originally intended. Moreover, reform initiatives are windows of opportunity to instigate change of various quality   frequently with little connection to the intended improvements of the original ills. In the case of the Commission the major part of the Kinnock proposals was conceived and adopted between 2000 and 2004. This administrative reform is the topic of a number of insightful studies (Bear"eld 2004; Coull and Lewis 2003; Kassim 2004a, 2004b; Levy 2004; Metcalfe 2000; Spence 2000; Spence and Stevens 2006; Stevens and Stevens 2006; Bauer 2001, 2002, 2008a, 2008b). While doubts have been raised as to whether the reform has been ef"ciently implemented and, even if so, whether it will boost organizational effectiveness or ef"ciency (Levy 2006; Ellinas and

Suleiman 2008; Bauer 2008a), it is fair to say that most observers see the reform as a kind of historic achievement — if compared with the up-to-then unimpressive reform record of that institution (Kassim 2004a, 2004b, 2008; Spence and Stevens 2006; Stevens and Stevens 2006). After all, the Kinnock reform was the "rst comprehensive overhaul of the organizational basis of the European Commission in the 50-year history of this institution (Bauer 2007b). However, current analyses usually take little notice of the fact that there have also been a number of smaller initiatives for organizational change in the past — arguably with little visible impact. Table 1 lists these initiatives for organizational reform since 1958. There should be no misunderstanding. Many of them are on a minor scale, others are more fact-"nding or screening exercises and those with broader implications — like the Spierenburg Report from 1979 — were not implemented. However, there is no denying that we lack information about these historical initiatives (failed or successful) and systematic accounts to analyse conditions and constellations favourable to or hampering managerial reforms in the Commission that would allow us to put recent changes into a broader perspective. The point is that so far we have not attempted to exploit the conceptional variance that these historical examples offer to sharpen and eventually answer our research questions. It is very likely that by studying organizational change in the Commission in a disciplined historical comparative fashion we would be able to learn a great deal about the conditions in which administrative reform initiatives at the supranational level emerge and when and how the implementation of organizational change in the supranational context may succeed or be doomed to fail.[5]

4. THEORETICAL PERSPECTIVES

Comparative historical analysis is one crucial dimension to put the study of administrative reforms within the European Commission into context. However, it is even more important to con"ne the appropriate heuristic tools and theoretical positions from which one starts conceptualizing and eventually interpreting observable organizational change. It should be recognized that studying public policy-making by putting the analysis of administrative reform centre stage makes sense if one accepts a plain epistemological position, namely that alterations of the organizational basis of a political actor impinge on this actor s capacities, and may subsequently affect directly or indirectly policy outputs to the production of which this actor contributes, and thus eventually also affect policy outcomes in general. As a consequence, studying administrative change is by no means a matter to be left exclusively to students of public administration alone but belongs to the core interests of political scientists or organizational sociologists who follow — however generally — a research agenda rooted in the new institutionalism (March and Olsen 1989; Koelble 1995).

Moreover, if one recalls the system-theoretical origin of the sub-discipline policy analysis, the importance of a focus on organizational change becomes

Table 1 Initiatives for organizational change within the European Commission 1958–2001

Initiative	Structures	Process	Personnel	Finance	Ethics
1959 Preliminary Report on the organization and functioning of the European Commission	X	X	X		
1959 Report on the organization and functioning of the European Commission	X	X	X		
1961 Ortoli Report (Committee of Rationalization)	X	X	X		
1970 Report of the Round Table of Eight on the Personnel Problems and Organization	X	X	X	X	
1970 Framework Programme of the Round Table of Ten on Personnel Problems and Organization	X	X	X		
1972 A-U-R-A Report on the Internal Functioning of the Services	X	X			
1973 Personnel Politics: Propositions and Guidelines			X		
1973 Audland Report on Information, Documentation and Internal Co-ordination		X			
1973 Report of the Screening Group on Organizational Functioning			X		
1979 Spierenburg Report	X	X	X		
1980 Ortoli Report: Report on Implementation of Spierenburg Report		X	X		

(*Table continued*)

Table 1 Continued

Initiative	Structures	Process	Personnel	Finance	Ethics
1986 Decision Commission on Modernization Politics		X	X		
1987 Programme for Creating Awareness of Management Questions – Seminars for Personnel		X			
1989 Set of Management Measures: Management, Mobilization and Information Programme		X	X		
1991 Guidelines and Programme on Personnel Training			X		
1995 Sound Efficient Management (SEM 2000)		X		X	
1997 Modernization of Administration and Personnel Policy (MAP)			X		
1997 Designing the Commission of Tomorrow (Decode)		X	X	X	
2001 Reforming the European Commission, White Paper	X	X	X	X	X

Source: Barbara Heisserer 2008.

even clearer. The heuristic credo of systems theory is summarized in Figure 1. Looking at this "gure it is easy to see why it is crucial, from the point of view of a modi"ed systems theory, to focus on the concrete organization of the throughputs (Luhmann 1964; Easton 1965; Scharpf 1977).[6] This is so because inputs (political missions and public demands) pass speci"c throughputs (legal and personnel resources, reality of internal organization, i.e. constellations, processes, management, etc.) to form particular organizational outputs. In other words, the relationship between speci"c inputs and throughputs conditions particular outputs   with outputs being the organizational product aimed at generating a desired policy outcome in the real world. The exact relationship

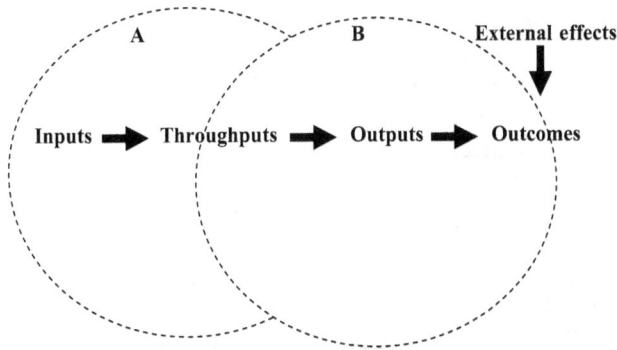

Figure 1 Two Perspectives on Organizational Change.

between speci"c outputs and the eventual outcomes is notoriously dif"cult to establish: "rst, because of long causal chains with each link constituting a challenge to causal analysis; and, second, owing to external effects which unavoidably and independently of the organizational outputs in"uence outcomes but remain dif"cult to anticipate, let alone control. As a pragmatic consequence, academic interest has privileged the study of inputs and outputs whereas to a lesser degree   or more precisely in a less systematic way   the triad of inputs, organizational throughputs and outputs has been the object of investigations.

Conceived in such a way, it becomes obvious why organizational change as an object of systematic study can basically assume two analytical purposes. Organizational change as the modi"cation of throughputs can be studied as an *explanandum*. Then organizational change per se is the phenomenon of which we seek a better understanding, i.e. the dependent variable. Or, organizational change can be conceptualized as part of the explanation for a speci"c phenomenon on which we focus with our research question. In this case organizational change is of interest as much and insofar as it causes changes to policy outputs and outcomes. Conceived in this way organizational change is (at least part of) the *explanans* or the independent variable in a respective research design (Bauer 2007a).

So far, both of these research agendas shape the scienti"c production about the reform of the European Commission (Bauer 2008a). The "rst, more basic set of questions aims at explaining administrative reform as such (in Figure 1 indicated by ellipse A). The second, perhaps more complex and more ambitious set of questions asks what difference this particular administrative reform actually makes   in terms of policy output or even outcome (ellipse B). Since the second set of questions regularly builds upon the "rst, and as it seems reasonable to take the "rst step before the second, it is no surprise that up to now we know much more about the triggers, scope and quality of the recent organizational change within the Commission in the context of the Kinnock reforms than about the effects these reforms have on the Commission s capacity to deliver EU policy output or on policy outcome.

At this point in our discussion it is important to note the existence of a major research gap. The pertinent sub-disciplines — international relations, organizational sociology, comparative public administration — have failed so far to engage in studying internal changes of international public organizations. As a consequence, there have been virtually no attempts to systematically put such international organizational changes into analytical contexts in order to explain policy outputs. The emergence of the study of the organizational impact of international bureaucracies as an interest of empirical social science research is a very recent trend (Barnett and Finnemore 2004; Liese and Weinlich 2006; Bauer and Knill 2007; Benner *et al.* 2007; Yi-Chong and Weller 2008; Geri 2001; Dijkzeul and Beigbeder 2003). It thus seems fair to emphasize that it is by no means clear whether these isolated scholarly endeavours will eventually add to the consolidation of a veritable research *agenda*, able to connect the pertinent questions from various approaches and to rally the various sub-disciplines behind a set of mature and salient research questions. In this respect, the recent work on organizational change within the European Commission seems much more advanced than that on any other international organization (Egeberg 1999, 2004; Trondal 2007; Suvarierol 2007; Bauer 2007b; Balint *et al.* 2008). Put bluntly, to better understand the case of reforming the European Commission little conceptual help can be expected from other research about international public organizations for the time being. At any rate, it is clear that the study of organizational change in the European Commission eventually needs to be put into context with this emerging and hopefully soon consolidating research agenda focusing on organizational issues of international and supranational bureaucracies.

Bearing this gap in mind, and agreeing that it is probably worthwhile to conceive the issue of reforming the European Commission as a case of management change in a public organization, the obvious thing to do is to turn to the comparative research on public sector reform. And indeed, here we "nd models that may help to depict the potential forces at work (Pollitt and Bouckaert 2004: 25). Such models are strong in providing descriptive categories about origins, processes, scope and intensity of managerial change in public organizations. They implicitly contain a heuristic to identify crucial factors worth looking at in order to disentangle international organizational change as a dependent variable. Unfortunately, so far comparative public administration accounts are less advanced in providing analytical explanations for the change we observe, let alone for the effects in terms of policy output that these changes may cause (but see Barzelay 2001; Barzelay and Füchtner 2003).

Reviewing this literature, there seem to be two major descriptive categories of interest: process and substance. Substance means that one has to ask for the speci"c quality, magnitude or intensity of change of a managerial modernization.[7] The process category contains the preconditions and origins of management change, like speci"c triggers, and also the internal politics and external demands of how management change was put on the agenda, how speci"c initiatives were designed, agreed upon and implemented. It is obvious that substance and process are descriptive categories. However, given the dearth of knowledge about managerial change in international bureaucracies in general and in the European Commission in particular, much might be gained if by using such merely descriptive schemata   we were able to produce, better systematize and qualify empirical observations about organizational change in the international and supranational sphere.

When looking for explanations for management reforms in the European Commission, a priori, i.e. before settling the exact research question, there are no limits to subsume the ongoing modernization processes to particular and distinct research programmes in the broader social sciences. For example, the analysis of management reforms of international organizations "ts well into the line of comparative public administration research attempting to understand the spread of new public management ideas (Osborne and Gaebler 1992; Peters and Savoie 1998; Wright 1997).

Administrative modernizations or reforms within international organizations can also be an issue for cultural theory (heterogeneous workforce, con"icting culturally loaded norms, styles and behaviour), discourse theory (role of media), organizational sociology (what leads staff to accept a reform?), management theory (how do organizations learn?), accountability theory (modernization as a means to legitimize organizational existence or expansion) and   most relevant for the research agenda pursued in this volume   policy analysis (how does reform affect policy output and outcome?; what is the role of policy networks, expert communities and the like?).

These approaches can be further distinguished as to whether their research programme focuses on external or internal factors. A "rst set of research programmes asks questions about how organizational procedures and styles become ever more homogeneous, how complex organizations learn from one another, how organizational solutions travel from one constituency to another, and what the factors facilitating the acceptance of alien solutions at home are (DiMaggio and Powell 1991; Dolowitz and Marsh 2000; Brooks 2005). Transfer, diffusion, lesson drawing, learning as well as bandwagoning and symbolic politics are the mechanisms which   although they cannot be discussed in detail here (see, however, Knill 2005)   appear to have great explanatory potential.

A second way to unpack organizational change within the European Commission is to look at the internal side of the story. The concepts of veto players (who can obstruct reform or how does reform redistribute veto power?), incrementalism (bounded rational actors), garbage can (contingent decision-making processes), policy entrepreneur (reform advocates), of"ce maximizing strategies (redistributive interests of top managers), principal-agent theory (reform pressure from constituencies   in particular those who "nance the budget of the organization), decoupling (jumping rhetorically at the modernization trend without implementing meaningful reform) are all approaches that focus on internal driving factors and appear promising in the attempt to disentangle the Commission s management reforms (Tsebelis and Kreppel 1998; Lindblom 1959; Kingdon 1995; Pollack 2003; Dunleavy 1992; Brunsson 1989).

Particularly important for the internal perspective is institutional context: decision-making rules, positional and policy-orientation power games and the like (North 1999). The institutional context in relation to (expected) power shifts between the affected administrative actors (as reform winners and losers) and reform advocates is crucial from that perspective. Moreover, looking at institutional relationships means focusing on the interrelatedness between internal and external factors.

In other words, organizational change in the European Commission is probably most fruitfully explored as a European public policy itself (Richardson 2006; Barzelay 2001). The particular importance of the study of organizational change derives from the fact that this kind of change not only affects the management of internal processes of the Commission, but may also in"uence virtually all policy output produced by this actor. Research questions within this context will probably remain as heterogeneous as the approaches, theories and mechanisms that shape the normal analysis of EU policy-making. The challenge thus is to synthesize perspectives in order to arrive at more comprehensive and complete explanations of causes and effects of management reforms in the European Commission.

5. APPROACHES, POSITIONS AND FINDINGS

The articles assembled in this volume attempt to take on the challenge of starting to think systematically about organizational change within the Commission. In seven studies one can obviously not pursue all possible research programmes, (some of) which have been mentioned in the previous section. Mirroring the yet unconsolidated nature of the topic under scrutiny, the following articles take distinct perspectives, use various research strategies and methods, and attempt to solve diverse empirical puzzles related to the Kinnock reform of the European Commission. However, by exploring their various research interests they address the two basic sets of questions outlined above. First, why was such comprehensive reform possible and how was it implemented (Kassim 2008; Knill and Balint 2008; Schön-Quinlivan 2008), and, second, what are the implications of these reforms for the role of the Commission or Commission of"cials (Peterson 2008; Ellinas and Suleiman 2008; Bauer 2008a), and how do the Kinnock reforms condition the reform capacity of that organization in the post-reform phase (Cini 2008). In other words, the two core research programmes outlined above are well represented and the reform of the European Commission is thus studied as both a *dependent* as well as an *independent* variable.

Hussein Kassim starts by revisiting the historical account of the Kinnock reform. He shows what the reform initiatives were all about and how they were implemented in a surprisingly short space of time. Kassim goes on to compare the particular path and the unforeseeable success (in terms of number of adopted reform measures) of the organizational change brought about under the leadership of Neil Kinnock with the standard approaches in comparative public administration used to explain management change. He shows that none of the pertinent theoretical traditions, be it approaches based on classical Weberian analysis, neo-institutionalism or principal-agent theory, can coherently and comprehensively account for the emergence of the Kinnock reform. By isolating three key puzzles, empirical characteristics of the Kinnock reform which contradict the classical explanations of public sector reform processes, Kassim points to highly important issues for further empirical research and theory development with respect to factors and conditions of organizational change in supranational and international organizations.

Christoph Knill and Tim Balint are also interested in the substance of reform and how to explain the organizational processes that led to administrative change. However, they focus on a particular part of the Commission reform endeavour (human resource management) and compare observable change in the European Commission with similar reform initiatives in the Secretariat of the Organization for Economic Co-operation and Development (OECD). They take as a benchmark a systematically stylized version of new public management principles and root their theoretical expectations in organizational isomorphism. Knill and Balint "nd that while the Commission brought its management structures with regard to many dimensions under scrutiny closely in line with new public management, the OECD, by contrast, still relies on classical Weberian bureaucracy procedures. Although it has the organizational mission to push for such kind of change in national administrations, Knill and Balint show how fruitful a structured comparison of international bureaucracies can be. They suggest that their results indicate that a more precise understanding of the scope conditions of the highly in"uential theory of isomorphism has to be developed. According to the isomorphistic expectations, the occurrence of change in line with new public management in the case of the OECD was over-determined. That this change did not materialize points to the fact that isomorphism theory needs to be complemented by arguments with regard to the conditions under which organizations adopt policy innovations which diffuse internationally (Knill and Balint 2008: 687). More important than these remarkable results per se are two achievements: "rst, Knill and Balint overcome the sui generis paradigm in the study of the Commission and show that one indeed can compare the Commission with other international organizations. The potential deriving from such a strategy for understanding the Commission better is self-evident. Second, they try to be systematic about comparing administrative reform by developing an interesting coding scheme for scoring administrative characteristics. We need more of such innovations if we are to theoretically and empirically advance our knowledge of organizational change in international constellations.

Emmanuelle Schön-Quinlivan also follows a comparative design. She takes the analysis of organizational change to a meso organizational level in order to give a more "ne-tuned account of the scope of change brought about by the Kinnock reform within the Commission. Rooting her analysis in the concept of translation (Campbell 2004), Schön-Quinlivan analyses the application of the Kinnock reform processes in two functionally distinct Directorates-General (DGs) of the Commission. Doing this enables her to disentangle the constellations and conditions of the varying implementation processes within these DGs. She is able to pin down distinctive reform cultures in the DGs under study and isolates supportive leadership of the individual Directors-General as the single most important variable to account for application differences in the organizational reform menu . Her study is remarkable because she points to bureaucratic leadership as an important element for study   which is unjusti"- ably neglected in most of the current policy-analytical literature.

The study of Antonis Ellinas and Ezra Suleiman and that of Michael W. Bauer take the Kinnock reform conceptually as an independent factor. The studies   which were conceived and conducted strictly separately   are based on extensive and systematic interviewing of the objects of reform: top managers (Ellinas and Suleiman) and heads of unit (Bauer). Both studies are interested primarily in the effects of the reform on the Commission as an organization, and both studies are theoretically as well as methodologically disciplined and generate important new data. And their bottom line is strikingly similar, too: intentionally or unintentionally, the Kinnock reform has curtailed the capacity of the Commission to deliver policy drafts as a policy initiator and a political entrepreneur. Following the assessment of the likely effects of the Kinnock reforms, these studies nurture serious worries about the Commission s post-reform capacities to reach organizational ef"ciency and provide creative policy entrepreneurship as we know it, and as perceived to be an important driving force within the European integration process.

Michelle Cini addresses an extremely under-researched topic, as she focuses on the post-reform period in public organizations and asks whether the reform capacity of the European Commission improved or decreased in the aftermath of the Kinnock reform. This is indeed a very important issue as the problem of reform fatigue after big organizational change initiatives have been adopted is one to which scholars have regularly failed to pay particular, let alone systematic, attention. Cini attempts to confront this gap by concentrating on the ethics chapter of the Kinnock reform and how these issues have been tackled since 2004   the year when the Commission reforms were said to be in operation. This case is well chosen, as the ethical part of the Kinnock reform was clearly aimed at cultural change in the Commission and was thus a long-term organizational challenge right from the beginning. Cini reveals that the post- reform drive in the context of ethics and transparency has little to do with sys- tematic organizational capacity-building or strategic decision-making but rather with incrementalism, coincidence, and thus a garbage-can style of policy- making. Her "ndings raise a number of questions about the possibilities of organizational learning in general, and about the missing post-reform manage- ment capacity within the European Commission in particular.

John Peterson, considering the combined impact of the two greatest organizational challenges confronting the European Commission recently, i.e. enlargement and Kinnock reform, asks the central question of how the Commission s role has changed since the Santer resignation in the context of such twofold organizational stress. The suspicion is that administrative reforms may have weakened the Commission s capacity for managing EU decision-making in the multi-level system. Concentrating on the relationship between the College of Commissioners and the administration of the Commission as well as on that between the Commission and the European Parliament and, "rst and foremost, the Council, Peterson "nds little evidence for the thesis of such an endemic organizational decline. Rather, he sees the Commission undergoing a thorough transformation. The Commission appears set to become a more normal organization in the sense that it adapts to the intergovernmental management and decision modes which have been reinforced by recent enlargements and more critical attitudes of the EU publics to an ever closer Union . After all, the Commission is potentially in the best position or perhaps even the only possible actor to co-ordinate policy-making within the emerging structure of the EU27+ multi-level network governance. In this respect, the positive result from enlargements and internal reform is that the dynamic of events has led to a better "t of the Commission s capacities with the changing necessities. In short, it may be true that the Commission has lost policy-making autonomy but at the same time it appears now to be a more reliable organization to manage the new presumably more intergovernmental way of governing the EU. Thus implicitly John Peterson rightly warns us that our analytical benchmarks to assess the effects of organizational change in the case of the European Commission are inevitably rooted in particular concepts about the integration process and the ontological characteristics of the EU and its institutions.

6. OUTLOOK FOR EMPIRICAL RESEARCH

Taken together, the "ndings leave no doubt that recent initiatives for administrative modernization have transformed the European Commission. The reality of working in the Commission has altered and the organizational environment has also simultaneously changed. This is particularly evident in the relationship between the Commission and the other main actors at the supranational level (Peterson 2008). In addition, the organizational roles of the Commission (further) diversi"ed. Thus it becomes increasingly dif"cult for analysts to refer to the Commission; rather, one has to differentiate more precisely than in the past between the various organizational roles of the Commission, such as co-policy-making, supervising the national implementation of European policies, adjudicating national policies in line with European law, and managing its own organizational functioning ef"ciently and effectively (Hooghe 2001; Cram 1994). Against the background of the conceptual considerations and empirical "ndings in this volume, some of the most promising areas for further research in the context of organizational change and managerial reform within the European Commission appear to be as follows.

The "rst topic involves comparing the Kinnock reform and the initiatives for administrative change succeeding it with past modernization initiatives. We know of a number of small and medium-size administrative reform attempts in the history of the European Commission (see Table 1). But we have not yet attempted to study these cases systematically, let alone identify conditions and constellations that may comprise comparative lessons to shed light on the current reform outcomes. Not to try to bring the historical dimension to current analyses would be worse than short-sighted; it would be to act negligently and to forgo the potential to advance theory-building with respect to the topic of reforming the European Commission.

Another set of questions to ask (simple to state but inherently intricate and challenging to settle) is which of the Kinnock reform innovations are working now and which are not, and whether it makes sense to take the Kinnock reform as a coherent and clearly distinguishable set of initiatives.[8] Implementing the Kinnock reform involved tremendous internal turmoil and it is far from clear how the organization as a whole is coping with it. Moreover, even after formally completing the reform as a conceptual undertaking in 2004, many un"nished items have been left on the agenda (Levy 2006). It appears appropriate in this context to recall an iron law of the study of public policy, namely that the adoption of a public policy is by no means a guarantee of subsequent implementation. Many seem to think that the Kinnock reform is indeed past and that the challenge is now to study the various processes of institutional innovation and power redistribution that this reform has initiated for good or bad. To decide whether to take the Kinnock reform as a conceptual yardstick or not is no trivial matter, since much depends upon it for individual research endeavours. In simple terms, taken as a pure yardstick for the analysis of organizational change, one would have to focus the analysis on the degree of its appropriate implementation. Conceptualizing organizational change exclusively against the background of Kinnock s reform programme thus means risking missing or misjudging the broader transformational potential that emerged within the context of a from many perspectives perhaps failed original reform. Moreover, somewhere alongside tackling the history and the yardstick question researchers have to "nd the means of reasonably clear measurement that can be operationalized across individual cases in order to determine in comparative terms the intensity of the observable organizational change.

A further challenge is to bring the European Commission and the study about organizational change within it out of its *sui-generis corner*. The Commission certainly has unique features that distinguish it from other international organizations. However, there seem to be more similarities than differences and certainly enough features to conduct meaningful comparisons between the Commission and its organizational peers (Knill and Balint 2008; Balint *et al.* 2008). Much could thus be gained if organizational change within the

Commission were put into the context of the emerging research agenda on international bureaucracies (Bauer and Knill 2007; Barnett and Finnemore 2004; Benner *et al.* 2007; Geri 2001; Liese and Weinlich 2006; Yi-Chong and Weller 2008).

Finally, there is an emerging consensus that the Kinnock reform has changed the internal politics within the European Commission. But how exactly, and with what effect, is still an unanswered question. The most interesting mechanism in this context is that the reform has apparently had a differential impact on the various organizational roles of the Commission (Schön-Quinlivan 2008). The challenge is thus to come to grips with this differential impact and to tell which particular effects are to be expected under which conditions and in which constellations. Empirical evidence to settle such questions is sparse and, at best, mixed. For example, there appear to be forces within the Commission who disliked Kinnock s auto-reform exercise and the administrative changes it brought about. However, once they have learned to cope with the inflicted organizational transformation, and once they have become confident in mastering the politics of this new administrative reality, they want to refocus what they see as their real mission. Hence, they want to keep to the new status quo (which they now know) rather than engage in further organizational engineering (to ends they ignore). We can thus safely assume that the original Kinnock reform, and those managerial elements which have been conceived since 2004, are now taken into consideration by the internal actors when pursuing their individual objectives. Following this line of argument, the reform has certainly produced winners and losers. A new internal dynamic appears to be the result, favouring change of one sort over change of another. Seen from this perspective a final assessment of the Kinnock reform appears difficult, if not pointless. The ongoing and lasting significance of the Kinnock reform for students of the EU in general and from an EU public policy-making perspective in particular rather stems from the new internal politics it produces (cf. Hartlapp 2007). To uncover these patterns and to identify the differential impact the reform generates is perhaps the single most important challenge for empirical research.

7. THE NEXUS BETWEEN ORGANIZATIONAL CHANGE AND POLICY OUTPUT

There are complaints from inside the Commission that the reform intensified instead of solved the silo problem , in particular by pushing for decentralization of operational tasks and in the context of the implementation of activity-based management procedures. The silo problem characterizes a situation in which individual DGs are run as political and organizational fiefdoms , and it hence remains more difficult than ever to integrate this multi-organization into a coherent line of policy-making. Moreover, the last progress report about the implementation of the administrative reform from 2005 (!) states that the Commission intends to further consolidate, streamline and simplify internal procedures and working methods in the interest of effectiveness and efficiency (Commission

2005: 19). In the same vein, the Commission leadership since 2004 has shown little or no interest in the administrative reform agenda inherited from its predecessors. At least, it is not easy to tell what exactly have been the measures adopted in order to strike a better balance between the level of risk and cost of control that was promised in the last of"cial document about the Kinnock reform (Commission 2005: 19). This can, and perhaps must, be read as evidence that the Kinnock reform remains un"nished. It is "tting that those who currently work on management issues within the Commission seem to see their ongoing mission precisely in further consolidating, streamlining, simplifying and obviously also somewhat safeguarding what has been achieved so far.[9]

As regards understanding management reform   and even more so from the perspective of theory-building about organizational change   the task is perhaps less to pin down what the Kinnock reform has formally and informally changed within the Commission. The challenge rather lies in unpacking the nexus between organizational changes in the Commission and deriving consequences for EU policy output as such. This volume goes some way in this direction. It develops a number of analytical instruments and theoretical perspectives to better understand this relationship between alterations of organizational throughputs and their direct, as well as indirect, consequences for policy output. However, far from being able to settle this discussion, it calls upon students of EU politics, comparative bureaucracy and organizational sociology to pay more attention to what can be called the throughput output nexus[10] in EU policy-making.

Biographical note: Michael W. Bauer is Assistant Professor (C1) for Comparative Public Policy and Administration at the Department of Politics and Management, University of Konstanz, Germany.

Address for correspondence: Michael W. Bauer, Department of Politics and Management, University of Konstanz, D 91, D-78457 Konstanz, Germany. email: michael.w.bauer@uni-konstanz.de

NOTES

1 See Kassim (2004a, 2004b); Levy (2004, 2006); Stevens and Stevens (2006); Spence and Stevens (2006); Balint *et al.* (2008); Bauer (2008a, 2008b) and Bear"eld (2004).
2 The reform is commonly named after Neil Kinnock, the vice-president in charge of implementing the administrative modernization. Furthermore, one can argue, if administrative change stretches over various areas as is usual, if it is appropriate to talk about *the Kinnock reform* or *reforms*. For simplicity, I will refer to the administrative reform packages initiated between 2000 und 2004 in the singular form as the Kinnock reform .
3 Cf. the public hearing governance in the European Commission , 3 and 4 October 2007 in the European Parliament, Brussels. (http://www.europarl.europa.eu/comparl/cont/site/auditions/governance_en.htm).

4 One can argue if it is indeed a new or just a renewed interest, cf. Coombes (1970) or Metcalfe (1992).

5 For an attempt focusing on actors constellation over time, see Bauer (2007b).

6 Throughputs are in this context perhaps best understood as a label for the internal organizational reality and a speci"c way to process particular tasks with the organizational resources at hand.

7 It is common in the "elds of comparative public policy and public administration to distinguish between three to four levels of intensity of such organizational change (Hall 1993; Sabatier and Jenkins-Smith 1993; Knill 2001; Pollitt and Bouckaert 2004). One may thus differentiate loosely between no change, optimization, reform and transformation. How to establish the intensity of an administrative reform is analytically as dif"cult as it is important if one wants to engage in cross-case comparisons.

8 It is remarkable and astonishing that, after "ve years of operation, the Commission itself has provided so little hard information about the effects of reform and how it works in practice. The European Parliament appears particularly disappointed about this continuing silence despite various formal demands for clari"cation of the picture. Recently, the Parliament complained that the Commission had archived the of"cial homepage about the reform. Moreover, some Members of the European Parliament from the Budgetary Control Committee have initiated several external research studies (about activity-based management and the effects of organizational decentralization) apparently in response to the restricted information policy of the Commission with respect to the effects of organizational reform.

9 That was the message conveyed by high of"cials in interviews between 18 and 20 December 2007.

10 For a more extensive discussion of the throughput output nexus in the context of administrative reform and its potential for policy-making on the empirical example of the recent management changes in the European Commission, see Bauer (2008b).

REFERENCES

Balint, T., Bauer, M.W. and Knill, C. (2008) Bureaucratic change in the European administrative space. The case of the European Commission , *West European Politics* 32(1) (forthcoming).

Barnett, M. and Finnemore, M. (2004) *Rules for the World. International Organizations in Global Politics*, Ithaca, NY: Cornell University Press.

Barzelay, M. (2001) *The New Public Management: Improving Research and Policy Dialogue*, Berkeley, CA: University of California Press.

Barzelay, M. and Füchtner, N. (2003) Explaining public management policy change: Germany in comparative perspective , *Journal of Comparative Policy Analysis* 5(1): 7 27.

Bauer, M.W. (2001) *A Creeping Transformation? The European Commission and the Management of EU Structural Funds in Germany*, Dordrecht: Kluwer.

Bauer, M.W. (2002) Limitations to agency control in EU policy-making the Commission and the poverty programmes , *Journal of Common Market Studies* 40(3): 381 400.

Bauer, M.W. (2006) Die Reform der Europäischen Kommission: Eine Studie zur Managementmodernisierung internationaler Organisationen , *Verwaltungsarchiv. Zeitschrift für Verwaltungslehre, Verwaltungsrecht und Verwaltungspolitik* 97(3): 270 92.

Bauer, M.W. and Knill, C. (eds) (2006) *Management Reforms in International Organization*, Baden-Baden: Nomos.

Bauer, M.W. (2007a) Introduction: Management reforms in international organiz-
    ations , in M.W. Bauer and C. Knill (eds), *Management Reforms in International
    Organizations*, Baden-Baden: Nomos, pp. 11 23.
Bauer, M.W. (2007b) The politics of reforming the European Commission adminis-
    tration , in M.W. Bauer and C. Knill (eds), *Management Reforms in International
    Organizations*, Baden-Baden: Nomos, pp. 54 69.
Bauer, M.W. (2008a) Diffuse anxieties, deprived entrepreneurs: Commission reform
    and middle management , *Journal of European Public Policy* 15(5): 691 707.
Bauer, M.W. (2008b) Der Throughput output nexus in der empirischen Verwal-
    tungswissenschaft , *Die Verwaltung* 41(1): 63 76.
Bear"eld, N.D. (2004) Reforming the European Commission. Driving reform from
    the grassroots , *Public Policy and Administration* 19(5): 13 24.
Benner, T., Mergenthaler, S. and Rotmann, P. (2007) International bureaucracies: the
    contours of a (re)emerging research agenda . Paper presented at the German Political
    Science Association (DVPW) IR section conference, Technical University
    Darmstadt, 14 July 2007.
Brooks, S.M. (2005) Interdependent and domestic foundations of policy change: the
    diffusion of pension privatization around the world , *International Studies Quarterly*
    49(2): 273 94.
Brunsson, N. (1989) *The Organization of Hypocrisy: Talk, Decisions and Actions in
    Organizations*, Chichester: Wiley.
Campbell, J.L. (2004) *Institutional Change and Globalization*, Princeton, NJ: Princeton
    University Press.
Christiansen, T. (1997) Tensions of European governance: politicized bureaucracy and
    multiple accountability in the European Commission , *Journal of European Public
    Policy* 4(1): 73 90.
Cini, M. (1996) *The European Commission. Leadership, Organization and Culture in the
    EU Administration*, Manchester: Manchester University Press.
Cini, M. (2008) European Commission reform and the origins of the European Trans-
    parency Initiative , *Journal of European Public Policy* 15(5): 743 60.
Commission of the European Communities (2005) Progress report on the Commission
    reform beyond the reform mandate, COM (2005) 669 "nal 21.12.2005, Brussels:
    Of"ce for Of"cial Publications of the European Communities.
Coombes, D. (1970) *Politics and Bureaucracy in the European Community: A Portrait of
    the Commission of the EEC*, London: George Allen & Unwin.
Coull, J. and Lewis, C. (2003) The impact reform of the staff regulations in making the
    Commission a more modern and ef"cient organisation. An insider s perspective ,
    EIPAScope 3: 2 9.
Cram, L. (1994) The European Commission as a multi-organization: social policy and
    IT policy in the EU , *Journal of European Public Policy* 1(2): 195 217.
Dijkzeul, D. and Beigbeder, Y. (2003) Introduction: Rethinking international organ-
    izations , in D. Dijkzeul and Y. Beigbeder (eds), *Rethinking International Organiz-
    ations. Pathology and Promise*, New York: Berghahn, pp. 1 26.
DiMaggio, P.J. and Powell, W.W. (1991) The iron cage revisited: institutional
    isomorphism and collective rationality in organizational "elds , in W.W. Powell
    and P.J. DiMaggio (eds), *The New Institutionalism in Organizational Analysis*,
    Chicago: University of Chicago Press, pp. 63 82.
Dolowitz, D. and Marsh, D. (2000) Learning from abroad: the role of policy transfer in
    contemporary policy making , *Governance* 13(1): 5 24.
Dunleavy, P. (1992) *Democracy, Bureaucracy, and Public Choice: Economic Explanations
    in Political Science*, New York: Prentice-Hall.
Easton, D. (1965) *A Systems Analysis of Political Life*, New York: John Wiley.
Edwards, G. and Spence, D. (1994) *The European Commission*, London: Longman.

Egeberg, M. (1999) The impact of bureaucratic structure on policy making, *Public Administration* 77(2): 155 70.

Ellinas, A. and Suleiman, E. (2008) Reforming the Commission: between modernization and bureaucratization, *Journal of European Public Policy* 15(5): 708 25.

Geri, L.R. (2001) New public management and the reform of international organizations, *International Review of Administrative Sciences* 67(3): 445 60.

Hall, P.A. (1993) Policy paradigms, social learning and the state. The case of economic policymaking in Britain, *Comparative Politics* 25(3): 275 96.

Hartlapp, M. (2007) Intra-Kommissionsdynamik im Policy-Making: EU-Politiken angesichts des demographischen Wandels, *Politische Vierteljahresschrift* 40 (Sonderheft): 139 60.

Heisserer, B. (2008) Management reforms in international organizations. A critical analysis of in"uencing factors on organizational change of the European Commission. Unpublished manuscript, University of Konstanz.

Hoffmann, S. (1966) Obstinate or obsolete? The fate of the nation-state and the case of Western Europe, *Deadalus* 95(3): 862 915.

Hooghe, L. (2001) *The European Commission and the Integration of Europe. Images of Governance*, Cambridge: Cambridge University Press.

Kassim, H. (2004a) A historic accomplishment. The Prodi Commission and administrative reform, in D.G. Dimitrakopoulos (ed.), *The Changing European Commission*, Manchester: Manchester University Press, pp. 33 63.

Kassim, H. (2004b) The Kinnock reforms in perspective: why reforming the Commission is an heroic, but thankless task, *Public Policy and Administration* 19(1): 25 41.

Kassim, H. (2008) Mission impossible , but mission accomplished: the Kinnock reforms and the European Commission, *Journal of European Public Policy* 15(5): 648 68.

Knill, C. (2001) *The Europeanization of National Administrations: Patterns of Institutional Change and Persistence*, Cambridge: Cambridge University Press.

Knill, C. (2005) Introduction: Cross-national policy convergence: concepts, approaches and explanatory factors, *Journal of European Public Policy* 12(5): 764 74.

Knill, C. and Balint, T. (2008) Explaining variation in organizational change: the reform of human resource management in the European Commission and the OECD, *Journal of European Public Policy* 15(5): 669 90.

Koelble, T.A. (1995) The new institutionalism in political science and sociology, *Comparative Politics* 27(2): 231 43.

Kratochwil, F. and Ruggie, J.G. (1986) International organization: a state of the art on an art of the state, *International Organization* 40(4): 753 75.

Levy, R. (2004) Between rhetoric and reality. Implementing management reform in the European Commission, *The International Journal of Public Sector Management* 17(2): 166 77.

Levy, R. (2006) European Commission overload and the pathology of management reform: garbage can, rationality and risk aversion, *Public Administration* 84(2): 423 39.

Liese, A. and Weinlich, S. (2006) Die Rolle von Verwaltungsstäben internationaler Organisationen. Lücken, Tücken und Konturen eines (neuen) Forschungsfelds, *Politische Vierteljahresschrift* 37 (Sonderheft): 491 524.

Lindblom, C.E. (1959) The science of muddling through, *Public Administration Review* 19(2), 79 88.

Luhmann, N. (1964) *Funktionen und Folgen formaler Organisation*, Berlin: Duncker & Humblot.

March, J.P and Olsen, J.P (1989) *Rediscovering Institutions: The Organizational Basis of Politics*, New York: Free Press.

Metcalfe, L. (1992) After 1992: can the Commission manage Europe? , *Australian Journal of Public Administration* 51(1): 117 30.

Metcalfe, L. (2000) Reforming the Commission: will organizational ef"ciency produce effective governance? , *Journal of Common Market Studies* 38(5): 817 41.

North, D. (1999) *Institutions, Institutional Change and Economic Performance*, Cambridge: Cambridge University Press.

Nugent, N. (1997) *At the Heart of the Union. Studies of the European Commission*, Basingstoke: Macmillan.

Nugent, N. (2001) *The European Commission*, New York: Palgrave.

Olsen, J. (2006) Maybe it is time to rediscover bureaucracy , *Journal of Public Administration Research and Theory* 16(1): 1 24.

Osborne, D. and Gaebler, T. (1992) *Reinventing Government: How the Entrepreneurial Spirit is Transforming the Public Sector*, New York: Plume.

Peters, B.G. (2001) *The Politics of Bureaucracy*, London and New York: Routledge.

Peters, G.B. and Savoie, D.J. (1998) *Taking Stock: Assessing Public Sector Reforms*, Montreal: McGill-Queen s University Press.

Peterson, J. (1999) The Santer era: the European Commission in normative, historical and theoretical perspective , *Journal of European Public Policy* 6(1): 46 65.

Peterson, J. (2004) The Prodi Commission. Fresh start or free fall? , in D.G. Dimitrakopoulos (ed.), *The Changing European Commission*, Manchester: Manchester University Press, pp. 15 33.

Peterson, J. (2008) Enlargement, reform and the European Commission. Weathering a perfect storm? , *Journal of European Public Policy* 15(5): 761 80.

Pollack, M.A. (2003) *The Engines of European Integration: Delegation Agency and Agenda Setting in the EU*, Oxford: Oxford University Press.

Pollitt, C. and Bouckaert, G. (2004) *Public Management Reform A Comparative Analysis*, Oxford: Oxford University Press.

Richardson, J. (2006) Policy-making in the EU. Interests, ideas and garbage cans of primeval soup , in J. Richardson (ed.), *European Union. Power and Policy-making*, London and New York: Routledge, pp. 3 29.

Sabatier, P.A. and Jenkins-Smith, H.C. (1993) *Policy-Change and Learning: An Advocacy Coalition Approach*, Boulder, CO: Westview Press.

Scharpf, F.W. (1977) Does organization matter? Task structure and interaction in the ministerial bureaucracy , *Organization and Administrative Sciences* 8(1): 149 68.

Schön-Quinlivan, E. (2008) Implementing organizational change the case of the Kinnock reforms , *Journal of European Public Policy* 15(5): 726 42.

Spence, D.B (2000) Plus ça change, plus c est la meme chose? Attempting to reform the European Commission , *Journal of European Public Policy* 7(1):1 25.

Spence, D.B. and Edwards, G. (eds) (2006) *The European Commission*, London: John Harper.

Spence, D.B. and Stevens, A. (2006) Staff and personnel policy in the Commission , in D.B. Spence and G. Edwards (eds), *The European Commission*, London: John Harper, pp. 173 208.

Stevens, H. and Stevens, A. (2006) The internal reform of the Commission , in D.B. Spence and G. Edwards (eds), *The European Commission*, London: John Harper, pp. 454 80.

Suvarierol, S. (2007) *Beyond the Myth of Nationality: a Study on the Networks of European Commission Of cials*, Utrecht: Eburon.

Trondal, J. (2007) The public administration turn in integration research , *Journal of European Public Policy* 14(6): 960 72.

Tsebelis, G. and Kreppel, A. (1998) The history of conditional agenda-setting in European institutions , *European Journal of Political Research* 33(1): 41 71.

Wright, V. (1997) The paradoxes of administrative reform , in W.J.M. Kickert (ed.), *Public Management and Administrative Reform in Western Europe*, Cheltenham: Elgar, pp. 7 13.

Yi-Chong, X. and Weller, P. (2008) To be, but not to be seen: exploring the impact of international civil servants , *Public Administration* 86 (forthcoming).

'Mission impossible', but mission accomplished: the Kinnock reforms and the European Commission

Hussein Kassim

INTRODUCTION

The European Commission presents a fascinating case for scholars of administrative reform. While national administrations in advanced industrial societies
have undergone periodic and often radical change since the 1950s, the Commission grew in size and complexity but did not undertake major administrative
reform. However, having changed little in terms of its main procedures for
over 40 years, it implemented a programme of far-reaching change, involving
the simultaneous overhaul of personnel, "nancial management, and planning
systems in six years between 1999 and 2005. The accomplishment of such a
wide-ranging transformation in such a short timeframe is unusual in the case
of any public administration (Pollitt and Bouckaert 2004; Sahlin-Andersson
2002). In those rare instances where far-reaching reform has been introduced
at the national level, as, for example, with the Next Steps in the UK, change
was implemented over a far longer period. At international level, meanwhile,

reform has generally been restricted to a limited number of speci"c areas (Bauer 2007a; Bauer and Knill 2007; Claude 1971; Geri 2001).

A pattern of continuity over four decades followed by a big bang of sudden and comprehensive reform is the "rst of three interrelated puzzles arising out of the Commission s experience. A second relates to the circumstances under which the reform came about and the Commission s response to it. Although the reform and elements of its content were externally imposed on the organization by the European Council and a Committee of Independent Experts (CIE) appointed by the European Parliament to examine the way in which the Commission detects and deals with fraud, mismanagement and nepotism (European Parliament 1999), the Commission leadership implemented a reform programme that went signi"cantly beyond what these bodies demanded. In particular, and acting on its own initiative, it extended the reform to sensitive aspects of staf"ng policy   the very areas in which earlier reform initiatives had foundered. Rather than reacting negatively or attempting to obstruct reform as might have been expected from an organization compelled by outside actors to introduce change, the Commission responded positively by expanding the scope of the reform.

A third puzzle concerns the Kinnock reforms as an instance of successful change.[1] The literature on bureaucracy and institutional and organizational change tends to be sceptical about the prospects of meaningful change, even more about far-reaching reform. Approaches to administrative reform inspired by historical institutionalism (HI) or sociological institutionalism (SI) (see, for example, Brunsson and Olsen 1993; Christensen 1997; Capano 2003), jointly considered as new institutionalism (NI) for the purposes of this article, among other things predict incremental or path dependent change.[2] They tend to assume that the impetus to reform comes from outside the organization concerned, that the pressure to reform is interpreted by the organization in terms of existing norms and values, and that any change is likely to be modest. Applied to the Commission, NI-informed theories of administrative reform would hypothesize at most incremental change, not the wholesale and simultaneous replacement of key systems and procedures.

Micro-level approaches, such as the Weberian orthodoxy (WO), and the classic principal agent model (CP A) meanwhile anticipate that change initiated by reform-minded politicians is likely to be blocked by bureaucrats. WO, essentially a theory of bureaucratic power, has been applied by several scholars to explain why reform efforts fail (see, for example, Kellner and Crowther-Hunt 1980; Suleiman 1974; Putnam 1974). Bureaucrats prefer the status quo, dislike uncertainty and will, and are able to, resist changes that threaten their status. CP A, by contrast, assumes that the preferences of principal and agent diverge, that bureaucrats are the bene"ciaries of power asymmetries vis-à-vis politicians (see, for example, Moe 1984, 1989; Weingast 1984), and that an agent instructed to reform will shirk. Both WO and CP A would hypothesize that the Commission would regard calls for it to reform as unwelcome and that it would attempt to obstruct any efforts to bring about organizational change.

As well as defying the expectations of leading theoretical approaches, the Commission s experience is at odds with the "ndings from comparative studies of administrative reform. Most empirical analyses emphasize the pitfalls. They highlight the extent to which reform is gradual, improvised and uncertain, how the original blueprints for change are unlikely to survive to the "nal stages of the reform process, and the many obstacles that lie in the path of would-be reformers (see, for example, Wright 1994, 1998). Unsurprisingly, they "nd very few instances of success (Pollitt and Boucrkaert 2004).

The three puzzles outlined above highlight features of the Commission case that make it so unusual. They also identify aspects of the reform that have been neglected in the existing literature. The puzzles are instructive in that they suggest an alternative image of the Commission and an alternative interpretation of its reform to that suggested by a casual reading of the Commission s history and the sequence of events that led to the Kinnock reforms. An organization that had remained essentially unchanged for four decades until forced to change by external action appears *prima facie* to be arrogant, powerful and oblivious to its failings. The analysis presented below, however, presents a somewhat different picture. It holds that the Commission leadership had in fact long been aware of the organization s weaknesses and attempted on several occasions from the late 1970s to address them (Bauer 2007b). Its lack of success reveals less a self-satis"ed and unself-conscious organization than an administration trapped in a reform predicament. The Commission is essentially a dependent institution. Not only are the rules that regulate its staf"ng and "nancial management and control procedures set out in legislation agreed jointly by the Council of Ministers and the European Parliament, but the Commission confronts formidable internal barriers that it has found impossible to overcome through its efforts alone. Reform of its administrative systems and procedures requires intervention on the part of member governments and, to a lesser extent the Parliament, but these actors are generally not interested in the Commission s internal administration.

How then to explain the changes introduced under Prodi? This article argues that the Kinnock reforms are best interpreted as a case of self-reform under delegation and best explained in terms of the predicament referred to above. The Commission s ability to undertake reform is constrained by its institutional setting and certain internal characteristics present formidable obstacles that can only be overcome with assistance from national governments. The crisis precipitated by the resignation of the Santer Commission in March 1999 compelled national governments to act and to insist that the Commission implement internal reform   a rare case of intervention in the Commission s administrative affairs by the member states. The European Council entrusted the task of modernizing the organization to the incoming College and thereafter played a limited role in the process. Meanwhile, the Commission took full advantage of the opportunity to act on an internal reform agenda developed over the course of two decades   the opportunist thesis   and to address other concerns raised by Commission of"cials.

A second argument is that the Commission's reform predicament and the very specific conditions under which it was able to implement change present a challenge to the existing theoretical literature. The leading theories begin from assumptions about the source of the desire for reform, the respective preferences of politicians and bureaucrats, and the constraints imposed by the political context that do not easily "t the Commission's case.[3] To the extent that the Commission's institutional setting is comparable to that of other international administrations, it suggests that a new theoretical approach may be needed to explain administrative reform in an international context of institutional dependence.

The discussion below is organized in four sections. The first describes the Commission's reform predicament. It argues that, in contrast to normal legislation where it can exert varying degrees of influence (see, for example, Pollack 2003; Schmidt 2000), the Commission is severely constrained in regard to the procedures and practices that govern its internal operation. It depends on the intervention of national governments and the European Parliament which only rarely show interest in the Commission's internal administration. The second section briefly discusses reform efforts by the Commission before that date. It argues that though the absence of an external impetus was a major constraining factor in limiting their achievements, the initiatives reveal the Commission leadership's desire to reform the administration and the evolution of an internal reform agenda. Backed by the mandate of the Berlin European Council which convened within two weeks of the Santer Commission's resignation, it argues that the Commission was finally able to undertake wide-ranging reform (the first puzzle).

The third part examines the content of the Kinnock reforms. It points to how the Commission extended the reform programme beyond the areas highlighted by the CIE (CIE 1999b)   the second puzzle   as evidence that the Commission leadership perceived the European Council mandate as a once-in-a-generation opportunity to modernize the organization and how it drew largely on internal diagnoses of the organization's weaknesses and prescriptions for reform. The fourth section considers the factors that account for the success of the Kinnock reforms against the pessimistic predictions of the theoretical and empirical literature (the third puzzle).

THE COMMISSION'S PREDICAMENT

The Commission faces a structural problem with regard to administrative reform, the identification of which is a key to understanding and resolving the three puzzles outlined above. This arises from two conditions which make external intervention a necessary condition for meaningful reform. The first is the presence of obstacles to managerial change inside the Commission itself. The second is the location of decision-making authority with regard to the rules governing staffing and financial management procedures in the hands of the Council and the European Parliament, bodies that show little interest in its internal operation.

Constraints, internal and external

The Commission leadership faces signi"cant impediments in efforts to bring about organizational change. First, the Commission s administrative culture places a high value on policy work, associated by of" cials with the Commission s role as the motor of integration and its mission to promote ever closer union. Management and managerial tasks, by contrast, have typically been regarded as mundane, insigni"cant, and a distraction from the institution s real work (Hooghe 2001; Laffan 1997; Abélès *et al.* 1993; Stevens and Stevens 2001). For much of its history, of" cials   and indeed members of the Commission have measured their career success in terms of the number and importance of policy initiatives for which they were responsible (Hooghe 1999a, 1999b, 2001). This hierarchy of values is reinforced by the priorities of member governments. They are concerned primarily with policy outputs and actions, not administrative processes. Second, the Commission s multinational composition has not been conducive to concerted action in regard to administrative change or to management more generally. Commissioners and of" cials drawn from national administrations with very different cultures and values have found it dif" cult to agree on a diagnosis of the organization s problems and the importance that should be attributed to them, still less on whether and what action should be taken to resolve them (Shore 2000: 198).

The staff unions have also proved to be an obstacle to reform   a third barrier. The Commission inherited the *paritaire* system from the French and German administrative traditions (Stevens and Stevens 2001: 56   60), where staff representatives play an important role in the running of the administration. The staff unions were well resourced and occupied a privileged position within the organization. Their representatives sat on myriad committees at various levels, taking decisions in regard to working conditions, personnel and other issues. Not only were the staff unions well placed to oppose initiatives which they considered as endangering their status or job security, but they have demonstrated a tendency towards militancy. They have on occasion been able to mobilize mass support among Commission of" cials to counter reform initiatives.

The dispersal of power within the Commission has been a hindrance   a fourth obstacle. The Commission is a pillarized and fragmented organization that lacks the strong leadership which analyses of reform highlight as important (Pollitt and Boucrkaert 2004: 50, 58   9). Its Directorates-General are baronies or " efdoms , formally equal, that have priorities and interests that they " ercely protect. Individual departments rather than the Commission as a whole are the focus of loyalty on the part of of" cials. In such an environment, co-ordination is dif" cult and leadership precarious. Moreover, the principle of collegiality has acted against an accumulation of power at the Commission s centre. Despite the strengthening of the Commission Presidency since the Treaty of

Amsterdam, the Commission President, unlike the head of government in national political systems, does not have the authority to impose organizational change.

The challenge presented by these internal barriers is compounded by the Commission s relative powerlessness in respect of the regulations that govern its staff and "nancial management procedures.[4] Authority to amend these rules lies with member governments, sometimes acting jointly with the European Parliament. The working conditions of Commission staff, their rights and obligations, are set out in the Staff Regulations, which were adopted in 1961 and codi"ed in 1968. These detailed rules apply to the of"cials of all European Union (EU) institutions (except the European Investment Bank and the European Central Bank) and cover all aspects of personnel policy. As Stevens and Stevens (2001: 46) observe, they impose a rigid, law-based framework ... on the scope for management to introduce change with any amendment requiring laborious procedures involving consultation "rst with staff representatives and then with the inter-institutional staff regulations committee before a proposal can be put to the Council of Ministers .

Salaries and the material conditions of EU of"cials are governed by a separate but also legally binding (and complex) formula, known as the method , which is set out in a Council Regulation. Under the method, which was introduced in 1976 to expedite and depoliticize the issue of pay, salaries are reviewed each year on the basis of an index prepared by the Statistical Of"ce in agreement with the national statistical of"ces in the member states (Stevens and Stevens 2001: 46) and adjusted annually in line with the purchasing power of remuneration in member state administrations. Decisions on staf"ng and recruitment, meanwhile, are made by the Budgetary Authority, which authorize[s], not only an overall appropriation for staff expenditure, but a speci"c number of posts at different levels (Commission 1979: 3). A further illustration of the Commission s dependence on outside bodies is the so-called geographical quota ,[5] which until the Prodi Commission was an important factor in making senior appointments. According to this convention, which though unwritten was rigorously observed, each member state could expect a certain number of its nationals in top jobs.

Finally, "nancial management and control are governed by the Financial Regulation adopted in 1970. This regulation establishes a framework that applies to all the EU institutions that receive funding through the budget the same that are covered by the Staff Regulations. It sets out rules governing the raising and spending of all EU funds, and in its original version, which followed the French model, divided responsibility between a "nancial controller, authorizing of"cer, and accounting of"cer. It also provided for the scrutiny of expenditure *ex post*. Though updated subsequently, its key features remained unchanged until the Regulation was amended in 2002 as part of the Kinnock reforms. Like the Staff Regulations, it is a legislative act that can only be amended by the Council and Parliament. Owing to its complexity and the number of parties it affects, it is costly and time-consuming to reform.

The perils of external dependence

The dif"culty for the Commission leadership was not only that its internal administration was governed by rules decided by other bodies, but that the latter had little reason to show interest in the internal management of the organization.

Member governments were concerned to safeguard their power of appointment over Commissioners and the presence of their nationals in the upper echelons of the services, but beyond this they had little incentive to invest time in matters that were complex, sensitive, and not salient to their domestic constituencies. Policy decisions and other decisional outputs at the EU level were far more consequential. It would take exceptional circumstances for the administration of the Commission to be suf"ciently important for governments to invest scarce political resources in seeking reform.

At the domestic level, governments can increase their political capital by talking of the need for, or proposing, administrative reform. As Pollitt and Bouckaert observe: [a]nnouncing reforms, criticizing bureaucracy, praising new management techniques, promising improved services ... help to attract favourable attention to the politicians who espouse them (2000: 6). In practice, the pursuit of reform is invariably dif"cult, but it is an undertaking that resonates favourably with citizens. The same is not usually true of the EU. Though the Commission may be a useful target and Brussels bashing a popular sport, calling for Commission reform, still less embarking on it, is not guaranteed to win votes. EU institutions (unlike many EU policies) operate out of the public gaze and are generally too distant for their inner workings to be of interest. Even if Union-level bodies are perceived as inef"cient or ineffectual, governments can deploy a variety of strategies to manage the problem short of committing scarce resources to the pursuit of reform.

Though the incentive structure facing the European Parliament differs from that confronted by national governments   Members of the European Parliament (MEPs) are much more likely to take an interest in Commission administration whether as part of an agenda to extend parliamentary scrutiny or in performance of their routine duties to control the executive   it does not have the same leverage as governments. It has the power to sanction the Commission, but whereas support from the European Council for an initiative of the Commission President to improve "nancial management procedures, to introduce greater accountability of technical assistance of"ces (TAOs) or to reward performance may strengthen the latter s hand, the European Parliament does not command the same authority.

The Commission in crisis

The lack of interest that governments had shown in Commission administration changed with the political crisis provoked by the resignation of the Santer Commission in March 1999. The Commission s demise was the outcome, first, of growing concern in relation to EU finances shown by the Parliament in the 1990s and, second, of suspicions of nepotism, notably in regard to Directorate-General (DG) XXII (Education, Training, and Youth) under the responsibility of Commissioner Edith Cresson, that were given apparent substance by documents delivered to a leading MEP by a disaffected Commission official. Although a censure vote called by the Parliament failed to muster sufficient votes in January 1998, the Commission agreed to create a CIE to investigate allegations of fraud, mismanagement and nepotism laid against it.[6] The Committee was asked to submit a first report by mid-March and a more wide-ranging review of the Commission s culture, practices and procedures in a second report within the context of issues arising in its first (CIE 1999a: 1.1.7).

When the Committee presented its findings in March 1999, the Commission voted to resign rather than face another censure vote. Although the report found no evidence that any member of the Commission had benefited from fraudulent dealings, it concluded that there had been instances where Commissioners or the Commission as a whole bear responsibility for instances of fraud, irregularities or mismanagement in their services or areas of special responsibility (CIE 1999a: 137). The CIE reported evidence of poor management in three programmes (tourism, MEDA, and Leonardo da Vinci), found problems in the award of contracts, and expressed general concerns in relation to the functioning of TAOs. In its controversial but widely quoted last line, the report concluded that [i]t is becoming difficult to find anyone who has even the slightest sense of responsibility. [7] After a tense debate within the College, the Commission tendered its resignation.

In the face of an institutional crisis, member governments were forced to take action. Heads of State and Government met in Berlin ten days after the Commission s resignation, and nominated Romano Prodi as Commission President-designate. They also issued the following reform mandate to the incoming Commission:

> The Commission should speedily put into effect the necessary reforms, in particular for the improvement of its organization, management and financial control. In order to do this, the next Commission ought to give urgent priority to launching a programme of far-reaching modernization and reform. In particular, all means should be used in order to ensure that whenever Community funds, programmes or projects are managed by the Commission, its services are suitably structured to ensure highest standards of management integrity and efficiency.
>
> (European Council 1999)

Prodi announced that a Commission Vice President   the post that would be occupied by Neil Kinnock   would be charged with leading the reform and undertook to abide by the recommendations of the CIE s second report, which was due for publication in the autumn.

In summary, the crisis of March 1999 compelled the European Council to address the questions raised by the European Parliament and the CIE about the Commission s management. The mandate from the Union s political leaders offered the Commission leadership an escape from its historic reform predicament and an opportunity to address the organization s shortcomings of which, as the discussion in the following section indicates, it had long been aware, but which it had been unable to remedy.

A HISTORY OF FAILED INITIATIVES, 1978–99

Members of the College and senior of"cials, particularly in the Secretariat General, had monitored the Commission s operation and been conscious of its weaknesses from its earliest days (Levy 2004). In the late 1970s, the Commission launched the "rst of what would be a series of reform initiatives. Though they largely ended in failure, these efforts showed the development of an internal reform agenda that anticipated many of the recommendations made in the CIE reports and that would inform the measures implemented by Kinnock.

A short history of administrative reform

Though Emile Noël, the Commission s " rst Secretary General, had commissioned reports on aspects of the administration in the 1960s, the "rst published review appeared in 1979, following the creation by Commission President Roy Jenkins of a committee under the chairmanship of Dirk Spierenburg to examine its internal operation. The Spierenburg report drew attention to a certain lack of cohesion in the College of Commissioners, an imbalance between portfolios, insuf"cient co-ordination among senior of"cials, a maldistribution of staff between departments, and shortcomings in the career structure of the civil service of the Commission (Commission 1979: para. 1.3.4). Although there was some attempt at follow up and some action taken, many of the weaknesses identi"ed in 1979 still needed to be addressed . . . in 2000 (Stevens and Stevens 2006: 434).

A second set of initiatives was launched in the 1980s by Henning Christophersen, Commissioner for Personnel and Administration, and Richard Hay, Director-General of DG IX. Their main aim was to improve the quality of management, to devolve greater responsibility to Directors-General and to develop a tier of middle management. At the same time, investment was made in information technology and training, an equal opportunities programme was developed, and efforts made towards bringing an end to irregularities in staff recruitment. An Inspectorate General was created to evaluate staff deployment, and a screening exercise launched to examine the use of human resources. These initiatives were not part of a sustained effort, however, and did not deliver major results.

Awareness of the organization s de"ciencies was further acknowledged towards the end of the third Delors Commission. First, an outgoing senior of"-cial, Philippe Petit-Laurent, reported in 1994 that few of the problems identi"ed by Spierenburg had been resolved (Stevens and Stevens 2006: 433 4). Second, the Schmidhuber memorandum, drafted by a departing Budget

Commissioner, highlighted problems in "nancial management and anticipated some of the criticisms that would later appear in the CIE s "rst report (CIE 1999a). It observed that the services paid too little attention to how policies were "nanced, that they were overly reliant on a centralized "nancial control function to detect problems, and that the evaluation of spending programmes was inadequate (Laffan 1997: 181). The document was adopted at the last meeting of the Delors Commission.

The Santer College was the "rst to make administrative questions a main Commission priority with Erkki Liikanen, Commissioner for Personnel and Administration, taking the lead in efforts to modernize the Commission administration. A series of initiatives aimed at introducing greater "nancial awareness and decentralizing responsibility for budgetary and personnel matters was launched under the rubric of Tomorrow s Commission . The "rst, Sound and Ef"cient Management programme (SEM 2000), launched in 1997, was directed at "nancial management (Stevens and Stevens 2001: 187 92; Levy 2002: 74 6). The second, Modernization of Administration and Personnel Policy (MAP 2000), sought to decentralize and simplify procedures for managing and organizing staff. A screening exercise to investigate how of"cials were distributed across the organization a third element was conducted between November 1997 and May 1999.

These efforts soon ran into dif"culties, however.[8] The proposals had been drawn up by a small circle of of"cials inside DG IX (Personnel and Administration). Though the ideas under discussion re"ected conventional wisdom in public administration, they were interpreted as a threat to the Commission s institutional autonomy by some within the organization. When the staff unions were informed in April 1998 that the College was to consider a reform programme in May and consult them about it the following month, they objected both to the plan to make the consultation documents available not just to themselves but to all staff, and to any discussion by the College of Commissioners until they had had their say (Stevens and Stevens 2006: 437). In an increasingly charged climate, the leaking of the Caston report , an internal discussion document which contained proposals for reforming the Staff Regulations, notably to replace the existing four-category career structure (A, B, C, D) with one based on two broad categories to end grade in"ation in the staff report system and to enshrine merit as the principal criterion for promotion, made it easy for the impression [to take] hold that the Commission was secretly planning a major assault on the cherished rights and independence of the European civil service (Stevens and Stevens 2006: 437).[9] The unions called for a strike on 30 April which attracted wide support among staff. As a result, the Caston report was disowned and a group representing management and staff convened under the chairmanship of David Williamson (Secretary General of the Commission, 1987 97) to discuss personnel issues. Its proposals, though agreed by both sides and reported in November 1998, were modest, traditional (Stevens and Stevens 2001: 192 3), and secured none of the changes originally proposed.

This brief survey shows not only that the view of the Commission as an organization unreflective about its internal operation is mistaken, but also that in its diagnoses and the issues that it targeted, the leadership anticipated criticisms made in the CIE report and prefigured many of the themes of the Kinnock reforms. These included procedures relating to promotion, appraisal and career structure, the undervaluation of management skills, weaknesses in financial management, and the inefficient allocation of resources to the Commission leadership. It also shows that the staff unions came effectively to exercise a veto power over personnel policy. In the absence of interest on the part of member state governments, moreover, the Commission leadership lacked the resources to affect significant change.

EXPANSION OF THE REFORM PROGRAMME: AN OPPORTUNITY SEIZED

Looking at the sequence of events in 1999 and 2000 it would be easy to conclude that the reform exercise and its content were imposed on the Commission by outside parties. While the European Council had instructed the Commission to undertake far-reaching modernization in March, the CIE set out its recommendations in its second report (1999b) in September and a chastened Commission presented its reform White Paper. Such an inference would, however, be mistaken. Closer inspection reveals the blueprint drawn up by the Commission, and still more the reform programme actually implemented during Prodi s tenure, to be more wide-ranging than the CIE s prescriptions (1999b). The use made of internal experience and expertise in the reform process, the specific targeting of areas that had proved to be a stumbling block in the past, and the incorporation of ideas that had featured in earlier reform initiatives suggest a different reading; namely, that the Commission leadership seized the opportunity to implement a wide-ranging modernization programme.[10]

The reform White Paper

The Commission s blueprint for reform, adopted by the College on 1 March 2000 (Commission 2000), set out 98 actions under four headings. The first heading, A Culture Based on Service, underlined the principles that informed the reform (independence, responsibility, accountability, efficiency, and transparency) and proposed measures covering conduct, interaction with citizens and access to EU documentation. The second proposed a new system for planning and organizing the work of the Commission. Based on activity-based management (ABM), it was designed to introduce greater predictability and better resource allocation. An annual Policy Strategy agreed by the College would form the basis of work programmes for each of the services and each DG would be required to evaluate its activities at the end of the cycle. A new framework for delegation to executive agencies, decentralized decision-making and a simplification of administrative procedures, were also proposed under this heading.

With respect to human resources   the third heading   the White Paper incorporated the CIE s recommendations on staff unions, national balances, training, mobility, career advice, and reform of the staff reports and promotions system, as well as those relating to clearer rules regarding professional incompetence, improved practice in the " eld of disciplinary responsibility, and better management performance. It also set out proposals on recruitment, mobility, underperformance, non-permanent staff, and discipline. However, the measures ultimately adopted in the area of staff policy went even further than those outlined in the reform White Paper. They were formulated within a special group chaired by Niels Ersbøll, a former Secretary General of the Council Secretariat, which included representatives of management and the unions, and which was created to discuss the most important changes concerning personnel, notably career structure, promotion and mobility.[11]

Finally, in the area of "nancial control and management, the White Paper proposed the creation of an entirely new architecture to replace the traditional system of centralized *ex ante* control. A key change was to make authorizing of"-cers in the services directly responsible for approval of expenditure. Accountability was further strengthened by a decentralization of "nancial responsibilities to Directors-General, who each year would be required to give their signed personal assurance af"rming that expenditure had been used appropriately. A new Central Financial Service, with a network of directors, was created with an oversight and advisory role, and the audit system overhauled, strengthened and separated from "nancial control. Auditing would be conducted by units inside each service, within the wider Commission by an Internal Audit Service, and externally by the Court of Auditors.

Broadening the reform

A close reading of CIE II reveals as evidence for the opportunist reform thesis an overlap with earlier Commission initiatives in terms of the problem areas that it had identi"ed. These included key aspects of personnel policy including linking promotion more closely to performance, improving the system of appraising staff, rationalizing the career structure, giving greater value to management, increasing mobility, and improving training and career guidance (see CIE 1999b: pt 6.114), as well as "nancial management, where CIE II contained echoes of the Schmidhuber memorandum and SEM 2000. It also shows the extent to which the Commission leadership expanded the scope of the reform beyond the report s 90 recommendations. For example, though CIE II (CIE 1999b: 108 39) discussed the conduct of of"cials, internal communication, and transparency at length, its recommendations were somewhat narrow. The reform White Paper, by contrast, called for action across a broad front and included proposals for a code on administrative behaviour, as well as action to improve consultation with representatives of civil society, the Commission s use of information technology, and the settlement of payments.

The new framework for priority-setting and resource allocation provides a further example of expansion by the Commission, since the measures set out in the reform White Paper were not pre"gured in CIE II, though they had been a recurrent theme of earlier reform attempts. CIE II made few prescriptions in this regard, but the Commission leadership made giving management a higher pro"le and improving managerial skills a key focus of the reform programme. Its actions under this heading provide a very clear illustration of the opportunist thesis : how the Commission used the opportunity to implement changes in dif"cult areas, where the room for manoeuvre had been limited in the past.

Perhaps the most dramatic example relates to personnel policy. Though discussion of staff measures in the main text of CIE II accounted for more than a third of the document (52 pages out of 140), the 13 recommendations it put forward were somewhat vague and not especially radical. Though, for instance, it called for reform of the staff reports and promotions system (recommendation 70), it stated explicitly that: What is really required is not an overhaul of the Staff Regulations . . . but simply correct application of the rules and principles set out therein (CIE 1999b: 19; see also section 6.2.4). Similarly, CIE II pointed to possible risks of stagnation and in"exibility in the Commission s career structure, but called only for solutions to be considered (CIE 1999b: 68).

In both instances, the Commission s ambitions and its ultimate achievements were more far-reaching. In the reform White Paper, the Commission called for both a new system of staff appraisal (2000: 27) and a more linear career system (2000: 26). As a result of negotiations within the Ersbøll group, it secured the replacement of the four-category structure with two   much like the Caston report had proposed a decade earlier   and reformed staff appraisal through the introduction of Career Development Review, which it linked to promotion and career management. It later added a series of measures designed to improve working conditions in the Commission, including family-friendly policies and allowances, and gender and sex equality rights   all introduced at the instigation of Commission leadership in areas where CIE II had been silent.

Finally, the Commission implemented measures that would feature among CIE II s recommendations prior to the latter s publication. While the caretaker Commission adopted codes of conduct on the behaviour of EU Commissioners and on relations between Commissioners and their departments, Prodi committed the Commission in July 1999 to introducing new rules for senior appointments, individual accountability of Commissioners to the Commission President, and reducing the size of *cabinets*, while increasing the multinationality of their composition.

Drawing on internal experience and expertise

As well as the overlap in content, the design of the reform strategy was devised explicitly to draw on internal expertise and experience. If the exercise had involved no more than a transposition of CIE II, the process would have been organized very differently. Instead, Kinnock created a Task Force composed of of"cials from all parts and all levels of the Commission. The idea was that, although it would attempt to learn as much as it could from other administrations that had implemented reform (see Bear"eld 2004: 17 18), the reform would be shaped to meet the speci"c and particular needs of the Commission. As well as working its way through earlier Commission texts, the Task Force utilized the services expertise and tested proposals against the insider experience of of"cials. A series of Planning and Co-ordination Groups composed of of"cials from relevant services worked on various sections of the reform programme. The Task Force, the Kinnock *cabinet*, and Kinnock personally invited and received suggestions and feedback from individual of"cials.

Furthermore, it is important to recall that leading "gures in the Kinnock *cabinet* and the reform Task Force had "rst-hand knowledge of the organization s strengths (notably, the calibre of its staff) and weaknesses (for example, its failure to reward merit and sometimes sti"ing procedures). This included Neil Kinnock himself, who had served as Commissioner for Transport in the Santer Commission, senior of"cials from DG Administration and Personnel, including some who had been associated with earlier reform initiatives,[12] and a number of other high "yers.[13] Their experience of the institution s shortcomings, in particular as regards personnel issues, was important in informing the reform agenda.

In summary, although the reform programme incorporated CIE II s recommendations, many addressed concerns of which the Commission leadership had been long aware or repeated proposals from earlier reform initiatives. Moreover, the drafting of the reform blueprint drew extensively on insider experience. Thus, the Kinnock reforms bear the imprint of a pre-existing internal reform agenda and responded to internal concerns.

EXPLAINING THE SUCCESS OF THE KINNOCK REFORMS

The third of the three puzzles casts the Kinnock programme as an anomaly for the main theories of administrative reform, which are pessimistic about change that is deliberate, successful, and radical. This section argues that key assumptions made by these theories do not apply in the Commission s case and that any plausible account of the Commission s reform experience must address the speci"c character of the organization s institutional setting, which imposes important conditions on reform possibilities and Kinnock s reform leadership, which was a model of change management.

Theorizing reform

An exhaustive critical survey of the relevant theoretical literature is beyond the limits of this article. However, it is possible to identify four dif"culties that the Kinnock reforms and more generally the Commission s reform predicament raise for the main theories of administrative reform. The "rst concerns the source of the reform agenda. A premise common to all the aforementioned theoretical approaches is that a reform agenda is developed outside an administration and imposed upon it. Although bureaucrats may temper and minimize (NI) or block reform initiatives (WO, CP A), these approaches do not generally expect a reform agenda to emerge and develop inside an administration. As the Kinnock reforms and the history of its earlier failed reform efforts show, this assumption does not hold in the case of the Commission.

A second problem concerns the motivations of those working for the administration and their attitudes towards change. The aforementioned theories treat bureaucrats as inherently conservative and perceiving reform as a threat to their status and able to mobilize resources to defend the status quo. Where politicians persist, bureaucrats either move to obstruct reform (WO, CP A) or to interpret it through pre-existing norms and values (NI), resulting in at most incremental change. However, the Kinnock reforms suggest that programmes envisaging genuine change can in fact be developed within the administration that is the subject of reform. The Commission case shows that when bureaucrats are entrusted with the task of designing and implementing reform,[14] they do not necessarily attempt to resist by blocking (WO) or shirking (CP A), nor do they necessarily interpret external pressure in terms of existing norms (NI). Indeed, they may extend and expand its scope signi"cantly beyond what was originally demanded. The experience of the Kinnock reforms suggests that the motivations of bureaucrats, particularly in senior positions, are more complex and may be more mixed than in the theories discussed here (John et al. 2005).[15] Some top-level bureaucrats may in fact be courageous risk-takers, entrepreneurs who are not only willing to accept change, but prepared to bring it about. In terms of motivation, they may be more concerned about the reputation of their organization than about their future career prospects.[16]

A third dif"culty concerns leadership. While national governments created the opportunity, effective leadership on the part of Kinnock was a crucial factor in its successful implementation (see Kassim 2004a, 2004b). However, most theories of administrative reform are silent on this issue. WO and CP A assume that leaders are to be found among politicians, not bureaucrats, but say little about how and what form leadership takes. NI, by contrast, offers compelling explanations as to why similar comparable institutions produce divergent outcomes, but both its HI and its SI variants proceed from structuralist premises that pay little attention to agency (Hay and Wincott 1998). This neglect is curious when empirical studies of reform show that leadership is a key factor (see Pollitt and Bouckaert 2004; Barzelay and Gallego 2006; for a discussion of leadership and change management, see Fernandez and Rainey 2006).

A "nal dif"culty concerns the terms in which the theories account for reform. WO and CP A approach reform as an interaction between two sets of actors, politicians and bureaucrats, while NI sees reform as an exogenous challenge to an organization conceptualized as a community bound by a commitment to common values. A dif"culty for both sets of theories is that of"cials do not necessarily share the same norms and that, even where they do, they may differ in their readings of what a given norm implies. Existing theories of administrative reform do not easily "t the case of an internally differentiated organization, where, like in the Commission, senior of"cials advocating change are confronted with resistance by staff unions.

An additional problem for WO and CP A is that the construction of reform as a confrontation between politicians and bureaucrats is not instructive for examining the Commission. The politicians bureaucrats dichotomy cannot be applied to the relationship between national governments and the Commission leadership. The composition, functions, and powers of the College disqualify it from categorization as a bureaucracy in the sense of a permanent, career civil service intended by both WO and CP A. In some circumstances, it may be a useful heuristic for understanding the interaction between the College and the services, but this is not so in the case of Commission reform, where a third actor (member governments) plays a crucial role.

CONCLUSION

The Kinnock reforms are an impressive achievement that have rightly attracted the attention of EU scholars and students of administrative reform more generally. However, as this article has shown, important aspects of the reform have been overlooked in existing accounts. This article has drawn attention to some of these neglected features and argues that they support a very different interpretation of the Commission, its awareness of its own failings and its willingness to address its shortcomings, than a simple reading of events might suggest. Rather than a complacent organization, the Commission s efforts between 1979 and 1999 reveal a body aware of its internal de"ciencies, but unable to correct them. In this context, the mandate issued by Heads of State and Government at the Berlin European Council was less an unwelcome imposition than a licence for the Commission leadership to overhaul systems and procedures that members of the College and senior of"cials had long known to be problematic. It seized the opportunity to implement an internal reform agenda that had been developing within the organization since the late 1970s and to address other aspects of its functioning that experience had demonstrated to be problematic. Neither the member states nor the European Parliament played a signi"cant role in the reform process.

The Commission s experience presents an anomaly for existing theories of administrative reform as they do not anticipate or predict that change will be led by the organization targeted for reform. Their assumptions about the source of reform initiatives, the respective preferences of politicians and bureaucrats, and the bureaucrats motivations do not easily "t the Commission s case. Similarly, their expectation that an external impetus to change will be emasculated, particularly if the advocates of reform stand aside after an initial intervention, is not ful"lled in the Commission s case. As an instance of self-reform by delegation, the Kinnock reforms thereby pose an important challenge to the leading theories.

Scholars contend that the structural or institutional context in which reform takes place is likely to condition reform opportunities and outcomes (see, for example, Pollitt and Bouckaert 2004). However, in the Commission s case the relationship between administration, politics, and society differs a great deal from the relationship that obtains at the national level and on which most theorizing about bureaucracy and bureaucratic behaviour is based. One possibility is that the Commission s predicament and the possibility of self-reform delegation arise from an opportunity structure closer to that faced by international administrations than by national bureaucracies. It might therefore be pro"table for future research efforts to be directed toward the experience of these underresearched organizations.

Bibliographical note: Hussein Kassim is Professor of Politics at the School of Political, Social and International Studies at the University of East Anglia, UK.

Address for correspondence: Hussein Kassim, School of Political, Social and International Studies, University of East Anglia, Norwich, NR4 7TJ, UK. email: h.kassim@uea.ac.uk

ACKNOWLEDGEMENTS

I should like to express my gratitude to the two former Commissioners and the many Commission of"cials who very kindly agreed to be interviewed over the past decade as part of the research on which this article draws. I also gratefully acknowledge the Faculty of Arts at Birkbeck, University of London, for the award of a College Research grant, and the British Academy for a small research grant which enabled me to undertake essential "eldwork. I should like to thank those who organized, participated in and attended the workshop Management Reforms in International and Supranational Organizations at the University of Konstanz, 30 June 1 July 2006, EU Consent workshops on the European Commission in Edinburgh and Paris on 15 16 February 2006 and 22 23 June 2006 respectively, and the panel Reforming European Organizations: Management Change in the European Commission and the European Parliament, EUSA Biennial Conference, Montreal, 18 May 2007, as well as "ve anonymous referees, and especially Michael W. Bauer for comments on earlier versions of this article. Special debts of gratitude are owed to Liesbet Hooghe, Peter John, Roger Levy, John Peterson, David Spence, Anne Stevens, and Handley Stevens, from whom I have learned a great deal in conversations over the years about the topics addressed in this article, and to Sara Connolly for useful suggestions. The usual disclaimer applies.

NOTES

1 In the limited sense that a reform programme was drafted, negotiated and adopted. The extent to which the reform has been successful in substantive terms is discussed by Coull and Lewis (2003) and Bauer (2008).

2 Historical institutionalism and sociological institutionalism are, of course, distinct approaches (see Hall and Taylor 1996). However, they share important commonalities with respect to how they explain the way in which organizations respond to external pressures to reform.

3 Nor without considerable contortion can theories of public policy change, such as Hall (1993) or Kingdon (1985, 1999), be made to "t the Commission case.

4 Nor does the Commission have any in"uence over the size of the College. The increasing number of Commissioners has compounded the dif"culty of managing the services, since each member of the Commission has responsibility for one or more Directorates-General associated with his or her portfolio(s).

5 The geographical quota disappeared with the Kinnock reforms, giving the Commission autonomy with regard to the appointment of its most senior of"cials (see Egeberg 2003).

6 See above. See Of"cial Journal C104, 11 April 1999 for details concerning the Committee s composition and terms of reference.

7 See Bulletin of the European Union 3, 1.10.12 for Santer s response.

8 This section draws extensively on Stevens and Stevens (2006: 436 7).

9 They included: partially linking pay and performance, setting cost effectiveness as an objective, and demonstrating that new policies should add value.

10 Interviews conducted with senior Commission of"cials in the mid- and late 1990s prior to the 1999 crisis revealed high levels of dissatisfaction with staf"ng practices, the staff report system and promotion procedures which gave greater emphasis to seniority and nationality than performance, as well as with the lack of management in the organization. See Hooghe (2001); also Coull and Lewis (2003: 8).

11 A strike was called by the unions for 19 March 2001, following the adoption of proposals on personnel management by the College, but was called off owing to lack of support.

12 Nicholas David Bear"eld is one example.

13 For example, Claude Chene, who chaired the Task Force, joined the Commission in 1976. He headed Karel Van Miert s cabinet (1992 94, 1997 99), was a member of Stanley Clinton-Davis s cabinet (1986 88), and in between was Director of Air Transport (1995 96) and Personnel (1995). Philip Lowe, who served as Kinnock s chef de cabinet for an important phase of the reform (2000 02), joined the Commission in 1973, had occupied the same role for Bruce Millan (1989 91), been Director of Rural Development in DG VI (1991 93), Director of the Merger Task Force (1993 95), been Neil Kinnock s chef de cabinet (1995 97) and Director General for Development (1997 2000).

14 During the entire reform process, the member states intervened only with regard to the personnel chapter and then only with respect to pensions, where future liabilities and expenditure were a concern. The European Parliament, by contrast, was concerned less with the substance of the changes to personnel and more with securing equal footing with the Council in regard to the Staff Regulations.

15 A similar charge can be made in regard to rational choice models (Niskanen 1971; Dunleavy 1991), though unfortunately there is insuf"cient space to develop this argument further here.

16 It is not at all clear, for example, if the individuals, members of the Commission or senior of"cials, who played a leading role were self-interested in the sense intended by Rational Choice Models (RCMs). Neither Prodi nor Kinnock stood to gain materially or to advance their careers. Senior of"cials, meanwhile, were risking their reputations among their peers by their association with an exercise that aroused considerable opposition within the organization, as correspondence to the staff magazine, Commission en Direct, and the protests of many of the staff unions revealed.

REFERENCES

Abélès, M., Bellier, I. and McDonald, M. (1993) Approche anthropologique de la Commission européenne, Brussels: Report for the European Commission, unpublished.

Barzelay, M. and Gallego, R. (2006) From new institutionalism to institutional processualism : advancing knowledge about public management policy change, *Governance* 19(4): 531 57.

Bauer, M.W. (2007a) Introduction: Management reforms in international organizations, in M.W. Bauer and C. Knill (eds), *Management Reforms in International Organizations*, Reihe Verwaltungsressourcen und Verwaltungsstrukturen, Baden-Baden: Nomos, pp. 11 23.

Bauer, M.W. (2007b) The politics of reforming the European Commission administration, in M.W. Bauer and C. Knill (eds), *Management Reforms in International Organizations*, Baden-Baden: Nomos, pp. 54 69

Bauer, M.W. (2008) Diffuse anxieties, deprived entrepreneurs: Commission reform and middle management, *Journal of European Public Policy* 15(5): 691 707.

Bauer, M.W. and Knill, C. (2007) Conclusions: Management reforms in international organizations, in M.W. Bauer and C. Knill (eds), *Management Reforms in International Organizations*, Baden-Baden: Nomos, pp. 191 99.

Bear"eld, N.D. (2004) Reforming the European Commission: driving reform from the grassroots, *Public Policy and Administration* 19(3): 13 24.

Brunnson, N. and Olsen, J.P. (1993) *The Reforming Organization*, London: Routledge.

Capano, G. (2003) Administrative traditions and policy change: when policy paradigms matter. The case of Italian administrative reform during the 1990s, *Public Administration* 81(4): 781 801.

Christensen, J.G. (1997) Interpreting administrative change: bureaucratic self-interest and institutional inheritance in government, *Governance* 10(2): 143 74.

Claude, I. (1971) *Swords into Ploughshares: The Problems and Progress of International Organization*, 4th edn, New York: McGraw-Hill.

Commission (1979) Proposals for reform of the Commission of the European Communities and its services (Spierenburg Report).

Commission of the European Communities (2000) *Reforming the Commission. A White Paper   Parts I and II*, COM (2000) 200 " nal/2, 5 April 2000.

Committee of Independent Experts (CIE) (1999a) *First Report on Allegations regarding Fraud, Mismanagement and Nepotism in the European Commission*, 15 March 1999.

Committee of Independent Experts (CIE) (1999b) *Second Report on Reform of the Commission. Analysis of Current Practice and Proposals for Tackling Mismanagement, Irregularities and Fraud*, 10 September 1999.

Coull, J. and Lewis, C. (2003) The impact reform of the staff regulations in making the Commission a more modern and ef"cient organisation: an insider s perspective, *EIPAscope* 3: 2 9.

Dunleavy, P. (1991) *Democracy, Bureaucracy and Public Choice*, London: Harvester Wheatsheaf.

Egeberg, M. (2003) *Organising Institutional Autonomy in a Political Context: Enduring Tensions in the European Commission s Development*, Oslo: ARENA Working Paper Series 04/02.

European Council (1999) Presidency Conclusions, Berlin, 24 and 25 March. Available: http://www.consilium.europa.eu/ueDocs/cms_Data/docs/pressData/en/ec/ACFB2.html (accessed 23 May 2008).

European Parliament (1999) *The Committee: Members, Terms of Reference and Organization*, press release, http://www.europarl.europa.eu/experts/press/mandaten_en.htm, accessed on 27 January 2007.

Fernandez, S. and Rainey, H.G. (2006) Managing successful organizational change in the public sector, *Public Administration Review* 66(2): 168 76.

Geri, L.R. (2001) New public management and the reform of international organizations, *International Review of Administrative Sciences* 67(3): 445 60.

Hall, P.A. (1993) Policy paradigms, social learning, and the state: the case of economic policymaking in Britain, *Comparative Politics* 25(3): 275 96.

Hall, P.A. and Taylor, C.R. (1996) Political science and the three new institutionalisms, *Political Studies* 44(5): 936 57.

Hay, C. and Wincott, D. (1998) Structure, agency and historical institutionalism, *Political Studies* 46(5): 951 7.

Hooghe, L. (1999a) Supranational activists or intergovernmental agents? Explaining orientations of senior Commission of cials towards European integration, *Comparative Political Studies* 32(4): 435 63.

Hooghe, L. (1999b) Images of Europe: orientations to European integration among senior Commission of cials, *British Journal of Political Science* 29(2): 345 73.

Hooghe, L. (2001) *The Commission and the Integration of Europe: Images of Governance*, Cambridge: Cambridge University Press.

John, P., Stoker, G. and Gains, F. (2005) Explaining bureaucratic attitudes to political control: the reform of the English local government executive in 2000. Institutional design and the political control of bureaucracy: the responses of bureaucrats to reform in English local government, Unpublished paper, available at http://www.ipeg.org.uk/staff/john/?PHPSESSID=5cbfbdf6add798776dea36ff66348d7d#publications.

Kassim, H. (2004a) An historic achievement. Administrative reform under the Prodi Commission, in D. Dimitrakopoulos (ed.), *The Changing Commission*, Manchester: Manchester University Press, pp. 33 62.

Kassim, H. (2004b) The Kinnock reforms in perspective: why reforming the Commission is an heroic, but thankless task, *Public Policy and Administration* 19(3): 25 41.

Kellner, P. and Crowther-Hunt, L. (1980) *Britain s Civil Servants: An Inquiry into Britain s Ruling Class*, London: Macdonald.

Kingdon, J.W. (1984) *Agendas, Alternatives and Public Policy*, 1st edn, Boston: Little Brown.

Kingdon, J.W. (1995) *Agendas, Alternatives and Public Policies*, 2nd edn, New York: HarperCollins.

Laffan, B. (1997) *The Finances of the European Union*, Basingstoke: Macmillan.

Levy, R. (2002) Modernising EU programme management, *Public Policy and Administration* 17(1): 72 89.

Levy, R. (2004) Critical success factors in public management reform: the case of the European Commission, *International Review of Administrative Sciences* 69(4): 553 66.

Moe, T. (1984) The new economics of organization, *American Journal of Political Science* 28(4): 739 77.

Moe, T. (1989) The politics of bureaucratic structure, in J. Chubb and P. Peterson (eds), *Can the Government Govern?*, Washington, DC: Brookings Institution, pp. 267 329.

Niskanen, W. (1971) *Bureaucracy and Representative Government*, Chicago: Aldine.

Pollack, M.A. (2003) *The Engines of Integration. Delegation, Agency and Agenda Setting in the EU*, Oxford: Oxford University Press.

Pollitt, C. and Bouckaert, G. (2000) *Public Management Reform. A Comparative Analysis*, Oxford: Oxford University Press.

Pollitt, C. and Bouckaert, G. (2004) *Public Management Reform. A Comparative Analysis*, 2nd edn, Oxford: Oxford University Press.

Putnam, R. (1974) The political attitudes of senior civil servants in Europe: a preliminary report , *British Journal of Political Science* 3(4): 257 90.

Sahlin-Andersson, K. (2002) National, international, and transnational constructions of new public management , in T. Christensen and P. Lægreid (eds), *New Public Management: The Transformation of Ideas and Practice*, Aldershot: Ashgate.

Schmidt, S. (2000) Only an agenda setter? The European Commission s power over the Council of Ministers , *European Union Politics* 1(1): 37 61.

Shore, C. (2000) *Building Europe. The Cultural Politics of European Integration*, London and New York: Routledge.

Stevens, A. and Stevens, H. (2001) *Brussels Bureaucrats? The Administration of the European Union*, Basingstoke: Palgrave.

Stevens, A. and Stevens, H. (2006) The internal reform of the Commission , in D. Spence and G. Edwards (eds), *The European Commission*, London: John Harper, pp. 454 80.

Suleiman, E. (1974) *Politics, Power and Bureaucracy in France*, Princeton, NJ: Princeton University Press.

Weingast, B. (1984) The Congressional-bureaucratic system: a principal agent perspective (with applications to the SEC) , *Public Choice* 44(1): 147 91.

Wright, V. (1994) Reshaping the state. The implications for public administration , *West European Politics* 17(2): 102 37.

Wright, V. (1998) The paradoxes of administrative reform , in W.J.M. Kickert (ed.), *Public Management and Administrative Reform in Western Europe*, Cheltenham: Edward Elgar, pp. 7 13.

Explaining variation in organizational change: the reform of human resource management in the European Commission and the OECD

Christoph Knill and Tim Balint

1. INTRODUCTION

Much scholarly attention has been devoted to investigation of the driving forces and consequences of the far-reaching national administrative reforms and changes in the public sector in the context of the global wave of new public management (NPM) that swept over Western countries from the early 1980s onwards (Hood 1991; Naschold and Bogumil 2000; Pollitt and Bouckaert 2004). Notwithstanding the fact that the pace and patterns as well as the "ne-tuning of NPM reforms vary across countries, there is hardly any doubt that there is a converging trend away from classical Weberian bureaucracies towards more market-oriented management principles and structures. This process of international diffusion was to a considerable extent fuelled by the communication activities of international organizations, such as the Organization for Economic Co-operation and Development (OECD) in the early 1990s (Hood 1995; Lægreid 2002).

In view of these developments, it is striking that management reforms within these international organizations themselves have so far hardly been subject to comprehensive investigations. We still have limited knowledge about the extent to which international organizations, often considered as crucial diffusion agents with regard to public sector management reforms, actually live up to the standards they promote. It is only recently that the role and functioning of international bureaucracies became a subject of growing importance (cf. Barnett and Finnemore 1999, 2004; Bauer and Knill 2007; Geri 2001; Hooghe 2001; Liese and Weinlich 2006).

In this article, we address this research gap by a comparative analysis of human resource management reforms in the European Commission and the Secretariat of the OECD. We analyse the extent to which both organizations reformed their human resource management structures and procedures in line with NPM principles. This selection of cases is based on the fact that the two organizations differ very sharply with regard to their reform record. While the Commission brought its management structures with regard to many dimensions closely in line with an NPM-like approach, the OECD, by contrast, still represents a more Weberian bureaucracy type when it comes to issues of human resource management.

Moreover, these "ndings are striking in light of the fact that the two organizations   notwithstanding their differences in terms of competences and nature (supranational versus international organization)   share many characteristics. Both organizations can be characterized as international bureaucracies where of"cials with similar educational backgrounds are employed. They were founded at around the same time and are based on legalistic structures and routines, re"ecting the Continental administrative tradition.

In our following analysis we "rst specify our dependent variable *reform of human resource management* (section 2). In a second step, we present our empirical "ndings and show why existing theoretical approaches derived from organization theory are not suf"cient to account for our empirical puzzle (section 3). Based on these considerations we consider in a third step alternative explanatory approaches and theoretical modi"cations of existing theories (section 4). Section 5 concludes.

2. EMPIRICAL FINDINGS: HUMAN RESOURCE MANAGEMENT IN THE EUROPEAN COMMISSION AND THE OECD

To assess the reform of human resource management in the European Commission and the OECD we consider formal changes with regard to the categories recruitment, career structure, staff appraisal, and training (Davies 2002; Vaanholt 1997). The OECD and the European Commission regulate their human resource management by staff regulations and staff rules. The staff rules specify the execution of the regulations and can only be changed by the Secretary General. Changes to the staff regulations are subject to the approval of the member states represented in the Council.

With regard to human resource management, we distinguish the ideal types of Weber s bureaucracy model (BM) (Vaanholt 1997) and the overall concept of NPM for human resource management (Liebel and Oechsler 1992; OECD 1995, 2005b; Pollitt and Bouckaert 2004). NPM is not a single and coherent reform concept and is differently de" ned, interpreted and implemented. Nevertheless, certain universal and internationally approved principles of NPM can be identi" ed, hence representing a general model for reforms in human resource management (Naschold and Bogumil 2000: 84; OECD 2005b: 181). The ideal types and respective indicators are summarized in Table 1.

We " rst consider the *range of reform* by comparing existing patterns of human resource management to an ideal type NPM approach for 1995 and 2007. This gives us an idea about the extent to which each organization moved towards NPM-oriented structures during the observation period. In a second step, we examine the *scale of reform* by comparing the distance to the NPM ideal type for both organizations in 1995 and 2007. In this way, we can judge which organization reformed its human resource management more, and also which organization is now closer to the ideal type.

The extent to which the different dimensions of human resource management re" ect either the BM or NPM ideal type is illustrated by an ordinal scale based on " ve categories, from 0 to 4. The value 0 means that a certain indicator is fully in line with the BM model, value 4 implies full conformity with the NPM ideal. The other values indicate constellations in between the ideal types. Category 1 means that reforms are more BM than NPM, category 2 refers to cases in which characteristics of both ideal types are similarly represented, and category 3 implies that indicators are closer to NPM than BM, although not fully in line with the latter. This distinction is needed because of the fact that empirically we often observe mixtures between BM and NPM elements with regard to the different indicators.

The reform of human resource management in the European Commission

In the European Commission, staff regulations and rules apply to 23,000 permanent of" cials, most of them with contracts for life. Aside from this, there are speci" c regulations for around 7,000 temporary agents, contract agents, seconded national experts, auxiliaries, and trainees, who, however, are excluded from our analysis.

As far as *recruitment* is concerned, the merit principle is the most important criterion in the selection procedure (European Commission 2007b). But in addition to this, a paragraph in the staff regulations ensures national balance, i.e. an appropriate representation of member states nationals. For senior managers, there is a very clear analysis of nationality in order to avoid over-representation or under-representation of certain nationalities, albeit without using a " xed quota (interview 12/05/2006). Furthermore, the standardized selection procedure is sometimes circumvented by parachutage , meaning that

Table 1 Operationalization of the dependent variable

Indicators	Value (BM)	Value (NPM)
Recruitment		
selection procedure in general	formal conditions (e.g. educational background), national balance	merit principle, sophisticated selection methods
selection procedure for senior staff	imprecise selection procedure, unrestricted length of appointment	formal selection procedure, length of appointment related to performance
profile of senior staff	expertise, limited responsibility for resources	management capabilities, responsibility for resources
Career structure		
entrance	usually first grade (salary class) of the respective career	every grade is open to competition
structure	horizontal and quite impermeable	vertical and permeable
basic salary	dependent on grade	dependent on task and responsibility
extra pay	paid automatically and related to seniority	performance-related pay for every official
merit bonus	none	cafeteria system (e.g. monetary and non-monetary incentives)
Staff appraisal		
performance appraisal	not obligatory and seldom	obligatory for every official, yearly target agreement
assessment of future potential	not obligatory and parallel to performance appraisal	obligatory for every official, independent of performance appraisal
senior staff appraisal	none	for every senior official at regular intervals
use of staff appraisal results	hardly connected to promotion (seniority principle) and incentives	directly connected to promotion and awarding of incentives
Training		
budget and hours of training	constant and low	increasing and appropriate
purpose	no explicit strategy	lifelong learning
management training for senior staff	voluntary and limited offer of courses	compulsory and variety of courses

ex-members of the Commissioners cabinets receive tenure more easily than other candidates. Another phenomenon is the submarine approach , where offi‑cials already in possession of "xed-term contracts receive tenure without any selection procedure (Stevens and Stevens 2001). Until the late 1990s, the selection procedure for senior staff was barely formalized and their pro"le was primarily based upon their expertise (Bauer 2008). Since 2001, however, senior staff are recruited by posting of the vacancy internally, rarely also externally. The recent reforms want the head of a unit to be more of a manager than an expert (interview 12/05/2006). For this purpose, the new selection procedure contains an additional layer, the assessment centre method , where candidates have to prove generic competences to become senior managers. The introduction of activity-based management also makes senior staff more accountable in ful"lling certain policy outputs. However, inde"nite contracts still limit personal responsibility and of"cials normally keep their positions until they retire.

The European Commission s *career structure* can be classi"ed as a typical career-based system. Entrance usually takes place at the "rst level (grade) of the respective career. However, the structure has changed considerably. In 1995 it has composed of four horizontal categories with four to eight grades, respectively. The professional staff belonged to category A, followed hierarchically by categories B, C and D. The translators and interpreters had their own career path named LA. At that time, it was dif"cult to be promoted more than two or three times so many of"cials reached the highest grade after 15 to 20 years of service (Stevens and Stevens 2001). The new system, by contrast, contains two function groups and 16 grades. The categories B and C are now classi-"ed as assistants (AST 1-11) and the categories A and LA as administrators (AD 5-16). This structure is more vertical and allows for more merit-based promotion than before (European Commission 2004; interview 12/05/2006). After the reform, of"cials with management responsibilities earn more than their counterparts in the grade without this responsibility, though basic salary is still not linked to the job, but to the grade a person holds. In addition to the basic salary, of"cials receive seniority steps that are paid automatically. During the period of investigation they were reduced from eight to "ve per grade in order to increase the weight of merit and reduce the weight of seniority (interview 12/05/2006). There are still overlaps between the grades, i.e. an assistant with higher seniority can earn more than an administrator. However, the salary increase now proceeds digressively. This means that, after the reform, an of"cial more quickly reaches a position where he does not receive any extra pay simply by staying in his job. This way, the Commission wants to motivate of"cials to make an effort for promotion. Finally, there is a merit bonus.

The *staff appraisal* system has also changed considerably. Now performance appraisal contains a target agreement and is conducted every year and independently of the new assessment of future potential. The appraisal of senior staff was introduced as a pilot scheme and is not yet institutionalized. An important goal during the reform process was to enhance the ef"cient use of staff appraisals as a basis for merit-based promotion. In 1995, almost all of"cials were promoted automatically because of the seniority principle. The performance appraisals did not serve as a valid instrument, because nearly all of"cials received the mark good (interview 12/05/2006). Therefore, a new catalogue of criteria and marks was introduced containing up to 32 merit and priority points. Of"cials can now accumulate their points and are promoted when they reach a certain threshold. However, for of"cials with average performance, automatic promotion still exists. See Table 2 for an overview.

In the 1990s, *training* was not an explicit priority of the Commission. The budget was decreasing and of"cials attended training on average less than three days a year (Stevens and Stevens 2001: 106). Since 2000, however, the budget has more than doubled so of"cials now receive training on more than nine days a year (European Commission 2005). Connected to this "nancial investment was the implementation of a new strategy for a culture of lifelong learning. The goal is to make a more "ne-tuned analysis of what each department or of"cial needs and how training can help to deliver that by coaching, internal consultancy, paying for external training, etc. (interview 12/05/2006). The approach to management training was also revised. Senior staff with responsibility for "nancial and personnel resources are under an obligation to

Table 2 Range of reform in the European Commission

Indicators	1995	2007	Change
Recruitment			
selection procedure in general	2	2	no change
selection procedure for senior staff	0	1	towards NPM, but still closer to BM
profile of senior staff	0	2	towards NPM, but still closer to BM
Career structure			
entrance	1	2	towards NPM, but still closer to BM
structure	0	3	towards NPM
basic salary	0	1	towards NPM, but still closer to BM
extra pay	0	2	towards NPM, but still closer to BM
merit bonus	0	0	no change
Staff appraisal			
performance appraisal	1	4	towards NPM
assessment of future potential	0	4	towards NPM
senior staff appraisal	0	1	towards NPM, but still closer to BM
use of staff appraisal results	0	2	towards NPM, but still closer to BM
Training			
budget and hours of training	0	4	towards NPM
purpose	0	4	towards NPM
management training for senior staff	0	4	towards NPM

attend management courses. On top of this, it is no longer possible to be promoted to a management position without having taken those courses.

The reform of human resource management in the OECD

The staff regulations and rules apply to the 2,000 permanent of"cials in Paris, of whom about 60 per cent have "xed-term and 40 per cent inde"nite contracts (OECD 2004). In addition, there are speci"c regulations for around 300 short-term employees like consultants, trainees and auxiliaries, who, however, are excluded from our analysis.

Starting with the dominant principles in *recruitment,* we "nd minor changes towards NPM during the observation period, with the merit principle playing a major role (interview 15/03/2006). Though the OECD tries to achieve a good mix of representation of member states (national balance), there is no institutionalized committee which controls adherence to this goal. In contrast to the strong merit-based recruitment of regular staff, peculiarities with regard to the so-called project staff have to be emphasized. The latter refers to OECD of"cials "nanced by voluntary contributions from member states for certain projects and positions. It is at the discretion of the OECD directorate that receives the contributions whether the position is advertised, and whether the applicants go through structured selection processes. When it comes to the recruitment of senior staff, it is at the discretion of the Secretary General whether these positions are advertised. However, in early 2000, the OECD adopted a policy that all senior staff are to be on "xed-term contracts. These contracts are only renewed if performance is satisfactory. Even internal appointees promoted through an internal process have to relinquish their inde"nite contracts if they have them. The pro"le of senior staff is still their expertise although, since the introduction of activity-based management, they are subject to strong performance discipline (interview 15/03/2006). This means that they are accountable and responsible for outputs laid down in the programme of work and budget. Nevertheless, there is no regulation that makes management skills a sine qua non for senior positions.

The *career structure* has remained almost unchanged since the establishment of the OECD. Every position is open to competition so that lateral entrance into the structure is the norm. This structure is composed of the categories A, L, B and C, each having again several seniority steps (OECD 2007). Category A is formed of professional staff (45 per cent), administrative and support staff are in category B, manual or technical staff are in category C, and linguistic staff belong to category L. This system is hierarchical and tends to make it dif"cult for of"cials to progress (interview 15/03/2006). Since the introduction of result-oriented budgeting, some member states have perceived increasing problems in deploying staff "exibly, i.e. in shifting them from one priority task to another (interview 17/03/2006). Some member states even believe that the actual system bars the OECD from attracting and recruiting the best specialists. Furthermore, basic salary is dependent on grade and not (necessarily) on the task or responsibility which a person has. In addition, OECD of"cials automatically receive extra pay by seniority steps. Seldom is this disbursement delayed for a determined period of time because of bad performance (interview 16/03/2006). Senior staff members (grades A7 and A6) account for six to eight possible steps, the other grades for ten to eleven. The higher a person rises, the more extra pay increases. In connection with basic salary, this leads to an over-lapping of grades so that a superior can earn less than his subordinate. Here is an example (interview 17/05/2006): it is only after ten years that a newly recruited superior in grade A5 would reach the salary level of his subordinate in grade A4, who has already received all possible seniority steps. The seniority principle is therefore quite important; performance-related pay does not exist. However, it is possible for the Secretary General to award an of"cial with one or more extra seniority steps in return for particular efforts (merit bonus).

Concerning *staff appraisal,* the whole system was reformed in 1999. Perform-ance appraisal is now binding on all of"cials and is conducted with target agree-ments on a yearly basis. The assessment of future potential is also compulsory. At the moment, in some directorates, there are optional 360-degree feedbacks for the appraisal of senior staff. It is planned to use the results as a basis for promotion and not length of service (interview 15/03/2006). However, the "ve-point scale and the written assessment as a set of criteria for staff appraisals are not suf"ciently linked to promotion or prolongation of contracts (interview 16/03/2006; interview 17/05/2006). From 1995 to 2004 the budget for *training* decreased considerably and reached a very low level (interview 14/03/2006).[1] At the moment, the OECD is rethinking its approach to training, because until now no clear strategy was pursued. See Table 3 for an overview.

The scale of human resource management reforms in comparison

In Table 4, we analyse the *scale of reform* by comparing the changes in the dis-tance to the ideal type NPM model for both organizations for 1995 and 2007. In 1995, we "nd that the human resource management of the OECD was clearly more in line with NPM principles than that of the Commission. Recruit-ment in general and lateral entrance into the career even corresponded to the NPM ideal type. By contrast, almost all indicators reveal an adherence to the BM model in the case of the Commission.

Ten years later, in recruiting staff, the OECD still corresponds more to NPM than the Commission. On the one hand, this is because of the fact that, contrary to the Commission, OECD senior staff members have exclusively performance-linked and temporary contracts. On the other hand, the merit principle is, despite recent problems with the recruitment of project staff, more important than in the Commission. By contrast, the Commission reformed its career structure, which is now based on two function groups. In comparison to the OECD, it provides more opportunities for advancement and less visible overlap of grades. In addition, managers in the Commission receive a basic salary that re"ects their duties more accurately than before. Only entrance to

Table 3 Range of reform in the OECD

Indicators	1995	2007	Change
Recruitment			
selection procedure in general	3	3	no change
selection procedure for senior staff	1	3	towards NPM
profile of senior staff	1	3	towards NPM
Career structure			
entrance	4	4	no change, yet NPM
structure	0	0	no change
basic salary	0	0	no change
extra pay	1	1	no change
merit bonus	1	1	no change
Staff appraisal			
performance appraisal	1	4	towards NPM
assessment of future potential	0	4	towards NPM
senior staff appraisal	0	1	towards NPM, but still closer to BM
use of staff appraisal results	1	1	no change
Training			
budget and hours of training	1	0	towards BM
purpose	1	1	no change
management training for senior staff	1	1	no change

the OECD s career structure is closer to the NPM ideal type, as is the case for the Commission.

Both organizations adapted their performance appraisals to NPM and conduct appraisals of senior staff on an optional basis. However, a fundamental difference is based on the fact that Commission of cials with consistently good performance are automatically promoted once they pass a certain threshold of points. In the OECD, performance appraisals are to a lesser extent formally connected to promotion or prolongation of contracts. Finally, different reform efforts are demonstrated most clearly with regard to training. While the Commission reformed substantially, for the OECD it is the weakest element of human resource management. There is no explicit strategy comparable to lifelong learning in the Commission and the number of training hours per employee decreased considerably.

To conclude, the Commission s human resource management was reformed further (*range*), and even more comprehensively (*scale*), than in the OECD. In the following section, we try to answer the question as to how this variation can be explained.

Table 4 Scale of reforms in the European Commission and the OECD (1995–2007)

Indicators	COM (1995)	OECD (1995)	closer to NPM	COM (2007)	OECD (2007)	closer to NPM
Recruitment						
selection procedure in general	2	3	OECD	2	3	OECD
selection procedure for senior staff	0	1	OECD	1	3	OECD
profile of senior staff	0	1	OECD	2	3	–
Career structure						
entrance	1	4	OECD	1	4	OECD
structure	0	0	–	3	0	COM
basic salary	0	0	–	1	0	COM
extra pay	0	1	–	2	1	COM
merit bonus	0	1	OECD	0	1	OECD
Staff appraisal						
performance appraisal	1	1	–	4	4	–
assessment of future potential	0	0	–	4	4	–
senior staff appraisal	0	0	–	1	1	–
use of staff appraisal results	0	1	OECD	2	1	COM
Training						
budget and hours of training	0	1	OECD	4	0	COM
purpose	0	1	OECD	4	1	COM
management training for senior staff	0	1	OECD	4	1	COM

3. HOW TO EXPLAIN THE EMPIRICAL PUZZLE? THE LIMITS OF ISOMORPHISM THEORY

When trying to account for the rather surprising empirical ﬁndings, we can generally differentiate between endogenous and exogenous factors. A ﬁrst approach would certainly be to focus upon endogenous, i.e. internal, characteristics within both organizations. In particular, one thinks of different internal problem pressures (owing to the perception and politicization of performance de"cits) in order to cope with the different scale of reforms. Performance crises especially, which attract considerable public attention, are emphasized as potential driving forces for administrative reforms (Bauer 2008; Pollitt and Bouckaert 2004). Indeed, both the European Commission and the OECD were confronted with internal corruption allegations in the late 1990s (Peterson 2004; Stevens and Stevens 2006). To be sure, the two crises were quite different in terms of media attention and politicization; the Santer Commission even resigned in the course of the developments, while the problems within the OECD hardly attracted much public attention. These differences, however, barely constitute a plausible explanation for the observed variation in organizational change at both Commission and OECD level, given that the crises concerned primarily antiquated and opaque accounting procedures. The topic of human resource management played only a minor role in this context. Moreover, though performance de"cits owing to existing staff rules and regulations were raised internally in both organizations (European Commission 2000; OECD 1999: 32; OECD 2001: 97; OECD 2003: 94; OECD 2006: 102 3), our analysis has shown that the adoption and formal implementation of respective reforms differ sharply in our cases.[2]

Apart from problem pressure, there are other endogenous factors like the nature of the organization and its organizational size that may offer an explanation (cf. Knill and Bauer 2007). But there seems to be no discernible connection between the size and the competences of an international organization and its reform efforts in human resource management. This is at least the case if organizations dispose of a minimum number of employees and cover a certain scope of tasks   like the European Commission and the OECD do.

In view of this, the crucial question is why similar internal arrangements and problems led to far-reaching reforms in the Commission but not in the OECD. Are there differences in the environment of each organizations that can account for our empirical results? To answer this question, institutional isomorphism emerged as a promising framework, as it accounts for the phenomena of the international spread and diffusion of policy innovations and reform concepts, not least with regard to public sector reforms (DiMaggio and Powell 1991; Levi-Faur 2002; Meyer and Rowan 1977; Meyer *et al.* 1997). The central argument advanced by DiMaggio and Powell is that legitimacy rather than ef"ciency is the major driving force of organizational change. To increase their legitimacy and ensure their persistence, organizations embrace rules, norms and routines that are widely valued in their organizational environment.

Hence, organizational change is essentially driven by external developments rather than intra-organizational concerns about the organization s ef"ciency. DiMaggio and Powell identify three mechanisms which drive isomorphic organizational change, namely coercive, mimetic and normative isomorphism. In the following text, these mechanisms will be investigated in closer detail.

Coercive isomorphism

An important driving force of isomorphic organizational change emerges from coercion. Organizations adjust their structures and procedures to be in line with organizations on which they are "nancially or legally dependent. According to these considerations, DiMaggio and Powell (1991: 74) hypothesize that the greater the dependence of an organization on another organization, the more similar it will become to that organization in structure, climate, and behavioral focus.

Looking at our cases of human resource management reforms in the European Commission and the OECD, this kind of dependence might especially result from potential pressures exerted by the member states. In both organizations, the member states could, in principle, exert "nancial and political pressure to adjust existing management structures, as they play a crucial role in de"ning the budget of these organizations. In this context, dependence with regard to introducing NPM-based human resource management structures is assumed to vary with three factors.

First, the budgetary contributions might vary across member states, implying that the OECD and the European Commission are not equally dependent on each member state. In view of our research question, it is of particular importance whether member states that can be characterized as NPM core countries, or member states that are laggards in introducing NPM reforms at home, are more in"uential in terms of political decisions and budgetary contributions. To account for this variation, we divide the member states of the OECD and the Commission into two groups of NPM core countries and NPM laggards, and measure the number of votes each group has in the Council as well as its respective budget contribution. This classi"cation is based on common distinctions in the respective literature (cf. Hood 1995; Kim 2002; OECD 1995; Pollitt and Bouckaert 2004). In this context, we assume that no signi"cant changes in the classi"cation of the member states occurred during the observation period 1995 2007. This assumption is supported by comparing respective assessments in the literature. The groups of NPM leader and laggard member states are summarized in Table 5.

Second, the budgetary pressures exerted by the member states might increase with the size of the personnel budget in relation to the overall budget. Third, the more an organization disposes of own resources which cannot be in"uenced by the member states, pressure on the personnel budget may be reduced.

Table 6 summarizes the characteristics which the OECD and the Commission display with regard to the three above-mentioned indicators (cf. European Commission 2006; OECD 2006, 2005a). On all indicators, it becomes apparent that we should expect more NPM-based changes of human resource management in the OECD than in the Commission. While in the European Union (EU), the share of Council votes of NPM laggards is more than twice as high as those of the NPM core countries, this difference is much less pronounced in the OECD. A similar picture emerges for the structure of the

Table 5 NPM leader and laggard states in the EU and the OECD

Group	EU	OECD
NPM leaders	Denmark, Finland, the United Kingdom, Ireland, the Netherlands, Sweden	Australia, Canada, Denmark, Finland, the United Kingdom, Ireland, New Zealand, the Netherlands, Norway, Sweden, Switzerland, the USA
NPM laggards	Austria, Belgium, France, Germany, Greece, Italy, Portugal, Spain	Austria, Belgium, France, Germany, Greece, Italy, Japan, Mexico, Portugal, South Korea, Spain, Turkey
Other (lack of data)	Luxembourg	Czech Republic, Hungary, Iceland, Luxembourg, Poland, Slovakia

budget and respective budgetary contributions. More than 50 per cent of the EU budget is "nanced by NPM laggards, such as Germany, France, Italy and Spain. In sum, it is obvious that we should expect more pronounced NPM-oriented reforms in the OECD than in the Commission. Our empirical "ndings, by contrast, show exactly the opposite pattern. This leads us to the conclusion that coercive isomorphism does not seem to play a signi"cant role in the reform process.

Mimetic isomorphism

Organizational adjustment to the environment is not only expected to take place as a result of coercive pressures, but may also occur in constellations of high

Table 6 Indicators of coercive reforms

Indicator	EU	OECD
Number of Council votes		
... of NPM leaders	32.1%	36.7%
... of NPM laggards	65.6%	43.3%
... of other member states	2.3%	20.0%
Relative budget contribution		
own resources	27.0%	7.3%
... of NPM leaders	19.6%	33.1%*
... of NPM laggards	53.2%	41.2%*
... of other member states	0.2%	1.0%
Relative size of the personnel budget	2.5%	47.2%

Note: * = plus voluntary contributions.

uncertainty; for example, ambiguous goals, uncertain means end relations or confrontation of new problems. In such constellations it is argued that organizations imitate the structures of other organizations which they perceive as particularly successful. Instead of a long-winded search for own solutions to existing problems, organizations strive to ensure their legitimacy by emulation (DiMaggio and Powell 1991: 75; Guler *et al.* 2002: 213).

With regard to potential uncertainty affecting human resource management reforms in the Commission and the OECD, we concentrate in the following text on the "nancial and personnel resources of these organizations. To what extent can they trust in the continuous development of their "nancial and personnel means? These factors are measured by three indicators, namely the length of the budgetary period as well as the development of the budget and staff numbers during the observation period (1995 2007). The more uncertain the situation of an organization with regard to these aspects (expressed by short budgetary periods and decreasing budget and staff size), the more we should expect the imitation of NPM-oriented management reforms. This expectation is based on the general observation that, during the last two decades, NPM has developed into a dominant reform approach around the globe, notwithstanding persistent differences in the speed and scope of adoption across countries (Pollitt and Bouckaert 2004).

When looking more closely at the different indicators, we arrive again at the conclusion that mimetic isomorphism is more likely in the OECD than in the Commission. This becomes apparent "rst in the fact that "nancial planning within the EU is based on a relatively long period; the member states decide every seven years on the "nancial framework for the yearly budget. In the OECD, by contrast, the budget is based on yearly and (from 2007 onwards) biannual decisions of the Council. Compared to the Commission, there is hence more uncertainty with regard to "nancial planning in the OECD.

Second, long-term "nancial planning in the EU at the same time implies that, during the observation period, both the size of the yearly budget and personnel resources within the Commission remain very stable. In the OECD, by contrast, on both indicators signi"cant decreases can be observed from the late 1990s onwards. Between 1996 and 1999, the member states decided to cut the OECD budget by 18 per cent, implying that the OECD had to cut 220 jobs (OECD 1997a: 93; OECD 1999: 32). This development was triggered by reductions in the "nancial contributions of the United States, which also induced other members to reduce their payments. As a consequence, staff numbers fell by 10 per cent between 1995 and 2005, although "ve new members joined the organization during this period (the Czech Republic, Hungary, Poland, Slovakia and South Korea). Moreover, the OECD s nominal budget in 2007 was below the 1995 "gures (OECD 1996, 2000, 2006), implying as one OECD of"cial states that you have to do the same amount of work with less money (interview 17/03/2006).

Hence, we "nd that the variation in human resource management reforms between the Commission and the OECD cannot be explained by mimetic isomorphism. Given much higher uncertainty with regard to "nancial and human resource planning, NPM-oriented reforms were much more likely to take place in the OECD than in the Commission.

Normative isomorphism

A further mechanism driving isomorphic organizational change is based on similar dominant normative orientations and the beliefs of staff members. In this context, the impact of similar professional backgrounds and the role of professional organizations and epistemic communities (Haas 1992) in spreading common understanding and perceptions of policy problems and solutions are emphasized in the literature (Hasse and Krücken 2005: 26).

In terms of professional standards (education, academic background), similar orientations can be assumed for the OECD and the Commission. In both organizations, staff are recruited from the best-educated academics in Europe (Hooghe 2001; Spescha 2005). Against this background, we consider it more appropriate to focus on the home country of the staff members rather than their educational background. This focus is also used by other studies, such as that by Hooghe (2001). In her study of decision-making within the European Commission, she found that the Commission bureaucrats, in many instances, de"ne their respective positions by taking account of the majority opinion in their home countries. For our concrete case of human resource management, we should therefore expect that the support of staff members for NPM-oriented reforms depends on the extent to which such developments were adopted or are supported in their home countries. The higher the number of staff from NPM core countries, the more the organization will adopt NPM-based reforms.

This argument, however, needs further explication. First, it can be assumed that the extent to which staff members perceive themselves as associated with the dominant beliefs and positions of their national context decreases over time. The longer the tenure of of"cials, the more socialization with the orientations and goals of the international organization will become dominant over their domestic socialization (cf. Hooghe 2001: 211). Second, the extent to which of"-cials might act as agents of diffusion within the international organization is dependent upon their degree of embeddedness in international discourses and networks in which issues of human resource management are debated.

To analyse the Commission and the OECD along the above-mentioned indicators, we concentrate on staff with academic backgrounds and top administrative of"cials in both organizations (European Commission 2007a; OECD 2004). For overall staff "gures, we focus on all of"cials within the career track A at the OECD level (906 individuals in 2004) and the new career track AD at the Commission level (10,184 individuals in 2007).[3] With regard to top of"cials, we consider the nationality of grades A6 and A7 (53 persons) in the OECD and of A1 and A2 (275 individuals) in the Commission. The staff composition of the Commission and the OECD according to these dimensions is shown in Table 7.

Table 7 Nationality of staff and top officials in the European Commission and the OECD

Indicator	COM	OECD
Whole staff with academic background		
... from NPM leaders	26.8%	48.5%
... from NPM laggards	73.8%	49.0%
... from other member states	0.4%	2.5%
Top officials		
... from NPM leaders	31.3%	56.6%
... from NPM laggards	68.6%	43.4%
... from other member states	0.1%	0%

Looking at top officials, we find that within the Commission around two-thirds of personnel are nationals of NPM laggard countries, basically from France, Germany, Belgium, Italy and Spain. Less than a third of the staff have the nationality of an NPM core country. This picture is even more pronounced when looking at all the staff with academic backgrounds. In the OECD, by contrast, top officials from NPM core countries make up 56.6 per cent, while for the entire staff the share of NPM leaders and laggards is almost equal. Based on these figures, mechanisms of normative isomorphism with regard to NPM-based reforms should be more pronounced for the OECD than for the Commission.

This expectation, which is contrary to our empirical results, is further supported when considering the length of time during which staff are typically employed in both organizations. In the OECD, only 30 per cent of the top officials and 45 per cent of the entire staff have time unrestricted working contracts, while in the Commission almost all staff members have tenure. Compared to the Commission, we can hence assume staff socialization in the OECD to be based much more on the national context rather than shaped by the organization itself. This should facilitate the transfer of dominant domestic ideas with regard to human resource management into the organization.

The same statement applies with regard to the involvement of staff members in international communities and networks in which NPM and human resource management reforms are discussed. While the Commission is predominantly concerned with issues of drafting and policy formulation, the OECD perceives itself primarily as a think-tank which, via its Public Management Committee (PUMA),[4] explicitly acted as *the* international promoter of NPM-based human resource management (OECD 1995; Sahlin-Andersson 2002). Against this backdrop, it is almost ironic that the OECD recently announced a new report on modernizing public employment in order to push respective reforms in its member states (OECD 2005b), while at the same time keeping rather old-fashioned structures at home.

In summary, we find that the different mechanisms of coercive, mimetic and normative isomorphism do not provide a sufficient explanation of the variation in human resource management structures found in the OECD and the European Commission. While isomorphic changes towards NPM-based structures should be more pronounced in the OECD than in the Commission, empirical "ndings reveal exactly the opposite pattern. Therefore, the central puzzle emerging from our analysis is: Why did the OECD not embrace, to a similar and even stronger extent, NPM-based human resource management reforms as the Commission did? We argue in the following text that this puzzle can be addressed by close investigation of the limits of the mechanisms of institutional isomorphism.

4. SCOPE CONDITIONS OF ISOMORPHIC CHANGE

It is an important achievement of isomorphism theory that it differentiates between the mechanisms that drive organizational change. Moreover, the theory identi"es the factors that affect the relative importance of each mechanism in a speci"c constellation; for example coercive isomorphism is more pronounced, the more an organization is dependent on other organizations. What is theoretically underdeveloped, however, is the fact that   in many instances   organizations will have multiple choices when striving to increase their legitimacy in their organizational environment. On the one hand, there might be more than one dominant model that could serve as a blueprint for change. On the other hand, and this is of special importance in our case, isomorphic change might refer to different dimensions, levels or aspects of existing organizational structures, routines and practices. In other words, it is unclear under what conditions an organization decides to reform, for instance, its formal structure, its decision-making procedures or its human resource management. Which parts of the menu of potentially legitimacy-enhancing reform models circulating in the international environment do organizations actually select and why?

We argue in the following text that organizations base these decisions upon the relative legitimacy gains to be derived from the varying options for isomorphic change. The case of the OECD shows that these potential gains are strongly affected by the speci"c legitimacy problems with which an organization is confronted. Given the OECD s rather fundamental crisis with regard to its self-identity and future development, isomorphic adjustments to its human resource management were not a suf"cient remedy to overcome this crisis.

First, since the 1990s the OECD has experienced a fundamental crisis with regard to the de"nition of its future objectives and mission.[5] As its then General Secretary Johnston emphasized in 1997: it has become clear that the OECD suffers from a lack of distinct identity ... Dealing with the full range of public policy issues it has become increasingly dif"cult to capture in a few descriptive words what the Organization actually does (OECD 1997b: 3). Notwithstanding this early diagnosis, the OECD still lacks a clear focus and decision as to what to do with which member states (interview 16/03/2006; interview 17/03/2006). The new Secretary General Angel Gurr'a assumed of"ce in

June 2006 and asked   again   the member states to better de"ne the OECD s role. He argued for a new and clear mandate; a mandate for relevance.

Con"icts about future goals are very dif"cult to resolve in view of internal decision-making structures based on unanimity. This is particularly true here, as the adoption of new goals in light of the tight budgetary situation would require a reduction in other activities. Such redistribution con"icts, however, are dif"cult to address within the existing structures (Chavranski 1997: 71; interview 17/03/2006). For the maintenance of the status quo, it is suf"cient that there is only one member state objecting to the dissolution of a certain working group or committee. Overcoming this crisis requires respective adjustments in the decision-making procedures, an issue discussed for years, albeit without any solution on the horizon as yet.

A second related problem is the unresolved con"icts with regard to potential enlargements of the OECD. There is an ongoing debate about whether the organization should integrate bigger players , such as Brazil, China, Russia or India, or focus on the accession of Central and Eastern European countries. The longer this con"ict over a more global or a more European focus lasts, the higher the risk that the OECD loses its pro"le or policy monopoly to other international organizations, such as the EU, the International Monetary Fund, the World Bank or the World Trade Organization in the "eld of foreign trade and economic policy (interview 17/03/2006). This problem is further aggravated by the fact that, among the general public, there is decreasing perception and knowledge of the activities and achievements of the OECD. For instance, in most member states, the general public is not aware of the fact that the highly politicized Programme for International Student Assessment (PISA) ranking was launched by the OECD.

In sum, we can observe a continuing identity crisis for the OECD that constitutes an important scope condition of isomorphic change. As the OECD s organizational environment is almost exclusively constituted by national governments and their civil servants attending respective meetings and working groups, the identity crisis also has an external dimension that can be termed a legitimacy crisis. Against this background, isomorphic adjustments to the OECD s human resource management were not a suf"cient remedy to overcome this crisis. On the contrary, the member states did not agree upon substantive management reform but upon the reduction of costs by downsizing staff and reducing the budget for training. As far as the European Commission is concerned, such fundamental con"icts over objectives and challenges could not be identi"ed. Owing to its seven-year "nancial framework and its political sovereignty, such problems are less likely to occur than in the OECD.

5. CONCLUSION

In this paper, we compared human resource management structures in the European Commission and the OECD, and their development towards NPM-based reform models between 1995 and 2007. Our results show that, overall, an orientation towards NPM models is more pronounced in the European Commission than in the OECD. This "nding is striking from both an empirical and a theoretical perspective. First, it appears paradoxical that the OECD   considered to be one of the most important international promoters of NPM   has a rather old-fashioned human resource management that needs to be further improved and reformed in the future. Second, our empirical results con"ict with theoretical expectations derived from institutional isomorphism: coercive, mimetic and normative pressures for NPM-based adjustments were stronger in the OECD than in the European Commission so that we should actually have observed opposite reform patterns. Against this background, our comparative analysis suggests that organizations are highly selective in terms of how to react to pressures for isomorphic change. Thus, we have argued that isomorphism theory needs to be complemented by arguments with regard to the conditions under which organizations adopt policy innovations which diffuse internationally. They seem to be contingent upon the speci"c problems with which an organization is confronted and the potential legitimacy gains for overcoming these problems.

Biographical note: Christoph Knill is Professor in the Department of Politics and Management at the University of Konstanz, Germany, and holds the Chair of Comparative Public Policy and Administration. Tim Balint is Ph.D. candidate at the same Chair.

Address for correspondence: Christoph Knill, Chair of Comparative Public Policy and Administration, University of Konstanz, Box D 91, D-78457 Konstanz, Germany. email: christoph.knill@uni-konstanz.de

ACKNOWLEDGEMENTS

We would like to thank Michael W. Bauer for organizing the inspiring conference on Management Reforms in International Organizations at the University of Konstanz, 30 June 1 July 2006, where we presented an early version of this article. We are also grateful to three anonymous referees for their excellent comments.

NOTES

1 Thanks to helpful co-operation with the OECD, the authors received detailed information about the variable training in order to validate the data (cf. Table 3). However, the speci"c content of these data cannot be made publicly available.
2 The OECD embarked on a major reform programme very recently. As this recent reform programme had not been completed and formally implemented at the time of this study, it is not covered in this article.
3 For the OECD, we relied on the most recent data available (OECD 2004). For the Commission, we took the 2007 data (European Commission 2007a) and excluded staff from the countries who joined the EU in 2004, assuming that the latter are of

limited importance in accounting for reform developments between 1995 and 2007. In both organizations the national composition of the staff has remained stable over the last decade.

4 PUMA was renamed Public Governance and Territorial Development (GOV).

5 See also various reports in *Financial Times*, 2 March 2003, 30 November 2005, 29 May 2006; *International Herald Tribune*, 29 November 2005, 10 February 2006, 10 May 2006; *Süddeutsche Zeitung*, 15 March 2003.

REFERENCES

Barnett, M.N. and Finnemore, M. (1999) The politics, power, and pathologies of international organizations , *International Organization* 53(4): 699 732.

Barnett, M.N. and Finnemore, M. (2004) *Rules for the World. International Organizations in Global Politics*, Ithaca, NY: Cornell University Press.

Bauer, M.W. (2008) Diffuse anxieties, deprived entrepreneurs: Commission reform and middle management , *Journal of European Public Policy* 15(5): 691 707.

Bauer, M.W. and Knill, C. (eds) (2007) *Management Reforms in International Organizations*, Baden-Baden: Nomos.

Chavranski, H. (1997) *L OCDE: Au cœur des grands débats économiques*, Paris: La Documentation Française.

Davies, M.D.V. (2002) *The Administration of International Organizations: Top Down and Bottom Up*, Burlington, VT: Ashgate.

DiMaggio, P.J. and Powell, W.W. (1991) The iron cage revisited: institutional isomorphism and collective rationality in organizational "elds , in W.W. Powell and P.J. DiMaggio (eds), *The New Institutionalism in Organizational Analysis*, Chicago: University of Chicago Press, pp. 63 82.

European Commission (2000) Reforming the Commission A White Paper Part I , document COM/2000/0200 "nal, Brussels.

European Commission (2004) Reforming the Commission. Human Resources . Available: http://ec.europa.eu/reform/2002/index_en.htm [2007, July/01].

European Commission (2005) Communication from the Commission to the European Parliament and the Council: progress report on the Commission reform beyond the reform mandate , document COM(2005) 668, Brussels.

European Commission (2006) The European Union budget at a glance . Available: http://ec.europa.eu/budget/budget_glance/index_en.htm [2007, July/01].

European Commission (2007a) Distribution of of"cials and temporary agents by nationality, category and grade (all budgets) . Available: http://ec.europa.eu/civil_service/docs/bs_sexe_nat_grade_en.pdf [2007, July/01].

European Commission (2007b) Staff regulations of of"cials of the European Commission . Available: http://ec.europa.eu/dgs/personnel_administration/publications_en.htm [2007, July/01].

Geri, L.R. (2001) New public management and the reform of international organizations , *International Review of Administrative Science* 67(3): 445 60.

Guler, I., Guillén, M.F. and Macpherson, J.M. (2002) Global competition, institutions, and the diffusion of organizational practices: the international spread of ISO 9000 quality certi"cates , *Administrative Science Quarterly* 47(2): 207 32.

Haas, P.M. (1992) Introduction: Epistemic communities and international policy coordination , *International Organization* 46(1): 1 35.

Hasse, R. and Krücken, G. (2005) *Neo-Institutionalismus*, Bielefeld: Transcript.

Hood, C. (1991) A public management for all seasons? , *Public Administration* 69(1): 3 19.

Hood, C. (1995) The new public management in the 1980s: variations on a theme , *Accounting, Organizations and Society* 20(2/3): 93 109.

Hooghe, L. (2001) *The European Commission and the Integration of Europe. Images of Governance*, Cambridge: Cambridge University Press.

Kim, P.S. (2002) Civil service reform in Japan and Korea: toward competitiveness and competency, *International Review of Administrative Science* 68(3): 389 403.

Knill, C. and Bauer, M.W. (2007) Theorizing management reforms in international organizations, in M.W. Bauer and C. Knill (eds), *Management Reforms in International Organizations*, Baden-Baden: Nomos, pp. 191 99.

Lægreid, P. (2002) Transforming top civil servant systems, in T. Christensen and P. Lægreid (eds), *New Public Management. The Transformation of Ideas and Practice*, Aldershot: Ashgate, pp. 145 72.

Levi-Faur, D. (2002) The politics of liberalization. Privatization and regulation for competition in Europe s and Latin America s telecoms and electricity industries, *European Journal of Political Research* 42(5): 705 40.

Liebel, H.J. and Oechsler, W.A. (1992) *Personalbeurteilung. Neue Wege zur Bewertung von Leistung, Verhalten und Potential*, Wiesbaden: Gabler.

Liese, A. and Weinlich, S. (2006) Die Rolle von Verwaltungsstäben internationaler Organisationen. Lücken, Tücken und Konturen eines (neuen) Forschungsfelds, in J. Bogumil, W. Jann and F. Nullmeier (eds), *Politik und Verwaltung. Politische Vierteljahresschrift Sonderheft 37/2006*, Wiesbaden: VS-Verlag für Sozialwissenschaften, pp. 491 524.

Meyer, J.W. and Rowan, B. (1977) Institutionalized organizations. Formal structure as myth and ceremony, *American Journal of Sociology* 83(2): 340 63.

Meyer, J.W., Frank, D.J., Hironaka, A., Schofer, E. and Brandon-Tuma, N. (1997) The structuring of a world environmental regime, 1870 1990, *International Organization* 51(4): 623 51.

Naschold, F. and Bogumil, J. (2000) *Modernisierung des Staates. New public management in deutscher und internationaler Perspektive*, Opladen: Leske + Budrich.

OECD (1995) *Governance in Transition. Public Management Reforms in OECD Countries*, Paris: OECD.

OECD (1996) *OECD Annual Report 1996*, Paris: OECD.

OECD (1997a) *OECD Annual Report 1997*, Paris: OECD.

OECD (1997b) The OECD challenges and strategic objectives: 1997 (Note by the Secretary General), document C(97)180, Paris.

OECD (1999) *OECD Annual Report 1999*, Paris: OECD.

OECD (2000) *OECD Annual Report 2000*, Paris: OECD.

OECD (2001) *OECD Annual Report 2001*, Paris: OECD.

OECD (2003) *OECD Annual Report 2003*, Paris: OECD.

OECD (2004) Staff pro" le statistics, document C(2004)48, Paris.

OECD (2005a) Financial statement of the Organization for Economic Co-operation and Development as of 31 December 2005. Available: http://appli1.oecd.org/olis/2006doc.nsf/linkto/exd-bc(2006)1 [2007, July/01].

OECD (2005b) *Modernising Government. The Way Forward*, Paris: OECD.

OECD (2006) *OECD Annual Report 2006*, Paris: OECD.

OECD (2007) Human resource management at the OECD. Available: http://www.oecd.org/document/8/0,2340,en_2649_34481_20008648_1_1_1_1,00.html [2007, July/01].

Peterson, J. (2004) The Prodi Commission: fresh start or free fall?, in D.G. Dimitrakopoulos (ed.), *The Changing European Commission*, Manchester: Manchester University Press, pp. 15 32.

Pollitt, C. and Bouckaert, G. (2004) *Public Management Reform. A Comparative Analysis*, Oxford and New York: Oxford University Press.

Sahlin-Andersson, K. (2002) National, international and transnational constructions of new public management , in T. Christensen and P. Lægreid (eds), *New Public Management. The Transformation of Ideas and Practices*, Aldershot: Ashgate, pp. 43 72.

Spescha, G. (2005) OECD und ihr Ein"uss auf die nationale Politik ein Streitgespräch , *Die Volkswirtschaft* 78(4): 29 33.

Stevens, A. and Stevens, H. (2001) *Brussels Bureaucrats? The Administration of the European Union*, Basingstoke: Palgrave Macmillan.

Stevens, H. and Stevens, A. (2006) The internal reform of the Commission , in D. Spence and G. Edwards (eds), *The European Commission*, London: John Harper, pp. 454 80.

Vaanholt, S. (1997) *Human Resource Management in der öffentlichen Verwaltung*, Wiesbaden: Deutscher Universitäts-Verlag.

Summary of interviews

Interviews	Place	Interviewees
14/03/2006	Paris	ambassador of OECD member state
15/03/2006	Paris	two employees of the OECD human resource department
16/03/2006	Paris	ambassador of OECD member state
17/03/2006	Paris	two representatives of the OECD Staff Association, ambassador of OECD member state, national expert in OECD personnel policy
12/05/2006	Brussels	seconded national expert for reform of EU staff regulations, two employees of DG Personnel and Administration
17/05/2006	telephone interview	ambassador of OECD member state, national expert in OECD personnel policy

Diffuse anxieties, deprived entrepreneurs: Commission reform and middle management

Michael W. Bauer

1. INTRODUCTION

Despite more than "ve decades in existence, the European Commission has engaged only recently in reforming its administration. This reform has been the subject of a number of insightful studies (Kassim 2004a, 2004b; Cini 2004; Levy 2004, 2006; Stevens and Stevens 2006; Spence and Stevens 2006; Balint *et al.* 2008). Apart from the intriguing question of why, given the new public management prominence of public sector reform in most of its national constituencies, the Commission was able to resist modernization for such a long time (Bauer 2007), scholars have been primarily occupied with describing the process as well as the content of the modernization, and assessing the internal consistency of individual reform chapters. In other words, the dependent variables have been primarily timing, implementation, substance and scope of the modernization of the Commission. Yet, since the reform has been in effect for some time, the challenge is increasingly to discover what difference, if any, it actually makes. *More precisely, one wonders what effects the reform has on the role of the European Commission as an actor within European public policy-making and, given the centrality of that organization for the EU system of govern-ance, eventually therefore on EU policy output.* Otherwise, why should one keep bothering   outside the small circle of EU public administration scholars   about the recent reform of the Commission?

In this article I attempt to tackle this effect question, hence turning the reform issue more towards the independent variable side of the story. The evi-dence presented will underline why one should perhaps bother more about the recent organizational change inside the Commission with regard to policy output. I will probably raise more questions than I am able to answer. Basically I argue that the reform, although in itself perhaps really an historic accomplish-ment and heroic task (Kassim 2004a, 2004b), will seriously change and even-tually limit the capability of the Commission to deliver policy and to shepherd its legislative drafts through the formal and informal stages of the EU policy process (Nugent 2001: 242)   at least to the standard as we know it.

To substantiate this claim, I will make two assumptions. The "rst is to centre this analysis upon the middle management   usually the heads of unit (HoU)   inside the Commission. Neither the rank and "le nor the top managers but the HoU are   in intellectual and administrative terms   the organizational backbone of the Commission. It is in the person of an HoU that policy expertise usually culminates and interlinks with the politics stream of EU public policy-making (Kingdon 1995; Richardson 2006). Below the HoU, individual power is too weak; above the HoU top managers   i.e. directors and directors-general   are too busy to engage intensively in the minutiae of an individual dossier while taking into account the various national and societal positions to identify viable lines of a satisfactory political compromise.

The second assumption is to qualify the dominant view that sees the Commission s strength in agenda-setting. There is a broad consensus that the Commission s (and the European Union s (EU s)) role is much more signi"cant in the early stages of the policy process than in later ones (Peters 1994, 1996; Bauer 2006). Given the growing importance of the presidency, the European Parliament, European-level lobbying and the usual contingencies of the modern policy process, the Commission s right of initiative constitutes in my view   in the "rst place a drafting rather than an agenda-setting power. Delivering concrete policy drafts, however, is usually the prime task of the HoU.

I will proceed as follows. In the next section I review the literature on the Commission which is relevant to the research question presented here   in order to show that my assumptions are plausible. I will then recall the content of the Kinnock reform (section 3). This can be done brie"y since I can draw on existing work and on those aspects of importance for the issues raised here. Section 4, the main section, reports on the results of a survey showing the misgivings and anxieties of middle managers as regards the general thrust of the reform, but also the endorsement of particular elements of the management change. The article ends with a short conclusion summarizing the main implications of the results for the Commission s future role in EU policy-making. In a nutshell, I conclude that the recent reform of the Commission does indeed comprehensively redefine the role of the HoU. The resource base (of the position) of a HoU to focus on policy drafting is hugely reduced. Negative consequences for the organization s potential to deliver a policy draft of high quality are therefore very likely.

2. THE ROLE OF THE COMMISSION IN EU POLICY-MAKING

The literature on the Commission fills libraries and is certainly too diverse to be summarized here (but see Cini 1996; Nugent 1997, 2001; Spence 2006; Bauer 2005). Beyond the debate about the Commission s autonomous capacity as a supranational actor inclined to influence the systemic development of regional integration according to its own preference (Smyrl 1998; Moravcsik 1998; Pollack 2003), it is probably fair to say that comparative policy analysis and public administration scholars have recently been most active and (arguably) most successful in coming to grips with this actor and its role in multi-level policy-making.

In my view, there is a broad consensus within the public policy and administration community that the Commission s strength lies rather in the early stages of the policy cycle (from problem definition up to, say, decision-taking) than in (supervising) policy execution and delivery (Bauer 2006). The concepts developed in this regard are agenda-setter, policy entrepreneur and subterfuge (Cram 1993; Peters 1994; Héritier 1997; Sabatier 1993).

Analysts usually treat the Commission (or an individual Directorate-General (DG) or service within it) as an actor itself, but they rarely specify under what conditions entrepreneurship — to take the most usual notion that conceptualizes the Commission as a purposeful political actor able to pursue an aim over long time periods and via astonishing detours — actually works inside the Commission administration. In this context it is perhaps useful to recall that the substantial competence behind entrepreneurship is the Commission s power of initiative, i.e. its monopoly to propose policy drafts. The EU may be an agenda-setting paradise (Peters 1994: 21; Rochefort and Cobb 1995) with the Presidency, Council, and Parliament constantly advancing (to the detriment of the Commission) their agenda-setting powers. However, in the end it is the Commission that delivers the policy draft and therefore sets the outlines for political compromise, i.e. where the final decision inside and between Council and Parliament may come to lie (Coombes 1970; Noel 1973; Peterson 1995; Cini 1996; Hix 2005). The crucial questions — which in my opinion have up to now not received their due attention — then become *who* are the entrepreneurs inside the Commission and *how* does this entrepreneurship actually work? In the following I will concentrate on the motivational and administrative implications of these questions.

Inside the Commission, reinforced through respective patterns of advancement and promotion, the noblest tasks have always been in conceiving new projects and pushing forward new initiatives for further integration (Hooghe 2001: 156). Consolidation, administration and management of tasks and initiatives already achieved are thought to be of secondary value (Ludlow 1991; Spence 2000; Bauer 2002). Moreover, in this fragmented and heterogeneous administration (Christiansen 2006), the individual level plays the crucial role. The aim is to get one s own proposal through   or at least to gain visibility with superiors by trying hard. In the end, successful policy drafts are the currency of prestige and the capital that returns in terms of career advancement, resource expansion or obtaining other interesting dossiers. Successful drafts re"ect on the Commissioner in charge, the director-general, the director and down the line of organizational hierarchy. However, policy formulation is a genuinely individualistic task (Peters 1996: 21). It is usually done at unit or section level guided by the respective HoU. The HoU occupies the pivotal position. As regards content, he used to be the acknowledged expert. At the same time he is an experienced insider who knows the Commission machinery, the informal side of the organizational hierarchy and the crucial policy pundits within the other European institutions, national administrations or relevant lobbies. The very fragmentation of the Commission and the de"cient horizontal and vertical co-ordination mechanisms reinforce the HoU s role and importance. In practice it is the rule rather than the exception that the sensible task of policy drafting lies in the hands of a single HoU as the central Commission of"cial (Peters 1994: 16). That trend as I would call it   of the *individualization of policy formulation* has not gone unnoticed. Other scholars have referred to it as the dossier or the rapporteur approach.

> This dossier approach is a way of working within the Commission that underpins much of the day-to-day life of of"cials, to the extent that it is taken for granted by those that have been socialised into Commission practice. The approach is essentially a juridical one, resting on the notion of individual responsibility for speci"c cases and on the technocratic expertise of of"cials who tend to become immersed in one small area of policy, becoming indeed experts in their own right.
>
> (Cini 1996: 153)

Neill Nugent describes the process of policy drafting, as it usually advances within the responsible DG, as even more pronounced:

> [Usually] a head of unit. . . assumes responsibility for what is known as a dossier ("le) on the proposal. This involves preparing the proposal and shepherding it through its decision-making stages. In working on the drafting of the proposal this of"cial   known as the rapporteur   has an absolutely crucial task since the legislation that is eventually adopted is likely to contain most of what is in the Commission s draft.
>
> (Nugent 2001: 242)

Hence, the rapporteur — usually the HoU — is in many respects the central individual behind a Commission legislative proposal. The HoU is crucially located between technical expertise and political management. He is the one who maintains the contact between his expert team and the increasingly politicized actors hierarchically above as well as within the speci"c expert community outside the Commission. The importance of the HoU in identifying potential for (technical) consensus and for the time-consuming and challenging task of guiding the proposal through the formalities and informalities of the Commission s internal decision-making process can hardly be exaggerated (Nugent 2001).

In sum, the entrepreneurship of the Commission has an individualistic basis which up to now has been somewhat — though, as the quotations above show, not completely — neglected. As a starting point, this individualistic basis of Commission entrepreneurship is in my opinion best conceptualized in terms of motivation and administration. The motivational side of the story refers to the congruence of interests between the individual and the organization, i.e. getting policy drafts positively decided upon, fostered by the standard incentives of career perspectives, quality improvement of future responsibilities (getting the high potential dossiers) or acquisition of other of"ce-maximizing resources. Unpacking the Commission as a public administration in this respect puts the HoU centre stage. From the perspective of analysing the effects of the recent Commission reform on policy output, the crucial question thus becomes whether and how the Kinnock reform modi"es the position of the HoU, thereby affecting the Commission s entrepreneurship capacity.

3. THE KINNOCK REFORM AND MIDDLE MANAGEMENT

The substance, scope and timing of the recent administrative reforms of the European Commission have been extensively dealt with elsewhere (Kassim 2008, 2004a, 2004b; Metcalfe 2000; Bear"eld 2004; Levy 2006). In this section it is thus unnecessary to go into detail. Instead, I would like to focus on two crucial aspects: the strategic planning and programming and personnel policy chapters of the reform. Both are not only regarded as most important, but also impact heavily on the HoU.

The chapter on Strategic Planning and Programming (SPP) is a cornerstone of the reform project. The traditional Weberian way of administrating was to be replaced by strategic priority-setting (on the basis of updated information about what is exactly done in the Commission and by whom), respective resource allocation, process monitoring, evaluation and inherently connected

redistribution of "nancial and personnel resources on the basis of that programming cycle. One should note that activity-based cost management (Cokins 1996) is still output-focused rather than outcome-focused. But it is a far cry from the input steering that the Commission applied in the past. The SPP cycle has run since 2003 and has put policy priorities at the heart of the decision-making... Managers are required to focus on the need to deliver on priority objectives and to report on achievements and performance (European

Commission 2004: 6). The SPP cycle is indeed a challenge. Means and needs have to be justi"ed in the light of targeted objectives. A detailed Annual Policy Strategy (APS) is drafted, discussed and agreed upon, involving virtually all layers of the internal administration in a huge communication and co-ordination exercise. The APS is translated into mission statements and work programmes for each Commission service, setting out speci"c objectives for directorates and units. In response Annual Activity Reports are required by each DG or service, which include strategic evaluations of activities and expenditure, and so on, up and down the hierarchy (Kassim 2004a: 48). Writing proposals for policy objectives, conceiving (measurable) progress and quality indicators, conducting impact assessment exercises, suggesting priorities, drafting respective reports, evaluating and communicating decisions to the rank and "le have become the bread and butter of the HoU s daily job.

The personnel chapter was the second centrepiece of the modernization blueprint since budgeting, programming and co-ordination aspects have personnel implications, and vice versa. The linearization of careers and the new pension regime were among the most contested issues among staff unions, the reformers surrounding Kinnock and the representatives of the member states (Kassim 2004a, 2004b; Bauer 2007). The aims were to keep staff motivated until very late in their individual careers (more but smaller promotion steps) and to keep the costs of salaries and pensions in check. The hotly discussed money and motivation issues distracted perhaps from the fact that the core of the managerial side of the new personnel strategy was a kind of extended leadership role for the HoU. According to the new personnel concept, it is the HoU who has to instruct, supervise and guide his unit staff so as to "t the human resource variable to the equation of the new priority-setting, programming and co-ordination approach. The aim was to make the Commission administration more accountable to the political College of Commissioners. In this sense the role of the HoU in motivating, managing and guiding staff is pivotal. A particularly dif"cult undertaking turned out to be the distribution of assessment points . Once an individual has accumulated a certain number of points, promotion becomes automatic. The distribution of points is an annual exercise and a highly competitive one, since the overall number of points is restricted. Some of these points are assigned by the directors-general, but the HoU distributes most of them.[1] At any rate, it is the HoU who implements the personnel strategy. He has to set annual job targets against which individual performance is assessed; he has to evaluate performance, and justify and report on his opinion; he has to negotiate the points, defend decisions, deal with more or less satis"ed managers, and so on. As an HoU who experienced the reform effects underlined: The HoU are now much busier with administrative stuff that comes with the reform. Personnel management things especially have been easier in the past. The reform has increased the responsibilities of the HoU substantially.[2] A Commission of"cial working in the team that conceived and implemented the reform put it somewhat more baldly: In the past you became HoU for writing good policy papers.

There was little interest in whether you were good at managing and guiding your team. [3]

All in all, the pressure on the HoU to develop and use staff potential in an optimal way — as de"ned by the SPP cycle — has increased dramatically. The good news is that HoU have gained in direct power over their personnel but the bad news is:

> that power over personnel comes with high bureaucratic costs and greater responsibilities as regards internal administration. Time for participating in working groups, circulating policy papers and engaging in negotiations is gone. In this sense, the reform means more management and in certain respects also more bureaucracy for the HoU. The point is that the traditional approach that the best policy expert should become HoU is still very much alive in the heads of the people. Especially in the Commission, the HoU are usually motivated by the content side of their job. Most of them are kind of political criminals [4] in an absolute positive sense; meaning highly motivated experts in their policy "elds who would just give anything for their dossier ... The reform means cultural change and that will take time.[5]

If the Kinnock reform thus utterly changes the role of the HoU, the obvious research question is how the HoU themselves assess the Kinnock reform with respect to their daily working life. To answer this question I conducted a survey whose results are presented below.

4. SURVEYING MIDDLE MANAGEMENT

In April 2007 the Commission employed 23,043 formal staff. According to internal sources, there are roughly 1,200 HoU, but only 800 have exclusively policy tasks. I used the information available from the organizational charts of the 13 DGs indicated by the Commission itself as policy DGs (e.g. those for agriculture, cohesion, environment, etc.) in order to create a list of HoU who are clearly engaged in policy-making. From this general population I randomly selected 200 as my survey population. In addition I also sampled some directors and directors-general as a control group. One hundred and sixteen telephone interviews with policy HoU were completed, a response rate of 58 per cent.

Almost 60 per cent said that the position of HoU had experienced the most dramatic changes in its pro"le owing to the Kinnock reform. The directors-general came second with 20 per cent. In the same vein and somewhat astonishingly — in respect of the short time span since the reform had been in operation — asked about the effects of the Kinnock reform with regard to their individual promotion, one-sixth of the HoU already saw an impact, shared equally between positive and negative.

Enabling the Commission to redistribute resources quickly and in accordance with changing priorities was a major concern for the reformer. Clearly, if this redistribution is only marginal it is questionable whether it pays to install new, painstaking, time-consuming and complicated procedures in the "rst place: policy ends would not change and neither would the distribution of means. The data put a big question mark over this crucial aspect. Asked about whether, as an outcome of the Kinnock reform, there had been a redeployment of personnel or "nancial resources because of changing political priorities, only a third of HoU saw such a redistribution while two-thirds did not see any.

As regards work pro"le, roughly 30 per cent of HoU considered promoting policies as their top priority, followed by providing internal management leadership (25 per cent), supervising implementation (16 per cent) and generating ideas (10 per cent). Two equally ingrained camps could be identi"ed: leadership and implementation, on the one hand, and promoting policies and ideas, on the other. But saying what is the most important aspect of your work as in the previous question is one thing, saying what the HoU really value most is something else. Asked whether the brightest policy innovators, irrespective of their level of seniority, should get more scope (and better career prospects) or whether fast-track, special arrangements for a small number of people should be avoided, two-thrids of the HoU replied that they would like to see more space given to the policy innovators, while only one-sixth objected.

The HoU were asked to assess the impact of the recent internal modernization (i.e. the so-called Kinnock reforms) in the light of their own experience by agreeing (or not) with seven statements (agree , disagree , or don t know). All the statements were taken from the Commission s own documents (White Paper and progress reports) on the reform. The overall assessment of the reform effects was negative. With the statement My unit/service has become more ef"cient and effective 59 per cent explicitly disagreed, and 15 per cent said they did not know (which is equally negative from the perspective of reform promoters). Personnel management has become leaner and more focused. I can concentrate more on the really important issues was contested by 86 per cent of the HoU. With The orders/instructions from superiors have become clearer, more transparent and more coherent 63 per cent disagreed, 12 per cent did not know. Similarly, little support can be found for I can work more autonomously because I can decide myself about important issues concerning the distribution of internal resources ; 71 per cent disagreed, 12 per cent did not know. However, with the statement The new tools and rules are applied in a formal and super"cial way. The majority of colleagues have yet to be convinced of their advantages 72 per cent explicitly agreed. The excuse offered by the following statement, i.e. that it is still too early to tell, was rejected by a huge majority. The phrase went The new tools and rules have yet to be applied coherently. Therefore, I do not have suf"cient information to draw conclusions. Fifty-"ve per cent disagreed, 29 per cent agreed, while 13 per cent did not know. At last the statement The new tools and rules do lead to more red tape and increase the internal administrative load elicited very clear reactions as 88 per cent of the HoU unambiguously agreed. In other words, the HoU think that their units have not become more ef"cient, personnel management has in their eyes become painstaking, and instructions from superiors appear to be barely transparent. In sum, there seems to be little behind the rhetoric of increasing the autonomy of lower levels, and there is consensus that red tape has rocketed as a consequence of the Kinnock reform.

The picture brightened when the HoU were asked about speci"c managerial elements introduced by the reform in the sphere of strategic planning and programming and the new personnel policy. Roughly, there was a persistent quarter of HoU who saw the reform elements negatively but   in stark contrast to the previous questions   now frequently relative and sometimes absolute majorities assessed the changes positively. As regards strategic programming in particular, reporting schemes and prospective management planning met with the approval of an absolute majority of HoU. They appeared to approve especially of the new rules allowing them to de"ne the responsibility of personnel individually and in advance. However, the setting of negative priorities was obviously seen as problematic. See Tables 1 and 2 for an overview.

HoU perceive the new personnel management even more positively than strategic programming. Ostensibly, they welcome the need to formulate detailed job descriptions, i.e. setting work-related personal targets and objectives. They are in favour of annual appraisal exercises and appreciate their power to decide on staff requirements and the related allocation of responsibilities. But they appear reluctant about the duties of leadership concerning (sometimes painful) decisions about the pay and promotion of their direct subordinates.

Finally, the survey included an open question. Out of 116 HoU 50 made sometimes lengthy   use of this last question to comment on the Kinnock reform. I coded these comments according to whether they indicated a positive, negative or neutral attitude towards the effect of the reform. Six were outright

Table 1 Strategic planning and programming: Which of the following elements improved your personal capacity to do your job?[6]

	Negative (%)	Positive (%)	Irrelevant (%)	Don't know (%)
Drafting the Annual Activity Report	34	40	24	2
Preparing the Annual Strategy Decision	32	46	20	2
Drafting the DG Annual Management Plan	29	55	14	2
Interim evaluation and monitoring of achievements	24	50	23	3
Defining the responsibilities of individuals	11	63	20	6
Setting negative priorities	37	27	32	4
New reporting duties	26	46	22	5

Table 2 Personnel management: Which of the following elements of personnel modernization improved your capacity to do your job?

	Negative (%)	Positive (%)	Irrelevant (%)	Don't know (%)
Detailed job descriptions	13	73	13	1
Annual appraisal exercises	36	50	11	3
Setting work-related and personal targets	13	68	17	2
Deciding on staff requirements and allocation of responsibilities	21	45	30	2
Promotion procedures	67	12	20	2
Setting objectives within your unit	11	74	12	2
Overseeing and assessing achievements	20	52	27	2
Reducing function groups and having a single pay scale with 16 grades	36	20	40	5

positive (somewhere along the lines of management should be a time-consuming activity or it was time for reform), and another six were neutral (in the sense of esprit est bon, la mise en oeuvre moins car elle crée un surplus de la bureaucratie ... parfois amène à la diminution de l effectivité). The vast majority of the HoU agreed that some kind of management reform of the Commission administration had been overdue. But 38 took the opportunity to convey a clear message: the Kinnock reform can be summarized in one word: bureaucracy . One of the more friendly comments in that category was many HoU feel they have to carry the heavy burden of bureaucratic, ineffective procedures that were introduced. Others were sharper: Kinnock is a disaster and a 300 per cent bureaucracy increase with form accounting for 80 per cent and substance just for 20 per cent , it is paperwork that nobody reads or just unproductive paper work . Others talk about control mania inside the Commission which creates a culture of fear ; control should be on a reasonable level: now it has gone mad . Many statements re"ect the fear that the Commission has lost its political duties , political priorities , political function and that the original mission is forgotten . The real problem is that process has become an aim in itself; there are lots of words, declarations, announcements which lead to nowhere; there is no increase in productivity . In the same vein: productivity is decreasing, internal procedures are the biggest constraints ; What has been done is a castration! Bureaucracy and security measures kill all the potential productivity . Or, with regard to the changing role of the HoU of major interest for my argument: avant les chefs d unité étaient les experts du domaine, maintenant ils ne sont que des managers . The point is that staff who were happy to have been reformed would probably have made different remarks. Considering the fact that the survey question did *not* directly invite comment on the de"ciencies of the Kinnock reform, this becomes even more worrisome.[7] The question was neutral: Do you wish to make a general or speci"c remark about the issues touched on in the survey? Therefore, politicians and managers at the top of the Commission are well advised to take such strong reactions from their middle management seriously.

Apart from this descriptive evidence, I conducted some simple regressions in order to test standard hypotheses   taken from Hooghe (2001)   which could be invoked to explain why an individual HoU supports or rejects administrative reform.[8] In other words, I took the expression of empathy or distaste of the HoU for the Kinnock reform as the dependent variable. Admittedly, Hooghe does not ask exactly the same research question as I do here. However, she investigates a number of mechanisms which may also hold analytical leverage in explaining the attitude of middle managers towards the recent reform of the European Commission, since she attempts to explain variance in the attitudes of managers as to whether they prefer a more managerial or a more political-entrepreneurial Commission. Arguably, this cleavage also lies at the heart of the relationship between middle management and Commission reform as discussed in this paper. I present the results in Table 3.[9]

Only with regard to the academic background hypothesis, i.e. that reform empathy correlates positively with an educational background in economics, do I "nd the expected relationship (though with a very low level of signi"-cance). The hypothesis that those HoU from a country with a continental

Table 3 Regression results

Sub-dimension	Dependent variable Additive index lnkin_positive
Reform aversion of initiative-oriented DG	−0.087 (0.84)
Reform aversion from idealist for European integration	0.128 (1.35)
Reform empathy owing to economic background	0.002 (1.81)*
Reform aversion of managers close to retirement	−0.001 (1.14)
Reform empathy/aversion as function of public management reform intensity in home country	0.029 (0.58)
Reform empathy owing to work experience within private sector	−0.180 (1.60)
Reform aversion because of huge staff responsibility	−0.024 (0.62)
Reform aversion owing to leftist political conviction	0.000 (0.14)
Constant	1.141 (5.24)**
Number of observations	116
R-squared	0.18

Note: Absolute value of t statistics in parentheses.
* significant at 10 per cent ** significant at 1 per cent.

administrative culture (as opposed to countries full-heartedly embracing new public management reforms) also shows a correlation. However, the nexus goes in the opposite direction. Those HoU from a country with a low tendency to implement new public management change think *more* positively about the Kinnock reform than those from a country with an outspoken new public management background. Also, I "nd an unexpected correlation between time to retirement and assessment of the Kinnock reform. The logic is that younger and still ambitious HoU, who know they will have to live with the new rules of the game brought about by the reform, will be more accepting, while those who have nothing to lose, i.e. those whose careers will not be affected by the changes, can afford to be critical. Therefore, the closer to retirement a HoU is, the more openly critical he may be as regards his attitude towards the Kinnock reform. However, managers close to retirement are more positive about the recent changes than young managers. Interestingly, Hooghe found the same negative correlations in her data (2001: 163ff.). The remaining hypotheses show no correlation pattern.

In sum, the survey results underpin the fact that the role of the HoU within the organization has been rede"ned by the recent administrative reform. At the very least, the results indicate huge feelings of anxiety, and sometimes even alienation, in their professional self-understanding as regards the effects of the Kinnock reform. According to the HoU, the general reform aims have not been met. What characterizes the current situation is an insuf"cient redistribution of resources, heavy red tape and heavy planning burdens, but not more autonomy. More speci"cally, the particular instruments introduced by the Kinnock reform   job descriptions, de"ning individual responsibilities, setting individual targets, annual appraisal exercises, systematically assessing achievements, monitoring and reporting duties   are evaluated more kindly, at times even very positively. This indicates a worrying level of alienation. The majority of HoU have misgivings about the reform and, more importantly, they dislike the new roles which the reform has assigned to them. Two-thirds still seem to prefer a role model as policy innovator and not one as public manager. However, as good public servants they accept their fate, and endorse in particular those reform elements which improve their capacity to do a proper job. In other words, they make an effort to function like managers, but in their hearts they still feel like policy entrepreneurs.

5. CONCLUSION: BETTER MANAGERS, DEPRIVED ENTREPRENEURS

Management reforms in the public sector (and elsewhere) usually have various effects   some may be intended, others unintended (Pollitt and Bouckaert 2004). In this article I attempted to gauge the possible implications of the recent Commission reform for EU policy-making. I assumed that the HoU, i.e. the middle management inside the Commission, is the crucial link between expertise and politics. And, further, I took for granted that the Commission s strength as an actor in EU public policy-making rests, to a large extent, on its ability to deliver concrete and substantial policy drafts of a high quality. From that perspective, I tried to "nd out what the recent Kinnock reform meant for the HoU. As it turned out, the Kinnock reform completely transforms the role of the HoU. It is probably not an exaggeration to think of the new role of the HoU as the centrepiece of the Kinnock strategy. This new role is displayed in the effort to make the Commission administration more accountable to the College, i.e. to subject policy output to central priority-setting and to increase the capacities at the organizational top for political steering. Taken together, this re"ects the usual new public management agenda of public sector reform (Bear"eld 2004; Schön-Quinlivan 2008). Note that I do not make any claims about the appropriateness or, indeed, about the long-term chances of success of the Kinnock reform to change the Commission administrative culture in that perspective (cf. Balint *et al.* 2008). Actually and paradoxically, in this respect the Kinnock reform may well work and reform advocates are probably correct in pointing out that modernization is, after all, a long-term endeavour, and that it is therefore too early to tell whether or not it is successful. However, from the point of view adopted as the analytical focus for this paper, *better internal management does not mean improved organizational capability for policy entrepreneurship.* To be clear: I have not investigated policy results and I did not develop a theory or an analytical framework, let alone apply it to empirical testing, which could lead to the conclusion that EU public policy output decreased in quantity or declined in quality since the adoption of the Kinnock reform. These are questions I would recommend researchers to engage in. *However, I do claim that the role of the Commission administration in the complicated equation of EU policy-making is weakened by the Kinnock reform.* The Commission will become more inward-looking, and crucial individuals will have less time for policy content than they used to have in the past. In a seminal article from 1997, Brigid Laffan saw the challenge for the Commission to change from a policy entrepreneur to a programme manager. The new challenge after the Kinnock reform may be to maintain decentralized entrepreneurship capability at the policy level in an organization subjected to burdensome management rules and a centripetal programming approach. There appears little need to fear an excessively entrepreneurial Commission for some time to come.

Biographical note: Michael W. Bauer is Assistant Professor (C1) for Comparative Public Policy and Administration at the Department of Politics and Management, University of Konstanz, Germany.

Address for correspondence: Michael W. Bauer, Department of Politics and Management, University of Konstanz, D 91, D-78457 Konstanz, Germany. email: michael.w.bauer@uni-konstanz.de

ACKNOWLEDGEMENTS

Earlier drafts of this paper were presented at the Connex RG1 Conference, 11 13 May 2006, Vienna, and at the EUSA Biannual Conference, 17 19 May 2007, Montreal. I am grateful for comments from Christoph Knill, Roger Levy, Liesbet Hooghe, Hussein Kassim and two anonymous referees. I am equally grateful for research assistance from Anna-Lena Beilschmidt, Dominik Bernauer, Michael Dobbins, Christina Eder, Elise Hadman, Dorota Tomalak, Jale Tosun, Natascha Warta, Stine Waibel und Alexander Wohlwender.

NOTES

1 This new system was designed to increase the transparency of individual perform- ance assessment and to ensure unbiased transmission of these results to the superiors responsible for deciding about promotion. The appraisal system is hugely unpopu- lar in the Commission. Its major de"ciency seems to be that HoU shy away from giving a very high or a very low number of points (so the whole exercise becomes ineffectual). DG Administration is currently working on improving this system. The intention is to reduce the number of points that an individual can receive and create a normal number of points for those who are doing a good, but normal job, which allows a normal career path without the current problem of comparative demotivation.

2 Explorative interview G, March 2005.

3 Explorative interview E, March 2005.

4 This interview was conducted in German; the term in the original is *Überzeugungs- täter*.

5 Explorative interview A, March 2005.

6 The HoU were given the options positive , negative and irrelevant and don t know/no answer .

7 To be sure, while the part directly before the open question was about reform issues, two-thirds of the questions asked in the survey had nothing to do with the Kinnock reform.

8 I conducted two regression analyses. First, I computed a multivariate ordinary least square regression. For that reason, I constructed an additive index with the answers obtained from the HoU when asked: If you assess the impact of the recent internal modernization (i.e. the so-called Kinnock reforms) in the light of your own experi- ence, which of the following statements can you agree with? Second, I conducted logit regressions. Unfortunately, the model "t is in general very low.

9 Reform aversion of initiative-oriented DG: this hypothesis relates to the different tasks that the Commission has to perform. One can distinguish three categories of policy DGs: implementation-oriented (e.g. agriculture, "sheries, cohesion policy), adjudication-oriented (competition, internal market, services) and initiat- ive-oriented (justice, freedom, security, health and consumer protection, the environment, education and culture). According to simple entrepreneurship logic, one should see the initiative-oriented as most affected by reform, and there- fore the HoU from these DGs would be most critical about the in"icted changes. Idealism aversion: this relationship concerns the original reason to join the Com- mission. The more idealism (usually associated with individual enthusiasm to help foster European integration) an individual expresses, the more likely it is that he or she sees the Commission as the creative pivotal actor embodying the European interest , and the more sceptical this individual might be that the Com- mission is changing into a managerial administration, as had been the outspoken

objective of the Kinnock reforms (reform aversion from idealists for European integration). Private sector experience: according to this hypothesis, work experience outside the Commission would make the HoU more open to the kind of change brought about by the Kinnock reform. Number of staff: furthermore, to what extent an individual HoU is affected by the Kinnock reform depends (in crucial respects) on the number of staff for whom he or she is responsible. The more staff, the greater the managerial responsibility and the higher the related administrative requirements (as regards individual target-setting, promotion procedures, reporting, etc.). Hence, one would expect that the more personnel a policy HoU has charge of, the more critical are seen to be the effects of the Kinnock reform (reform aversion because of huge staff responsibility). Leftist aversion: "nally, new public management reforms are ideologically closer to liberal and conservative political points of view. Hence, managers with a leftist political conviction should display aversion to such marketizing organizational change (reform distaste owing to leftist political conviction).

REFERENCES

Balint, T., Bauer, M.W. and Knill, C. (2008) Bureaucratic change in the European administrative space. The case of the European Commission , *West European Politics* 32(1) (forthcoming).

Bauer, M.W. (2002) Limitations to agency control in EU policy-making   the Commission and the poverty programmes , *Journal of Common Market Studies* 40(3): 381   400.

Bauer, M.W. (2005) The European Commission , in P.M. van der Hoek (ed.), *Handbook of Public Administration and Policy in the European Union,* London and New York: Taylor & Francis, pp. 149 76.

Bauer, M.W. (2006) Co-managing programme implementation: conceptualizing the European Commission s role in policy execution , *Journal of European Public Policy* 13(5): 717 35.

Bauer, M.W. (2007) The politics of reforming the European Commission administration , in M.W. Bauer and C. Knill (eds), *Management Reforms in International Organizations,* Baden-Baden: Nomos, pp. 54 69.

Bear"eld, N.D. (2004) Reforming the European Commission. Driving reform from the grassroots , *Public Policy and Administration* 19(5): 13 24.

Christiansen, T. (2006) The European Commission. The European executive between continuity and change , in J. Richardson (ed.), *European Union: Power and Policy-making,* London and New York: Routledge, pp. 99 117.

Cini, M. (1996) *The European Commission. Leadership, Organization and Culture in the EU Administration,* Manchester: Manchester University Press.

Cini, M. (2004) The reform of the European Commission; an ethical perspective , *Public Policy and Administration* 19(3): 42 54.

Cokins, G. (1996) *Activity-based Cost Management. Making It Work,* New York: McGraw-Hill.

Coombes, D. (1970) *Politics and Bureaucracy in the European Community: A Portrait of the Commission of the EEC,* London: George Allen & Unwin.

Cram, L. (1993) Calling the tune without paying the piper? The role of the Commission in European Community social policy , *Policy and Politics* 21: 135 46.

European Commission (2004) *Completing the Reform Mandate: Progress Report and Measures to be Implemented in 2004,* COM (2004) 93 "nal, 2 February 2004, Brussels.

Héritier, A. (1997) Policy-making by subterfuge: interest accommodation, innovation and substitute democratic legitimation in Europe   perspectives from distinct policy areas , *Journal of European Public Policy* 4(2): 171 89.

Hix, S. (2005) *The Political System of the European Union*, 2nd edn, Basingstoke: Palgrave.

Hooghe, L. (2001) *The European Commission and the Integration of Europe. Images of Governance*, Cambridge: Cambridge University Press.

Kassim, H. (2004a) A historic accomplishment. The Prodi Commission and administrative reform , in D.G. Dimitrakopoulos (ed.), *The Changing European Commission*, Manchester: Manchester University Press, pp. 33 63.

Kassim, H. (2004b) The Kinnock reforms in perspective: why reforming the Commission is an heroic, but thankless task , *Public Policy and Administration* 19(3): 25 41.

Kassim, H. (2008) Mission impossible , but mission accomplished: the Kinnock reforms and the European Commission , *Journal of European Public Policy* 15(5): 648 68.

Kingdon, J.W. (1995) *Agendas, Alternatives and Public Policies*, New York: Longman.

Laffan, B. (1997) From policy entrepreneur to policy manager: the challenge facing the European Commission , *Journal of European Public Policy* 4(3): 422 38.

Levy, R. (2004) Between rhetoric and reality. Implementing management reform in the European Commission , *The International Journal of Public Sector Management* 17: 166 77.

Levy, R. (2006) European Commission overload and the pathology of management reform: garbage can, rationality and risk aversion , *Public Administration* 84(2): 423 39.

Ludlow, P. (1991) The European Commission , in R.O. Keohane and S. Hoffmann (eds), *The New European Community. Decision-making and Institutional Change*, Boulder, CO: Westview Press, pp. 85 132.

Metcalfe, L. (2000) Reforming the Commission: will organizational ef"ciency produce effective governance? , *Journal of Common Market Studies* 38(5): 817 41.

Moravcsik, A. (1998) *The Choice for Europe. Social Purpose and State Power from Messina to Maastricht*, Ithaca, NY: Cornell University Press.

Noel, E. (1973) The Commission s power of initiative , *Common Market Law Review* 10: 123 36.

Nugent, N. (ed.) (1997) *At the Heart of the Union. Studies of the European Commission*, Basingstoke: Macmillan.

Nugent, N. (2001) *The European Commission*, Basingstoke: Palgrave.

Peters, B.G. (1994) Agenda-setting in the European Community , *Journal of European Public Policy* 1(1): 9 26.

Peters, B.G. (1996) Agenda-setting in the European Union , in J. Richardson (ed.), *European Union: Power and Policy-making*, London and New York: Routledge, pp. 61 76.

Peterson, J. (1995) Playing the transparency game: consultation and policy-making in the European Commission , *Public Administration* 73(3): 473 92.

Pollack, M.A. (2003) *The Engines of European Integration: Delegation, Agency and Agenda Setting in the EU*, Oxford: Oxford University Press.

Pollitt, C. and Bouckaert, G. (2004) *Public Management Reform   A Comparative Analysis*, Oxford: Oxford University Press.

Richardson, J. (2006) Policy-making in the EU. Interests, ideas and garbage cans of primeval soup , in J. Richardson (ed.), *European Union. Power and Policy-making*, London and New York: Routledge, pp. 3 29.

Rochefort, D.A. and Cobb, R.W. (eds) (1995) *The Politics of Problem De nition: Shaping the Policy Agenda*, Lawrence, KS: University Press of Kansas.

Sabatier, P.A. (1993) Advocacy-Koalitionen, Policy-Wandel und Policy-Lernen: Eine Alternative zur Phasenheuristik , in A. Héritier (ed.), *Policy Analyse. Kritik und Neuorientierung*, Opladen: Westdeutscher Verlag, pp. 116 48.

Schön-Quinlivan, E. (2008) Implementing organizational change   the case of the Kinnock reforms , *Journal of European Public Policy* 15(5): 726   42.

Smyrl, M.E. (1998) When (and how) do the Commission s preferences matter? , *Journal of Common Market Studies* 36(1): 79   100.

Spence, D. (2000) Plus ça change, plus c est la meme chose? Attempting to reform the European Commission , *Journal of European Public Policy* 7(1): 1   25.

Spence, D. (2006) The DGs and the services: structures, functions and procedures , in D.B. Spence and G. Edwards (eds), *The European Commission*, London: John Harper Publishing, pp. 128   55.

Spence, D. and Stevens, A. (2006) Staff and personnel policy in the Commission , in D.B. Spence and G. Edwards (eds), *The European Commission*, London: John Harper Publishing, pp. 173   208.

Stevens, H. and Stevens, A. (2006) The internal reform of the Commission , in D.B. Spence and G. Edwards (eds), *The European Commission*, London: John Harper Publishing, pp. 454   80.

Reforming the Commission: between modernization and bureaucratization

Antonis Ellinas and Ezra Suleiman

INTRODUCTION

Seven years after the administrative storm caused by the Eurocleaners of the Prodi Commission, the dust has started settling. It is a good time, then, to take stock. Have the ambitious reform efforts yielded the ef"ciency gains that the reformers sought to achieve? And have they set in place suf"cient controls against fraud? Answers to these questions vary substantially depending on who you ask. The Prodi Commission, which laid the groundwork for the most radical administrative transformation since the creation of the organization, boasts that within "ve years it completed all the reform-related measures set out in its 2000 White Paper (European Commission 2005). But Commission whistleblowers and auditors have argued that although the reforms are impressive on paper, in practice the organization remains exposed to fraud and mismanagement. Moreover, unions representing Commission of"cials have delivered damning appraisals of the reforms, blaming them for demoralizing staff and for creating a dog eat dog atmosphere within the organization. Scholarly observers have been more cautious in their analysis. Some have noted the unprecedented pace and scope of the reform (e.g. Kassim 2004) while others have pointed to its pathologies (e.g. Levy 2006).

This article utilizes and extends the insights of earlier scholarly work to present the views of top European of" cials on the reform initiative. Rather than relying on the claims of the modernizers and their outspoken critics, the article reports the beliefs of those who experienced the reform at "rst hand nearly 200 top managers whom we surveyed in 2005 through personal interviews. The timing of the interviews could not have been more opportune: by early 2005, the Commission completed all 98 measures included in its ambitious programme and started considering ways to push the reform beyond its original mandate. During this critical time, we asked of" cials to re" ect on the administrative reform and to evaluate its impact on their working environment. Top managers responded to a battery of questions about the structure of the Commission, about the recent changes in personnel policy and about their preferred course of future reforms.

The emerging view from the top management is that the Commission is caught between two con" icting trends, modernization and bureaucratization . This challenges the dominant view that the reform project was largely a move toward the institutional paradigm set by new public management (NPM). Based on the views of top Commission of" cials, the reforms can best be described as a marriage of NPM and Weberian-bureaucratic principles. The former sought to improve the ef" ciency of the Commission through the promotion of individual responsibility, managerial autonomy, and output-based orientation. The latter aimed to increase the accountability of the organization through the introduction of elaborate control and veri" cation procedures. The expanded body of rules and regulations has strengthened the bureaucratic elements of the organization at the expense of productivity and autonomy.

The set of administrative reforms initiated by Vice-President Neil Kinnock were a direct response to the legitimacy crisis that led to the fall of the Santer Commission. The "rst section of this paper examines the crisis that catalysed the modernization efforts. The second section provides a brief overview of the reform programme and the third offers an on paper assessment of the reform. The fourth and "fth sections report the views of the Commission s top management on the reforms. The article ends with some concluding thoughts on the future of administrative reform in the Commission.

CRISIS AND CHANGE

For nearly two decades the European Commission resisted calls for administrative reform. As Hussein Kassim nicely outlines in his contribution to this volume (2008), repeated efforts to improve the workings of the organization brought about either incremental or no change (see also Spierenburg 1979; Hay 1989; European Commission 1990, 1998, 1999; Stevens and Stevens

2001; Metcalfe 1999; Kassim 2004). Given this long organizational inertia, the radical transformation of the past few years cannot be understood in isolation from the crisis that led to the resignation of the Santer Commission in March 1999. The crisis exposed two main pathologies of the internal workings of the organization, highlighted by the Committee of Independent Experts which set out to investigate the allegations of fraud, mismanagement and nepotism raised against the Commission by the European Parliament (EP). The "rst problem was ineffective management: commissioners lost control of their departments, failed to respond effectively to chronic problems of understaf"ng, and avoided penalizing those responsible for irregularities. The second problem was inadequate control owing to the failure of internal audit and control procedures. The prescribed solution, then, was the enhancement of the managerial capacity of the Commission and an improvement in the allocation and control of its resources.

The prescriptions were taken up by the incoming Prodi Commission, which was given a strong political mandate to modernize the workings of the organization. Only a few months after taking of"ce, the Commission published a White Paper that detailed its reform proposals. The modernization effort drew from the "ndings of the two reports published by the Committee of Independent Experts and on a series of internal reports, including that of the Williamson group and the DECODE assessment. This gave a sense of continuity between the Kinnock and earlier reforms (Christiansen 2004: 112 13) as a number of the proposed measures had been either initiated or suggested by previous Commissions. But, as the White Paper rightly noted, the scope and ambition of the Prodi initiative far exceeded that of any previous reform exercise (European Commission 2000b: 6). For not only were some of suggestions novel, but they also came with tight deadlines for completion and clear assignments of tasks to the various directorates or units. More importantly, though, the Kinnock reforms were part of a comprehensive and cohesive reform strategy that was driven by a political vision to change the workings of the Commission.

THE KINNOCK REFORMS

The reform initiative of the Prodi Commission was launched in March 2000 with the approval and publication of the White Paper. The overall reform strategy of the Commission was divided into four themes set out in the "rst part of the White Paper. The second part detailed an action plan of 98 measures, deadlines for their implementation and the actors responsible for their execution (European Commission 2000a, 2000b). The "rst and overarching theme of the modernization push was the development of a culture based on service . As soon as it took of"ce the Prodi Commission agreed on new standards of behaviour for Commissioners and on a code for good administrative behaviour . Moreover, it sought to enhance public access to European Union (EU) documents, to improve the dialogue with civil society, to speed up payments to contractors and to build up the technological infrastructure of the organization. There was also an effort to codify relations with the EP, in light of institutional changes brought about by the Amsterdam Treaty. Most of the 11 measures detailed under the culture theme were improvements on actions initiated by previous Commissions. As Kinnock admits, the emphasis on culture was largely a convenient, spray-on label to summarize inherited organizational custom (Kinnock 2004: 8).

The second theme focused on the ef"cient allocation and use of resources based on the prioritization of policy outputs. Echoing NPM-type ideas implemented earlier in Anglo-Saxon countries (e.g. Hood 1991; Suleiman 2003), the White Paper proposed a reassessment of existing Commission priorities and the establishment of new ones. This would set the basis for the diversion of resources to those areas where they were likely to give the best policy outputs. The overall goal was to encourage the various directorates and departments to focus more on results, rather than procedures   what the White Paper termed   activity-based management . To facilitate this, the Commission would formulate an annual policy strategy to set the basis for the work programme of each individual administrative unit. The assignment of work programmes would help to decentralize decision-making and promote personal responsibility. It would also make it easier to determine the amount of resources required to achieve speci"c policy outputs. To encourage the more ef"cient allocation of resources, the White Paper proposed the formulation of a comprehensive framework for externalizing activities   for example, outsourcing.

The third theme of the reform initiative was the improvement of "nancial management and control as well as the establishment of more robust audit procedures. This part of the modernization project was tightly connected to the previous one. Activity-based management would facilitate the determination of a work programme for each of"cial, specify output expectations and devolve responsibility for their completion. Those of"cials making operational decisions involving expenditure would also assume "nancial responsibility. To deal with criticism about lack of responsibility and to address problems related to the increasing number of "nancial transactions   which doubled to 620,000 per year in "ve years   the Commission proposed the decentralization of "nancial control. Directors-General would be made responsible for adequate controls of their departments and managers would be held accountable for the "nancial decisions they take. According to this scheme, each unit would develop an independent audit capability. Moreover, the Commission proposed to set up two additional bodies, the Central Financial Service and Internal Audit Service, to advise and assist the managers and directors with "nancial control. In addition, an Audit Progress Committee would control audit processes, oversee the implementation of audit recommendations and assess the quality of audit work. Finally, there would be measures to maximize the prevention of "nancial irregularity through improvements of existing procedures.

The last and lengthiest theme of the reform project related to the modernization of human resources policy from recruitment to retirement. In line with its earlier proposals, the Commission sought to strengthen middle management by granting Heads of Unit autonomy for operational and "nancial decisions. Moreover, it identi"ed management ability as the most important criterion for appointments. With regard to recruitment, the White Paper proposed to improve the organization of open competitions and tests by taking into account the best practices in national and international administrations. One of the most notable suggestions regarded the establishment of a more linear career structure that would increase the incentives for improving performance. Appraisals would be made with the attribution of points and, consequently, promotion would depend mostly on merit, rather than seniority. Over-performance would be rewarded and under-performance would be dealt with more systematically. To improve the working environment, the Commission would grant the right to family leave, introduce more "exible working hours and strengthen the existing equal opportunities scheme. The White Paper also suggested improving the disciplinary and whistle-blowing systems.

The Commission hoped to complete the 98 reform-related actions outlined in the White Paper within two years and to review the progress of the reform in 2002. By February 2003, when it published its "rst comprehensive analysis of the reform effort, it could claim the completion of 87 out of the 98 actions. The few delays related to the development of the new procurements and accounting systems. There was also some lag with work programmes, internal controls and project management. Unsurprisingly, personnel policy proved to be the most contentious issue causing signi"cant tension between the Commission and the unions. The new set of Staff Regulations was adopted in May 2004 after a prolonged period of negotiations with staff representatives. Nevertheless, some of the most innovative aspects of the reform, like the new appraisal system and the new structure, were adopted much earlier. By 2005, the Commission claimed the completion of all 98 actions (see Table 1).

ASSESSING THE REFORM

The swift completion of the action plan has largely been taken as a mark of its success. The Kinnock reforms have come to be regarded as a historic

Table 1 Progress in implementing the 2000 action plan

	2000*	2003	2004	2005
Service-based culture	11	9	9.5	11
Priority-setting and resource allocation	9	8	9	9
Financial management, audit and control	42	38	42	42
Human resources	36	32	35	36
Total	98	87	95.5	98

Source: European Commission; various reports on reform.
Notes: Number of actions completed.
*Actions planned.

accomplishment (Kassim 2004: 33) or as a remarkable achievement that far exceeds previous modernization efforts (Bauer 2007: 52). Indeed, on a number of fronts the Commission has managed to make substantial progress. For example, the average number of days it took for the Commission to make a payment decreased from 54 in 1999 to 42.9 in 2003. And in 2003, between 80 and 90 per cent of public mail was replied to within the standard deadline compared with 70 per cent in 2002. Moreover, the number of days spent on employee training increased from 6.9 in 2001 to 8.3 by 2003. During that year, 7,000 Commission of"cials participated in "nancial training and 500 middle managers took management courses. There was also progress in the implementation of the equal opportunities scheme: the number of female top managers increased from 22 in 1998 to 39 in 2003 and the proportion of incoming female A-grade of"cials increased from 27.6 per cent in 2002 to 33.3 per cent (European Commission 2003, 2004).

But apart from the progress achieved in these speci"c areas, the overall impact of the reform on the workings of the organization is harder to assess. This is largely because a considerable number of reform-related tasks involved the drafting of proposals, reviews or rules and setting up new institutions, systems or committees. The completion of such tasks set the basis for change, but it did not necessarily improve the workings of the Commission. Moreover, despite the emphasis of the reformers on output, there is a peculiar absence of speci"c indicators for measuring the relative success of the reform. The few indicators used by the Kinnock team to assess progress in the implementation of the reforms were mostly put in place after the reform was well on its way. Using different criteria, Levy (2006) presents a strikingly different picture of the modernization effort than the one given by the Commission. He argues that the reform increased the workload of the of"cials and created more dependency relationships through the establishment of new processes. His on-paper analysis suggests that by 2004 the Commission implemented fully or partly only half of the actions it claimed it had completed. This negative assessment of the modernization effort con"rms insiders claims that the reform failed to bring about the desired effects. One of them, former chief accountant Marta Adreasen, was suspended in 2002 after blowing the whistle on the Commission s "nancial control mechanisms. Her claims were substantiated by a leaked report from the internal auditor that noted many procedural or systemic de"ciencies on reform-related tasks marked, in the 2003 review, as completed (European Commission 2004: 63 9). Further doubt about the effectiveness of the reforms was cast by the "nancial irregularities discovered in Eurostat during 2003.

THE VIEW FROM THE TOP

Our survey of nearly 200 top Commission of"cials presents a different view of the reform effort. The survey was carried out between March and

December 2005 through semi-structured interviews and it sought to build on the "ndings of Liesbet Hooghe s impressive work on the Commission (e.g. Hooghe 2001). It complements and extends the "ndings of Michael Bauer s survey of middle-ranking of"cials, presented in this issue (2008). All top of"cials were asked in writing to participate in the survey and a representative sample   68 per cent of Directors-General, 59 per cent of Depute Directors-General and 52 per cent of Directors   granted us interviews of up to one hour. To this notable pool of 133 top managers, we added a convenience sample of 55 middle managers or Heads of Unit to explore if views about administrative reform vary across managerial levels.[1] The total sample includes of"cials from all directorates and from most of the Commission s general and internal services (see Appendix). The geographical distribution of the sample is also balanced. More than half of the of"cials come from the "ve most populous member states: Britain (13 per cent), France (13 per cent), Spain (11 per cent), Germany (10 per cent) and Italy (10 per cent). The Belgians make up 10 per cent of the sample, the Dutch 6 per cent and the Greeks another 6 per cent, while only 2 per cent come from the ten new members states. The overwhelming majority of the of"cials we interviewed had worked for the Commission for at least ten years: 40 per cent joined the Commission between 1986 and 1995; 28 per cent joined in the preceding decade; and 17 per cent before 1976.

The survey asked top of"cials about their professional experience, the organizational culture of the Commission and their vision of the EU. A battery of "ve questions dealt speci"cally with the organizational structure of the Commission and with the Kinnock reforms. The survey followed the completion of all reform-related actions and anticipated the internal deliberations about the future of the modernization drive. Top Commission of"cials had experienced at "rst hand the intense efforts to change the workings of the organization and were best placed to assess its outcome. Along with the middle management, top of"cials bore the heaviest burden of the modernization drive: they had to follow new appraisal procedures, implement "nancial controls in their units and oversee the shift to activity-based management. The survey sought to tap into their "rst-hand knowledge by asking them to comment on the overall workings of the Commission and to assess the most contentious aspects of the Kinnock reforms, those relating to the management of human resources. During a time when the Barroso Commission was discussing the future of the reform initiative, the survey also asked of"-cials to sketch the contours of future reforms. The remainder of this section records their responses.

Not a hierarchical beast

Overall, top of"cials do not seem to share the commonly held view that the Commission is hierarchically structured, along the lines of the French and German bureaucracy. Out of the 189 of"cials who responded to this question,

110 or 58 per cent disagreed or strongly disagreed with the notion that the Commission is too hierarchical . Views about the structure of the Commission cut across rank, but not across length of service. Unsurprisingly, newer employees are more likely to view the Commission as being hierarchical than those who have worked for the Commission longer (see Table 2). Interestingly, while many of"cials despise the hierarchical nature of the institution, others think it is a necessary evil , as there is no other way to run a big complex organization . Moreover, many of"cials share the view that the Kinnock reforms pushed the Commission towards NPM, noting that the Commission has become less hierarchical over time. Out of the 100 of"cials who commented extensively on the question about hierarchy, 13 noted an improvement, mostly in terms of accessibility to the top as well as "exibility. None of the of"-cials suggested that the Commission had become more hierarchical (see Table 3).

Merit-based recruitment

Apart from their views on the overall structure of the Commission, the survey sought to tap into the experiences of top managers in the implementation of personnel reforms. To do so, it focused on one of the most sensitive components of the reform package: the new staff appraisal and promotion system. By 2005, when we conducted the survey, the Prodi Commission had completed two full exercises of the new system. Owing to the resistance that these exercises met from staff, in March 2004 it commissioned an in-depth external evaluation of the system, with a view to improving, in particular, the link between merit and promotion (European Commission 2005: 7). Our survey, then, sought to examine exactly this: the capacity of the new system to reward merit. After a quick reference to the Kinnock reforms, we asked top of"cials whether the promotion system was fully merit-based. As a control, we asked a similar question about a much less sensitive issue: the recruitment of new of"cials.

Table 2 Question: Some say the Commission is too hierarchical. Do you agree? (%)

Position (N= 183)	No	Yes
DG/DDG	58	42
D	63	37
HoU	50	50
Total	58	42
Length of service (N= 172)	No	Yes
0–10 years	46	54
11–20	53	47
21–30	71	29
>30	72	28
Total	60	40

Table 3 Supplementary remarks to question if Commission is too hierarchical (*N* = 100)*

Less hierarchical than (national) administrations	6
As hierarchical as (national) administrations	10
More hierarchical than (national) administrations	6
Improved from before	13
Same as before	1
Depends on Directorate	8
Depends on D/DG/Commissioner	11
Hierarchy is necessary	10
Easy access to top	8
Flexible	6
Others	30
Total	109

Note: *Some respondents touched on several themes, and their remarks were counted more than once.

The views of top of"cials on the recruitment procedures of the Commission are generally positive. More than half of the respondents think that recruitment is fully merit-based and another 40 per cent think that it is mostly merit-based . Only 7 per cent think that recruitment is not merit-based at all . Interestingly, the views of top of"cials vary considerably depending on their rank and experience. The higher up in the hierarchy and the longer their years of service in the Commission, the more likely they are to think that the recruitment process is fully merit-based. Hence, only 36 per cent of Heads of Unit consider recruitment to be fully merit-based compared to 73 per cent of Directors-General; and only 40 per cent of the newest of"cials think so compared to 72 per cent of the of"cials with the longest service (see Table 4). Although most of"cials think that recruitment is based on merit, many think that the open competitions might be rewarding the wrong types of merit. As one of the respondents noted, Recruitment is fully merit-based, but the wrong merit is being tested. People who are recruited can often lack the skills necessary to complete particular tasks . Moreover, many interviewees distinguished between recruitment for lower and higher ranks: The higher you get, the less merit-based the system becomes, and the more important political and nationality considerations become . For many top of"cials, there is a signi"cant element of randomness in the procedure, as the Commission hires only a tiny fraction of the 50,000 people who take its exams. And for others, the process is too bureaucratic and rigid, causing delays in resourcing units.

Promotion: mixed picture

The responses of top of"cials to the question about promotion paint a less rosy picture than the one given by their thoughts on recruitment. Whereas half of the

Table 4 Question: One of the most important set of reforms in the recent past, the Kinnock reforms, dealt with the issue of recruitment/promotion. Do you think recruitment/promotion in the Commission is fully merit-based?

Recruitment merit-based (%)			
Position (N = 83)	*Fully*	*Mostly*	*Not at all*
DG/DDG	73	27	0
D	56	35	9
HoU	36	55	9
Total	52	40	7
Length of service (N = 172)	*Fully*	*Mostly*	*Not at all*
0–10 years	40	48	12
11–20	49	42	9
21–30	55	39	6
>30	72	28	0
Total	53	39	8
Promotion merit-based (%)			
Position (N = 183)	*Fully*	*Mostly*	*Not at all*
DG/DDG	29	68	3
D	17	74	9
HoU	10	69	21
Total	16	72	12
Length of service (N = 66)	*Fully*	*Mostly*	*Not at all*
0–10 years	8	68	24
11–20	17	69	14
21–30	14	80	6
>30	36	57	7
Total	18	70	12

survey respondents think that recruitment is fully merit-based, only 16 per cent view promotion to be so. The vast majority of them or 72 per cent think that promotion is mostly merit-based, while 12 per cent think that the process is not merit-based at all. Naturally, the percentage of those who hold positive views of the promotion process decreases along with rank and length of service. The higher of cials are on the ladder, the more favourable their view of the process that got them there. Hence, while 29 per cent of Directors-General view promotion as being fully based on merit, only 10 per cent of Heads of Unit think so. Interestingly, 21 per cent of middle managers think that the system is not merit-based at all, compared to a mere 3 per cent of top managers (see Table 4).

Many top of cials think that, apart from merit, various other considerations are taken into account when promotion is decided. Among those who gave extensive responses to the question about promotion, a signi cant number noted that seniority is still important, in part because of the concessions that

Kinnock had to make to the trade unions. Many others suggested that politics or nationality is still important, especially for high-ranking of‟cials (see Table 5). As a Head of Unit noted, I know I will never be a Director-General because there are already three Spaniards . A large number of the respondents (55) responded to the question by comparing the current state of affairs with the previous one. The majority of them (31) noted an improvement, 16 said that things had stayed as before and only eight of them said that things had become worse.

Commenting on speci‟c aspects of the new appraisal and promotion system, top of‟cials painted a mixed picture. Many of them said that the new system increased transparency and helped to make top managers more accountable for their decisions. A typical response was that the Kinnock reforms made things more transparent but at the top of the organization nationality still counts . Another respondent noted: Yes to Kinnock! The system is more transparent now and it is easier to explain decisions to the staff . Similarly, another remarked: Indeed, it is more merit-based now than in the past. The old system wasn t that bad. But this one is more transparent . But many of‟cials also noted negative aspects of the new promotion system. Many were particularly critical of the point-based appraisal system. The words and phrases used to describe it should suf‟ce to give the overall picture: stressful, awful, demotivating, poisonous, tension-creating, bad for teamwork, etc. Moreover, a number of of‟cials pointed out that the increase in transparency came at the cost of cumbersome

Table 5 Responses to question whether promotion is merit-based ($N = 140$)*

Mostly merit-based but ...	
... nationality also important	10
... connections also important	7
... seniority also important	19
... politics also important	16
... gender also important	1
... visibility also important	3
... only up to a certain rank	9
Comparison across time	
Improved from before	31
Same as before	16
Worse than before	8
Positive and negative aspects	
More transparency/more accountability	18
Point system has negative effects	14
More rigid/cumbersome/bureaucratic/complicated	28
Other	34
Total	214

Note: *Some respondents touched on several themes, and their remarks were counted more than once.

procedures that overburden managers. Now the system is clean and clear. But the exercise is very complicated and heavy and the process has become very time-consuming . Others think that the administrative cost has come at no extra bene"t: The Kinnock reforms did not improve things. They haven t really changed things ... The old system was merit-based; the new system just made things more cumbersome. Yet others were even more negative: This Anglo-Saxon, private-sector system is probably making things less ef"cient. It is making things worse, much more cumbersome. Most private companies are abandoning this system.

More rules and procedures

The misgivings of top European of"cials about the cumbersomeness of the new personnel policy are largely in line with their views about the expanding body of rules that governs the Commission s workings. The vast majority of our inter-viewees (60 per cent) strongly agree or agree with the statement that the Com-mission is too bound by rules . As shown before, this contrasts with their views on the overall structure of the Commission. The cross-tabulation of their responses on rule-boundedness shows that they tend to cut across rank or length of service (see Table 6). Top of"cials criticize the tendency toward the bureaucratization brought about by the Kinnock reforms, especially with regard to "nancial rules. As a Director-General complained, Financial controls were weak; now they are too strong. Regardless of whether you are a big or a small spender, you have the same rules . According to some of"cials, the Kinnock reforms have brought about an administrative overdrive that has led to the proliferation of controllers and put of"cials on guard to protect themselves. As one of"cial noted in exasperation, It has gotten out of hand! There are too many cooks. There s a security mania. Everybody is afraid of taking risks. Some of"cials see the expansion in the body of rules as

Table 6 Question: Some say the Commission is too bound by rules. Do you agree? (%)

Position *(N = 183)*	No	Yes
DG/DDG	38	62
D	37	63
HoU	45	55
Total	40	60
Length of service (N = 66)	*No*	*Yes*
0–10 years	25	75
11–20	44	56
21–30	42	58
<30	36	64
Total	39	61

necessary, in order to thwart pressures from member states against the Commission, particularly after the Santer resignation. But although they understand this as a necessary step to respond to public criticism, they complain that the reform pendulum swung too far and that exaggerated controls have been put in place to overcompensate for the previous crisis .

BETWEEN MODERNIZATION AND BUREAUCRATIZATION

Overall, the view emerging from the top of the organization is that the Kinnock reforms have achieved progress in some areas but at the cost of introducing burdensome rules and cumbersome procedures. The top management thinks that the Commission is not as hierarchical as it is often portrayed and that in recent years it has become less hierarchical. The vast majority of the 200 interviewees also think that the Commission uses recruitment and promotion systems that are largely meritocratic, despite the various national or political considerations that it is compelled to take into account. But this general push towards modernization of the Commission in line with NPM-style ideas should not conceal a parallel trend towards the bureaucratization of the Commission. The vast majority of surveyed of" cials think that the organization is too bound by internal rules to the detriment of individual initiative. They view the procedural turn of the past few years as an administrative overdrive that risks undermining the willingness of of" cials to take risks. Moreover, the growing body of rules and regulations is thought to undermine the ef" ciency gains that the modernization effort sought to achieve. An example is the introduction of the new promotion system, which created lengthy bureaucratic procedures.

While the push towards modernization has been welcomed by the top management, the trend towards bureaucratization has generated strong demands for simplifying and streamlining the expanded body of rules that have been set in place over the past few years. This demand was expressed unequivocally when we asked of" cials which reforms they would like to see implemented in the future. Out of the 242 suggestions we recorded, more than a third (35.4 per cent) were about the simpli" cation of the rules or procedures governing the organization. Another 14 per cent regarded the streamlining of the organization and its rules (see Table 7). The extensive remarks of some of" cials tell of their exasperation: In the future, the Commission has to simplify procedures. I can t go to a meeting without getting 50 signatures! We need to simplify things a lot! Much more simpli" ed, logical, practical rules are needed. To control one euro you spend a lot of money, it s ridiculous. According to top managers of the organization, the administrative reforms of the past years are not only threatening ef" ciency but, more importantly, they seem to be undermining the capacity of the Commission to take risks and to innovate. Many of" cials note that the introduction of so many rules has made people obsessed with risk . They believe that there is a tremendous amount of risk aversion in the Commission . People have become afraid of fraud and this fear is paralysing as fewer are willing to take initiatives. We need to be able to take risks. We need to distinguish between

Table 7 Question: What kind of reforms, if any, would you like to see implemented in the future? (*N* = 182)

	Reforms mentioned	%
Simplifying	86	35.5
Streamlining	34	14.0
Devolve responsibility/More autonomy	23	9.5
None	23	9.5
Don't know	14	5.8
Flexibility	9	3.7
Co-ordination	8	3.3
Outsourcing	8	3.3
Resourcing/Increase resources	4	1.7
Other	33	13.6
Total	242	100.0

errors and fraud. We now want zero errors, which can t work. At the same time, the enforcement of lengthy procedures seems to diffuse responsibility and to undermine individual autonomy. This might explain why 9.5 per cent of the suggestions were about empowering employees by granting them more autonomy. In thinking about future reforms, many of" cials noted that The responsibilization or the empowering of of" cials is the way forward. For others, though, this might still be a risky approach. A considerable number of of" cials argued that no more reform should be undertaken before the organization is given time to digest the previous changes. As one of" cial characteristically put it, The past eight years have witnessed permanent reform. The behavioural rules of the game are changing every two years. The biggest future reform, then, would be to have a pause in the reform process. We need to stop for a while.

CONCLUSION

The view from the top of the organization is that the Commission is caught between two contradicting trends modernization and bureaucratization. This challenges the dominant view that sees the Kinnock reforms as a one-sided push towards NPM. The experiences of these top managers suggest that the introduction of NPM ideas such as the promotion of individual responsibility, managerial autonomy, citizenship orientation, and output-based assessment was accompanied by Weberian-type measures. Such measures included more robust "nancial controls and more stringent veri"cation rules; they also included more elaborate and more transparent personnel assessment procedures. The introduction of these measures has strengthened the bureaucratic elements of the organization at the cost of administrative ef"ciency and bureaucratic autonomy. In this sense it has undermined some of the aims the Prodi Commission sought to achieve.

The schizophrenic nature of the Kinnock reforms should not come as a surprise to close observers of the reform effort. The contradictions highlighted by the experiences of the top management merely re"ect the paradoxical objectives that the Commission set out to achieve. On the one hand, the reformers sought to bene"t from the modernization experience of many Western countries by introducing measures to enhance the ef"ciency of the Commission. On the other hand, though, they had to respond to the legitimacy crisis caused by the allegations of fraud and nepotism. The crisis created political demands for making the Commission more accountable, responsible and transparent (European Commission 2000a: 3). This led to a mixture of contradictory measures, some pushing the organization towards NPM-type modernization and others towards Weberian-type bureaucratization. This mixture of incompatible measures might be frustrating for those who saw the reform effort as an opportunity to enhance the ef"ciency of the organization. It is probably comforting, though, for those who understood it as a way to boost the waning legitimacy of the organization and to eliminate the democratic de"cit which the Commission was thought to exacerbate. In this sense, the trend towards bureaucratization is not the unintended consequence of the reform drive, as the frustration of top managers seems to imply. It is, rather, the intended effect of the political process that sought to limit the discretionary power of the Commission in order to re-establish its legitimacy.

Is this dual and contradictory course towards modernization and bureaucratization reversible? Can the organization be made more ef"cient without risking the loss of accountability? The Barroso Commission seems to think that it can, if it reverses the trend towards bureaucratization. In a recent report to the EP on the reform beyond the reform mandate , the Commission states that it wants to strike a better balance between the costs and bene"ts of control . It sets the simpli"cation of procedures and working methods as its cross-cutting objective and wants to streamline some of the newly introduced controls to achieve productivity gains (2005: 12). It is doubtful, though, whether the Commission can convince its political patrons to substantially alter the turn of the organization towards bureaucratization. Rising levels of Euro-scepticism and growing public anxieties over the loss of national sovereignty are likely to be strong impediments to any such change. In this sense, bureaucratization might be the price that international institutions have to pay when confronted with a crisis of legitimacy.

Biographical notes: Antonis Ellinas is a post-doctoral fellow at the Reuters Institute of Oxford University, UK. Ezra Suleiman is IBM Professor of International Studies and Professor of Politics at Princeton University, New Jersey, USA.

Address for correspondence: Antonis Ellinas, Department of Politics and International Relations, Reuters Institute, 13 Norham Gardens, Oxford OX2

6PS, UK. email: antonis.ellinas@politics.ox.ac.uk Ezra Suleiman, Princeton University, Politics Department, 130 Corwin Hall, Princeton, NJ 08544, USA. email: esuleiman@princeton.edu

ACKNOWLEDGEMENTS

We would like to thank the American Academy in Berlin, the Netherlands Institute for Advanced Study, Princeton University s Research Committee, Princeton s European Politics and Society Program and the Reuters Institute at Oxford University for their generous support for this project. We are indebted to Caspar van den Berg, Lisbet Hooghe, Michael W. Bauer and three anonymous referees for their useful and constructive critiques of an earlier draft, and to Quinton Mayne and Mai a Cross for their invaluable contributions during the various phases of the project.

NOTE

1 At the time of the interviews, there were 868 Heads of Unit. We randomly contacted 227 in the 17 largest Directorates-General   all those who had their contact details (fax numbers) on the EU website. The response rate was 24 per cent. Although there is no systematic bias that we know of in this convenience sample, the 55 respondents do not constitute a representative sample. Comparisons across rank, then, should be treated with some caution.

APPENDIX: INTERVIEWEES BY DIRECTORATE/SERVICE*

Name of Directorate-General	Number	%
Directorate		
Agriculture and Rural Development	17	9
Competition	8	4
Economic and Financial Affairs	7	4
Education and Culture	3	2
Employment, Social Affairs and Equal Opportunities	8	4
Enterprise and Industry	10	5
Environment	14	7
Fisheries and Maritime Affairs	4	2
Health and Consumer Protection	3	2
Information Society and Media	16	8
Internal Market and Services	6	3
Joint Research Centre	2	1
Justice, Freedom and Security	4	2

(*continued*)

Appendix Continued

Name of Directorate-General	Number	%
Regional Policy	7	4
Research	13	7
Taxation and Customs Union	3	2
Transport and Energy	3	2
Development	3	2
Enlargement	6	3
Europe Aid – Co-operation Office	17	9
External Relations	11	6
Humanitarian Aid Office – ECHO	3	2
Trade	7	4
Services		
European Anti-Fraud Office	2	1
Eurostat	0	0
Publications Office	0	0
Secretariat General	7	4
Press and Communication	0	0
Budget	4	2
Informatics	0	0
Interpretation	0	0
Legal Service	0	0
Personnel and Administration	2	1
Translation	0	0
Bureau of European Policy Advisers	0	0
Infrastructures and Logistics	0	0
Internal Audit Service	2	1
Total	192	100

Note: *Missing data for two interviewees.

REFERENCES

Bauer, M. (2007) The politics of reforming the European Commission , in M. Bauer and C. Knill (eds), *Management Reforms in International Organizations*, Baden-Baden: Nomos, pp. 51 69.

Bauer, M. (2008) Diffuse anxieties, deprived entrepreneurs: Commission reform and middle management , *Journal of European Public Policy* 15(5): 691 707.

Christiansen, T. (2004) The European Commission: the European executive between continuity and change , in J. Richardson (ed.), *European Union: Power and Policy-making*, London: Routledge, pp. 99 121.

European Commission (1990) *The Commission s Approach to the Management of Resources*, Sec(90) 1876 " nal, 10 October.

European Commission (1998) *General Report on the Activities of the European Union, 1997*, Brussels: European Commission.

European Commission (1999) *General Report on the Activities of the European Union, 1998*, Brussels: European Commission.

European Commission (2000a) *Reforming the Commission: White Paper, Part I*, COM(2000) 200 " nal/2.

European Commission (2000b) *Reforming the Commission: White Paper, Part II*, COM(2000) 200 " nal/2.

European Commission (2003) *Progress Review of Reform*, COM(2003) 40 " nal/2, 7 February.

European Commission (2004) *Completing the Reform Mandate: Progress Report and Measures to be Implemented in 2004*, COM(2004) 93 " nal, 2 February.

European Commission (2005) *Progress Report on the Commission Reform beyond the Reform Mandate*, Com 668 " nal, 21 December.

Hay, R. (1989) *The European Commission and the Administration of the Community*, Luxembourg: Of" ce for Of" cial Publications of the European Communities.

Hood, C. (1991) A public management for all seasons? , *Public Management* 69: 3 19.

Hooghe, L. (2001) *The European Commission and the Integration of Europe. Images of Governance*, Cambridge: Cambridge University Press.

Kassim, H. (2004) A historic accomplishment: the Prodi Commission and administrative reform , in D.G. Dimitrakopoulos (ed.), *The Changing European Commission*, Manchester: Manchester University Press, pp. 33 62.

Kassim, H. (2008)   Mission impossible , but mission accomplished: the Kinnock reforms and the European Commission , *Journal of European Public Policy* 15(5): 648 68.

Kinnock, N. (2004) Reforming the European Commission: organizational challenges and advances , *Public Policy and Administration* 19(3): 7 12.

Levy, R. (2006) European Commission overload and the pathology of management reform: garbage cans, rationality and risk aversion *Public Administration* 84(2): 423 39.

Metcalfe, L. (1999) Reforming the Commission , *EIPAScope* 99(3): 3 9.

Spierenberg, D. (1979) *Proposals for Reform of the Commission of the European Communities and its Services*, 24 September.

Stevens, A. and Stevens, H. (2001) *Brussels Bureaucrats? The Administration of the European Union*, Basingstoke: Palgrave.

Suleiman, E. (2003) *Dismantling Democratic States*, Princeton, NJ: Princeton University Press.

Implementing organizational change – the case of the Kinnock reforms

Emmanuelle Schön-Quinlivan

INTRODUCTION

After decades of more or less substantive administrative reforms in member states (Pollitt and Bouckaert 2004), the pressure was on the Commission to demonstrate that it could also reform itself, and commit to more administrative ef"ciency and better "nancial and human resources management, particularly in light of the largest and most costly enlargement since the creation of the European Economic Community. In the context of theoretical literature dominated by accounts of problematic administrative reforms and unanticipated consequences (Pollitt and Bouckaert 2004; Christensen and Lægreid 2001; Bauer and Knill 2007; Lipsky 1971; Pressman and Wildavsky 1973), Kassim (2008: 648) rightly insists on the accomplishment of such a wide-ranging transformation in such a short timeframe as laid out in the 2000 White Paper *Reforming the Commission* (European Commission 2000a) and implemented under Kinnock s leadership (see Bauer 2007).

Building on Kassim s study of the Kinnock reforms (2004a, 2004b, 2008) and the reasons which explain their wide-ranging scope as well as their near-entirety implementation, this article will ask two questions in order to further nuance the analysis of administrative reform in the Commission and the level of change it brought. Having detailed the four headings structuring the Kinnock reforms, Kassim (2008) takes a macro-level stance and states that the Commission, in its organizational and institutional structure, has undergone radical change. First, this paper will question whether Kassim s conclusions can be validated using a meso-level approach, given the organizational nature of the Commission. Second, the reform in action will be examined through an analysis of its scope and dynamic. Looking at two speci"c Directorates-General (DGs), the concept of translation (Campbell 2004) will be used to understand the transition from ideas to practice, from policy to action.

This paper explores how DG Transport and Energy (TREN) and DG Regional Policy (REGIO) have translated the Kinnock reforms into local prac-tice. It argues that translation of the reform ideas has depended on three key elements   local organizational environment, power struggles and leadership   and that it has resulted in signi"cant varying degrees of change in each DG. In order to develop this argument, the paper is divided into three sections. First, the heterogeneous and complex nature of the European institution will be brie"y stated and used to expose why it is essential in the understanding of the translation of the Kinnock reforms and the resulting change. Second, a compara-tive account of the scope of change in DG TREN and DG REGIO will be given, drawing on of"cial Commission documents as well as 32 semi-structured inter-views carried out between July 2006 and March 2007, mostly with Heads of Unit, who are the key daily implementers of the reform, but also with a few Direc-tors and Desk Of"cers. Finally, this detailed summary of change in the DGs will be revisited in the light of the concept of translation. It will help in exploring the dynamic of reform as it goes into practice and in highlighting how human agency and leadership have been crucial in getting of"cials to internalize and therefore own change.

A MULTI-ORGANIZATION: THE SIGNIFICANCE OF A MESO-LEVEL APPROACH

Neither an international secretariat nor a government of the European Union (EU), the European Commission is often described as a *sui generis* institution where political administrative relationships are particularly complex. Even though it does not escape comparison, it has become a cliché to say that the Commission has found no match in the world of international or national administrations (Cram 1999; Nugent 2000; Peterson and Shackleton 2002; Hooghe 2001; Stevens and Stevens 2001; Cini 1996; Page 1997; Edwards and Spence 2006; Shore 2000). A quick observation of the Commission highlights the multinational, multicultural and multilingual aspects of the organization which led Cram (1994, 1999) to call into doubt the homogeneous nature of the Commission and refer to it as a multi-organization (see also Caremier 1997: 238).

In order to develop this argument of a multi-organization, two points can be made. First, the Commission is composed of horizontal and vertical services. The former, such as the Secretariat-General or the Legal Service, co-ordinate the activities of all DGs and provide support to all the DGs. The latter, namely the DGs which represent the bulk of the organizational structure of the Commission, are divided into policy-making DGs, whose main activity revolves around policy outputs, and operational DGs or programme-managing DGs which deal with managing policies and programmes adopted by the EU. Second, the EU counted 15 member states when the Kinnock reforms were launched in 2000 and was facing the largest enlargement of its history, which brought the number of member states to 25 on 1 May 2004 and then to 27 on 1 January 2007. The House has always been a cauldron of nationalities and cultures. Despite a certain degree of socialization into a European spirit (Shore 2000), there is no evidence of a European administrative culture whereas national cultures are still very much alive among of"cials everyday interactions. The predominance of one or several similar nationalities in a DG is also often used to explain the way of doing business in this DG. Beyond the cultural aspect, Christiansen (1997) highlighted the diversity of the Commission s organizational components when he analysed the intra-institutional con"icts amongst DGs and their socialization into different modes of decision-making, political for DG IV as opposed to bureaucratic for DG XVI. Similarly, Ross (1995) insisted on the in"ghting between DGs and their Commissioners as well as between the Commission President and particular DGs.

As a result, the image of the Commission which has emerged in the literature is that of a heterogeneous organization with con"icting interests and cultures. Many national administrations are also heterogeneous in some ways. However, this aspect is magni"ed in the case of the Commission owing to the institution s functions and the diversity of nationalities, languages and cultures. In this regard a macro-analysis of the reform implementation can only lead to the conclusion of an historic achievement (Kassim 2004a) or the accomplishment of mission impossible (Kassim 2008). Yet this wide lens used to assess the success of the implementation of administrative change arti"cially erases the complex and multiple organizational nature of the Commission and hides the reality of change in practice.

In order to study the level of institutional change in the Commission, two DGs which reveal the Commission s organizational complexity were chosen: DG TREN and DG REGIO. They differ in function, size and budget. DG TREN s tasks involve a signi"cant share of policy work. It is the "rst DG to implement externalization with the creation of an executive agency, the Intelligent Energy Executive Agency (IEEA). Staff numbers approach 1,100, including the new category of contractual agents. Finally, it has a relatively small budget compared to other DGs in the Commission   close to €1.5 billion   and operates entirely on the basis of direct "nancial management. The responsibility for managing European monies is therefore not shared with member states.

In comparison, DG REGIO focuses mainly on policy management and has little role in policy conception. It is responsible for a sizeable part of the EU budget but its management is shared with the member states. This makes the issue of responsibility for fraud or mismanagement quite problematic, which explains why it has been at the centre of the Committee of Independent Experts report (1999) and is still at the core of the discussions between the European Court of Auditors (ECA) and the Commission. Finally, owing to this shared "nancial management and signi"cant delegation to member states, it is smaller than DG TREN, with staff reaching 722 in 2007, including contractual agents. Table 1 summarizes the key characteristics of each DG.

After setting up the context of this paper the Commission in its multi-faceted organizational nature and de"ning the two case studies, DG TREN and DG REGIO, which will be used to understand the scope and dynamic of change in the Commission, the speci"c object whose translation is at the heart of this paper should be brie"y outlined. Kassim (2004a, 2004b, 2008) as well as Levy (2003, 2004; see also Stevens 2003) have detailed and discussed the White Paper s ideas and measures in previous works so this summary will serve only as a reminder.

The Kinnock reforms were outlined in the White Paper under four headings:

- A cross-cutting issue, namely a culture based on service. The measures listed, which aim to achieve this cultural change, are very eclectic. The most signi"-cant element of this "rst chapter is the identi"cation of underpinning principles of the reforms which are meant to infuse the whole reform programme and become enshrined in of"cials ways of doing business: independence, responsibility, accountability, ef"ciency and transparency.
- The second chapter of the White Paper created a new system of planning and programming called activity-based management in order to match resources with Commission policy priorities. It is an umbrella concept integrating the Strategic Planning and Programming cycle (SPP), the Commission s

Table 1 Comparative characteristics of DG TREN and DG REGIO

	Activity	Staff	Financial management	Budget	Key objectives
DG TREN	Policy-making	1,100	Direct	€1.5 billion	Policy outputs
DG REGIO	Programme-managing	722	Shared	€347 billion	Managing regional programmes with member states

legislative work programme, which leads each DG to draft its own Annual Management Plan (AMP) and then monitor, evaluate and report on its activities in an Annual Activity Report (AAR). The emphasis in this new ambitious cycle was to think of policy priorities when engaging resources and setting up monitoring, evaluation and reporting mechanisms.

- The third chapter dealt with changing the human resources management system, creating a new semi-linear career system and a merit-based system of staff appraisal — the Career Development Reviews (CDRs) — which would be at the heart of a new promotion system. Many other measures were also mentioned (see Kassim 2004a, 2008), among which mobility and training were crucial.
- The fourth and final chapter focused on financial control and management whose flaws had led to the Committee of Independent Experts (CIEs) inquiry and the Commission's subsequent resignation. The new system aimed to decentralize financial responsibility and segregate audit from control. The key tenet of this new financial system was enhancing responsibility and accountability among all levels of officials.

THE REFORM IN ACTION: AN ACCOUNT OF TRANSLATION OF POLICY INTO ACTION

After defining the context and the specific object of this research, this section will focus on assessing the scope of institutional change as a result of the translation of the White Paper into action in DG TREN and DG REGIO. It will give a comparative account of change in both DGs as a result of the Kinnock reforms following the DGs' three institutional components (Bulmer and Burch 1998): their organizational structure, their processes and procedures, and their cultural and normative dimensions.

Organizational structures

Owing to their function and type of financial management, DG TREN and DG REGIO did not go through the same organizational restructuring. Two elements are discussed in this section: the first is common to the two DGs, namely the financial restructuring and auditing structure; the second, the creation of an executive agency, has only happened in DG TREN.

The main reform measure at the heart of the Kinnock reforms package has been the financial restructuring of DGs. As a result, DG TREN and DG REGIO have shifted from completely centralized financial management where DG Financial Control gave the *ex ante* visa on all Commission financial transactions — to a system which is fully decentralized with a counterweight, called Model 3 in the White Paper (European Commission 2000b: 63), also referred to as the Four Eyes principle. In DG TREN, this model of financial circuit has meant the creation of financial cells in each directorate which work on the financial aspects of projects, whereas DG REGIO has opted for financial assistants seconding the Director and carrying out *ex ante* verifications. The Director heads his or her Directorate and is a key manager, co-ordinating Heads of Units (HoUs) and acting as authorizing officer by subdelegation as a result of the Kinnock reforms. The Four Eyes principle is, however, applied in both DGs:

- The desk officer handles the operational side of the project and checks its financial soundness. His or her HoU has a second look at it before sending it to the financial unit.
- There, a financial initiating desk officer checks the financial accuracy of the transaction.
- A verifying officer then validates the financial transaction.
- It ultimately comes back to the line manager, the Director, who is the subdelegate authorizing officer for payment.

For more efficiency, since it handles a considerable number of financial transactions, DG REGIO has added one more step: before the payment procedure is launched by the desk officer, there is a first technical verification by the financial unit.

Even though the same model of financial circuit is used in both DGs, it was received better in DG REGIO than in DG TREN. All DG REGIO officials interviewed considered that the financial restructuring had increased the sense of responsibility at all levels, whereas in DG TREN it was often pointed out that the new financial structure relieved operational directors of their responsibility and recreated centralization at a lower level with total dependence on the financial unit.[1] This has produced a real bottleneck in DG TREN and it is felt that the change the reform has brought about is management by accountants rather than management by objectives.[2] The central financial unit has been criticized for rejecting projects without any explanation, which further isolates financial cells. In contrast, a DG REGIO desk officer commented, you can always go there [to the financial unit] and ask for your dossier to be scrutinized quickly because it s urgent.[3] DG REGIO s financial structure was reinforced in 2005 with an efficient information technology tool, the work flow system (WFS), which computerizes internal procedures and payments following a checklist, and therefore builds consistency and coherence across the DG.

Financial reform also involved the segregation of the control and audit functions. Internal Audit Capacities (IACs), directly accountable to the Director-General, were set up to carry out internal audits to the DG and assist the Director-General in the declaration of assurance which he or she has to sign in the AAR and which makes him or her financially responsible in case of irregularities. DG TREN s IAC performs about seven audits a year, mostly operational and financial audits, whereas DG REGIO s IAC, which has been christened Internal Audit and Advice Unit (IAA), carries out around 20 audits a year, which can be audits of compliance, on the internal control standards, risk assessments or operational audits. But its remit also includes consulting work with a wider reflection on the DG s tasks and its efficiency. In 2006, for example, the IAA launched a study on the role and responsibility of desk officers in order to identify how their influence in the field could be increased.

The second aspect of change with regard to organizational structure applies specifically to DG TREN since it is mainly a policy-making DG operating on the basis of direct financial management. The 2000 White Paper replaced the Bureaux d Assistance Technique with public law entities specialized in programme management, namely executive agencies. DG TREN was the first DG to implement externalization with the creation of the IEEA, which is accountable to its parent DG and established for a set time corresponding to the lifespan of the programme it runs.[4] The agency gives visibility to the programme, guarantees a better use of resources, and allows the parent DG to focus on its core task, policy-making. Since DG REGIO is a policy-managing service which works on the basis of shared financial management with the member states, it does not need to create an executive agency to manage its programmes, which is done by national authorities.

When it comes to restructuring, change took different forms in DG TREN and DG REGIO. Both altered their financial structures, following the Four Eyes system, the abolition of DG Financial Control, and the enforcement of segregation between control and audit. Yet, DG TREN put in place a rather cumbersome structure of financial cells and financial unit, which is further compounded by the rigid approach of the financial unit in everyday dealings with the units. This has led many interviewees to talk about a bottleneck and the re-creation of centralization at DG level. In comparison, DG REGIO set up assistants to the Directors rather than financial cells, and the financial unit seems to be always accessible to HoUs for advice or urgent matters. The DGs diverge on a further structural issue: the executive agency. But this can be explained by their difference in tasks and type of management. It does not reflect a differentiated implementation of the reform.

Processes and procedures

The main process which the White Paper introduced was the activity-based management cycle, a new strategic approach which is used to set priorities, define objectives, allocate and manage resources, and monitor and report on performance across the Commission. Both DGs have a horizontal unit in charge of the strategic planning process, referred to as the SPP cycle. The unit prepares two main documents, the AAR and the AMP, and has an input into the Commission s Legislative Work Programme (CLWP).[5] Figure 1 summarizes the sequence of documents which each DG has to produce as part of the SPP cycle.

The AAR is a political and budgetary assessment of the past activities of the DG which is signed off by the Director-General and the Director of Resources, who are personally financially responsible for the declarations made in the report. This written declaration of assurance, which can be qualified with reservations, is a clear sign, given by Directors-General, of their responsibility and

| November 2006 | February 2007 | July 2007 | September/October 2007 | January 2008 |
| December 2006 | March 2007 | | September 2007 | December 2007 |

| Start of the SPP cycle. Road map from Directorates | Draft Annual Policy Strategy | Secretariat-General sends a directive of preparation for the CLWP | CLWP finalized by Secretariat-General after discussion with Cabinets and Directorates | Adoption of CLWP by College |
| | Preparation of the 2006 AAR | | Preparation of the 2008 AMP | |

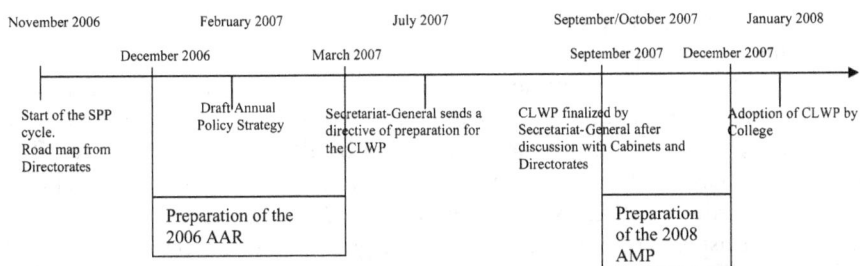

Figure 1 Preparation for the 2008 SPP cycle in DG REGIO and DG TREN

accountability. The AMP is compiled from contributions sent by each Directorate listing their priorities for the year to come. The DG ultimately drafts a document integrating its "nancial and human resources needs. DG TREN s and DG REGIO s AMPs main sections list each DG s operational activities which are then divided into objectives. Each objective is explained and output indicators as well as impact indicators are attached in order to help *ex ante*, mid-term and *ex post* evaluations of projects.

DG REGIO even introduced a mid-term assessment of the AMP and the AAR. There is also an intense effort of co-ordination in the DG regarding the implementation of the objectives stated in the AMP. Directors meet every week in order to keep themselves informed of the implementation process and take the necessary decisions to speed up programme implementation. Moreover, the Commissioner meets with the Director-General on a weekly basis. Finally, the Director-General is kept informed through bimonthly " nancial reports, bimonthly activity reports, discussions with the Audit Directorate, weekly meetings with the IAA and with the Resource Director on human resources issues (European Commission 2007).

Two main types of procedure are discussed in this section: the evaluation and monitoring procedures and the CDRs. Evaluation and monitoring have been at the heart of the reform process. As demonstrated in the AMP, the focus on measuring impacts and outcomes of policies and monitoring their implementation is central to of" cials work. Of" cials in both DGs have pointed out that " nding relevant indicators can be dif" cult and that they can be quite arti-" cial. Yet, as a DG REGIO HoU put it, l insistance sur les indicateurs et les *targets* est une conséquence de la réforme. [6] In order to help with the monitoring of the programme s implementation progress, DG REGIO put in place an electronic tool of checklists which computerizes internal procedures and payments, the WFS. Even though some of" cials still criticize it for its mechanical aspect and the lack of qualitative appreciation of the situation, a majority have accepted it and acknowledge that it has been bene" cial for the coherence which it has brought to the work. DG TREN has also set up a computer database, ADONIS, in which each request with a deadline is entered and monitored. Yet it is only used for administrative matters.

The second procedure concerns human resources management and represents a signi"cant departure from the old system of personal assessment. The new merit-based promotion system wanted by Kinnock is based on the CDRs. The CDRs involve a yearly one-on-one discussion between the of"cial and his superior. This procedure is launched by the HoU via computer. The civil servant has ten days to evaluate him or herself. Then the superior evaluates the self-assessment and gives a mark out of 20 based on three criteria: ef"ciency, ability and aspects of conduct. This mark goes to the Director who has to validate it. The mark given by the HoU is translated into merit points. The Director-General has then a certain number of priority points (a maximum of ten points per of"cial) to allocate to the staff he or she considers to have performed best. The CDRs are at the centre of a system which links promotion with merit and have been severely criticized in both DGs.

Interestingly, processes and procedures were implemented in the same way in DG TREN and DG REGIO. Both services complied with the different stages of the SPP cycle and the monitoring procedures, but still commented on how formal and cosmetic, rather than programmatic and strategic, these tools were. The CDRs, which applied to both DGs, are the perfect example of the bureaucratization of a "exible procedure which both DGs criticized in similar terms. Overall, processual and procedural change did not vary between DG TREN and DG REGIO. However, the study of norms and cultural change resulting from the Kinnock reforms is most revealing when it comes to differentiated change.

Norms and culture

DG TREN and DG REGIO have not experienced the same type of normative change. Interviews with HoUs have revealed an emphasis on different norms depending on the DG. Financial norms have been implemented in a similar way in both DGs, whereas training and mobility, for example, were approached differently. The Kinnock reforms insisted on a normative system built on "nancial responsibility and accountability. In both DGs, the AAR with its declaration of assurance and reservations, the AMP with the output indicators and the monitoring involved, as well as the new "nancial structure, have created an adequate environment for of"cials to internalize these norms of responsibility and accountability and integrate them in their daily way of doing business.

Mobility has also been promoted as a norm which should be taken into account by of"cials when thinking of their careers. It is obligatory for any of"cial in a sensitive post to move after "ve years. Some HoUs in DG TREN, as in DG REGIO, complain that mobility is counterproductive because it generates a loss of institutional knowledge. However, DG REGIO of"cials were more vocal about it because there is a strong divide in the DG on the issue between HoUs involved in horizontal work, who are in favour of the process, and those heading a geographic unit, who are more reticent. Two hundred and "fty desk of"cers and HoUs out of 722 have sensitive posts. This implies a high turnover every "ve years for units whose work is planned over a seven-year programmatic period and involves speci"c language skills. Therefore, several exceptions to the principle of mobility have been granted, which leads some HoUs in horizontal directorates to point to a lack of normative consistency.

Finally, nine and a half days training per year have been introduced as a means of socializing staff into the processes and practices of the reform. General "nancial training was mentioned in particular by DG TREN civil servants. However, DG REGIO has developed a tailor-made training programme which makes HoUs feel well equipped to do their speci"c work in a changing environment. The work of the human resources unit in this regard has also carved out a speci"c identity for DG REGIO, bringing some cohesion to the DG and support to of"cials.

DG TREN and DG REGIO are in a similar situation with their Directors-General having been replaced in the last two years. In terms of cultural change resulting from the Kinnock reforms, the replacement of French Director-General Lamoureux by German of"cial Ruete has had a signi"cant impact in DG TREN, whereas the departure of English Director-General Meadows and the appointment of German *fonctionnaire* Ahner demonstrated a continuity in supportive views of the reform. The fracture line between Lamoureux and Ruete rests on a question of management style between those who belonged to Lamoureux s *réseau* and those who did not. Lamoureux did not rate the activity-based management cycle very highly because of a lack of interest in management matters[7] and general distrust for a reform he regarded as too Anglo-Saxon.[8] The transition from Meadows to Ahner was ideologically smoother. The cultural environment of DG TREN is important because it frames the nature of social reality for of"cials, and consequently their beliefs and value structure when evolving in an administratively changed context.

The Kinnock reforms have generated an increased number of procedures. The lack of integrated processes, combined with a changed systemic environment where the European Parliament and the Council spend more time scrutinizing the Commission s work, has generated an intense culture of control denounced by DG TREN and DG REGIO of"cials. Of"cials argued that even though control mechanisms were in place before the Kinnock reforms, they have been strengthened and multiplied to the point that the feeling of being constantly controlled and audited has become part of of"cials common understanding of how their institution works. However, DG REGIO of"cials insist on a dual culture of control and responsibility which infuses all units. Owing to the circumstances in which the Commission had to resign and the political scrutiny exercised by the Parliament and the member states, DG REGIO of"cials are obsessed with obtaining a positive Declaration d Assurance (DAS).[9] As a consequence, concepts of "nancial responsibility and value for money are embedded in their reference frameworks.

Differentiated change was most noticeable in its normative and cultural dimension. This can be explained mainly by the difference in leadership between DG TREN and DG REGIO. The former s Director-General did not buy into the reforms philosophy and even actively resisted it for some time. As a result, DG TREN staff do not demonstrate a sense of ownership of the Kinnock reforms. In contrast, DG REGIO s Director-General supported the reforms. Despite staff criticism of how cumbersome and time-consuming they can be, they also highlight the positives. They always point out that the Kinnock "nancial reforms, more speci"cally, have allowed them to be without reproach *vis-à-vis* other institutions and to regain some legitimacy. As a result, it can be concluded that practical change was much wider in DG REGIO than in DG TREN because of a genuine internalization of normative and cultural aspects which helped staff to make sense of the reforms.

Institutional change in every aspect of the institution s dimensions has been a reality. Yet this change has been more uneven across DG TREN and DG REGIO than a Commission-wide reform programme would lead us to think. Each DG developed its own implementation of the reform which can only be understood through an identi"cation and analysis of the constraints surrounding the translation process in both DGs.

DELVING INTO THE INNERMOST PARTS OF THE ORGANIZATION: EXPLAINING DEGREES OF CHANGE THROUGH THE CONSTRAINTS OF TRANSLATION

The previous section gave an account of the scope of change as a result of the Kinnock reforms in DG TREN and DG REGIO. This section will now analyse varying degrees in the dynamic of change which can be observed in both DGs through the lens of translation and its constraints. The concept of translation comes from the institutionalist literature (Campbell 2001, 2004; Scott 2001; Hirsch 1997) and a re"ection on the conditions under which organizations adopt new practices, or not. It serves to identify the causal processes which explain the local implementation of principles and policies, and how organizations interpret the institutional pressures surrounding them. Translation is therefore the indispensable tool to analyse the dynamic of change when studying policy implementation from the macro-level to the meso-level, from Commission level to DG level.

Three essential factors conditioning the translation process have to be analysed to uncover why, and to what degree, change was different in DG TREN compared to DG REGIO:

- the DG s organizational context. Looking at the formal organizational context, two characteristics speci"cally relevant to the DG s governance arrangement, namely its function and its "nancial management structure, are isolated;
- the power struggles in which the DG is involved;
- the leadership support demonstrated by the Director-General.

Comparing DG TREN s and DG REGIO s organizational function brings to light their very distinct positions in the European institution. DG TREN is concerned with policy-making and has very few dealings with policy management, whereas DG REGIO s tasks are mostly about managing EU programmes and getting them implemented by member states. This functional opposition is reinforced by the DGs "nancial management structure. DG TREN works with a small budget, close to €1.5 billion in 2007, but operates entirely on the basis of direct "nancial management. On the other hand, DG REGIO s 2007 13 funding programme bene"ts from a €347 billion budget, yet its management is shared with member states.[10]

Whereas DG TREN itself has to account for the ways in which it spends EU money, DG REGIO is ultimately "nancially responsible for member states actions since they manage 99 per cent of the DG s funds. This puts the two DGs in very different positions regarding the translation of the Kinnock reforms. Owing to the size of its budget and its shared "nancial management, DG REGIO had already developed practices on planning, programming, evaluation through indicators, and monitoring before 2000. The Kinnock reforms forced it further in this direction, even leading to the indirect consequence of tougher supervisory procedures with member states. DG TREN s function and "nancial management structure meant that constant evaluation and monitoring of its activity was not at the forefront of the DG s preoccupations. Compared with DG TREN, DG REGIO s organizational context was more receptive to the ideas and measures included in the Kinnock reforms since some of them mirrored existing local practices.

The second element that affects the translation process is the power struggles in which the DGs are involved. Owing to the circumstances in which the Commission resigned in 1999 and the CIE s (1999) subsequent damning conclusions on the issue of the institution s responsibility in shared management instances, DG REGIO has been engaged in intense political opposition with the ECA which has raised political mobilization across the service. The ECA is responsible for auditing the collection and spending of European monies. Examining the legality and regularity of the transactions and the reliability of the Community accounts, every year it delivers a DAS, the French acronym for statement of assurance. Since 1975, it has empowered the European Parliament, through its report and recommendations, to give the Commission "nal discharge for the execution of each annual budget. In 2005, for the twelfth successive "nancial year, the ECA issued a DAS which was quali"ed for payments relating to all parts of the general budget of the EU except administrative expenditure. The quali"ed DAS re"ects the complexity met by the Commission in implementing the EU budget, and the challenge that DGs like DG REGIO face in providing satisfactory audit evidence to the Court, particularly regarding member state management of European monies. As a result, the ECA has refused to issue a positive DAS, highlighting year after year the continuing weaknesses in member states management and control systems and the Commission s supervisory role (European Commission 2007: 27). As a consequence, the Commission and the ECA have been at loggerheads over the positive DAS. In its 2006 AAR, DG REGIO clearly states its fundamental disagreement with the Court over the effectiveness of the supervisory controls carried out by the Commission:

> It considers that the Court fails to give suf"cient weight to the multi-annual aspect of the control arrangements for the Structural Funds that enables them to correct or compensate the material de"ciencies over the entire programming period, and that its conclusions are too generalised given the small size of the sample and the lack of homogeneity between Funds, Member States and systems.
>
> (European Commission 2007: 27)

Since the Commission has linked obtaining a positive DAS to an increase in its legitimacy in the institutional triangle, DG REGIO HoUs are acutely aware of the importance of the practical translation of the Kinnock reforms in order to present an irreproachable front to the outside world and the ECA speci"cally. DG TREN, however, does not seem to be entangled in similar disputes with outside European institutions, which means that its translation of the reform programme was not in"uenced by any speci"c political mobilization.

Finally, looking at the type of leadership which shaped the DGs manage-ment style and cultural environment gives the best understanding of the different dynamics at work and explains how human agency affected staff intern-alization of change. The lack of leadership support from the French Director-General Lamoureux, in post from 1999 to 2006, considerably slowed down the substantive implementation of the reform. Kinnock himself acknowledges that there was some friction with Lamoureux who was the "rst Director-General to organize resistance to some reform measures which he deemed Anglo-Saxon.[11] A look at the DG s organigramme leads to the conclusion that there was an over-representation of of"cials from southern European member states. It is also interesting to note that DG TREN is a very francophone administrative service since Lamoureux insisted on using French as the working language. At the end of Lamoureux s term there was not a single British, Irish or Swedish HoU.[12] A German civil servant who did not agree with Lamoureux s methods gives a vivid description of the atmosphere in the DG:[13]

> Mr Lamoureux was like Louis XIV. He knew it all. He was dictatorial, had his own *réseau*. This obviously comes from the French culture which puts the emphasis on hierarchy and power ... Lamoureux did extreme micro-management, circumventing people to get to the person he wanted. He preferred to deal directly with a B grade colleague of the same nationality rather than approach his or her hierarchy if it was not French.

As a result, when Mr Lamoureux was head of DG TREN, the activity-based management cycle was not considered very highly because of a lack of interest in management matters.[14] The new German Director-General Ruete is more supportive of the reform process but his impact has not yet been felt.

DG REGIO also experienced a recent change in leadership with German of"cial Ahner replacing Englishman Meadows as Director-General in January 2007. Yet the context is exactly the opposite to that of DG TREN, since both of"cials have been ideologically sympathetic and committed to the reforms and have supported and facilitated their translation into the DG s existing working practices. A deputy HoU[15] took the example of mobility to demonstrate the smooth transition between both Directors-General.

> The previous Director-General Graham Meadows experienced a lot of resistance from Directors when promoting mobility. When restructuring the DG, he constrained 30 people to move but he wanted to turn mobility into a norm which of"cials would integrate into their career development. Owing to Meadows departure, there was a pause in the implementation of the mobility programme. The new Director-General Ahner has taken up where Meadows left it but with caution since 2007 is a pivotal year when seven-year national programmes are negotiated and adopted.

This has resulted in a substantive practical implementation of reform measures in DG REGIO as well as a genuine ownership of the reform by its HoUs.

The three elements framing and constraining translation of the Kinnock reforms explain why DG REGIO has undergone a more effective translation of the Kinnock reforms in practice, with of"cials internalizing reform measures and their rationale rather than formally implementing them. DG REGIO s organizational environment, power struggle with the ECA over a positive DAS, and its supportive leadership all favoured substantive and internalized change. In contrast, the reform does not seem to "t DG TREN s everyday business as well and has created extra work for HoUs who do not accept it as readily as in DG REGIO since they consider it more super"uous.

CONCLUSION

Change in the Commission as a result of the Kinnock reforms cannot be denied. In this respect, Kassim (2008) is right in questioning the existing academic literature which focuses on the obstacles to change and the stickiness of institutions. It does not help in understanding the case of the Commission. But this article has gone beyond the statement of organizational change at macro-level and looked at the innermost parts of the organization at meso-level. This has revealed that despite being a Commission-wide reform programme, the translation of the White Paper has generated signi"cant varying degrees of change in DG REGIO compared with DG TREN. Far from being homogeneous, the translation process has had to adjust to speci"c local organizational environments, power struggles and different types of leadership which have constrained practical change in the way of"cials have internalized the reform. It follows that Kassim s emphasis on the signi"cance of exemplary reform leadership in the extensive implementation of the reform can be validated.

At a macro-level, leadership can be used as an explanation for the far-reaching implementation of the White Paper. Yet when the same argument is used at a meso-level, it sheds light on the discrepancies in ownership of the reform by staff and the resulting uneven practical change.

Bauer (2006: 27; see also Bauer 2008) argues that following the Kinnock reforms, the Commission will probably become more inside looking, and the responsible individuals will have less time for policy content than in the past. It is true that analysis of the Kinnock reforms demonstrates how cumbersome and time-consuming many of the new procedures are and the increased workload that HoUs, more speci"cally, are facing. Yet this paper claims that the local implementation of the reforms has revealed some room for manoeuvre when it comes to putting in place structures or training programmes suited to DG needs.

If, at "rst, the reforms inspired fear among staff, who felt the weight of "nancial responsibility and accountability, a second phase has now started with the use of the reforms as a legitimacy-reclaiming tool towards the outside world. It could be argued that the reforms, through stricter impact assessments, indicator-based monitoring, strategic programming, will improve the quality of policy outputs. The risk of a Commission sti"ed by procedures and centralized management has been threatened since the 1960s (Schön-Quinlivan 2006). Yet the European administration has enjoyed periods of policy entrepreneurship despite an ever-increasing workload and the concomitant procedures. Only future research will tell if the reforms have transformed the Commission into an administration of control too slow to invest the policy-making domain, therefore leaving this political space to the Council.

Biographical note: Emmanuelle Schön-Quinlivan is a Ph.D. student at University College Dublin, Ireland. Her work has been "nanced by the Irish Research Council for the Human and Social Sciences Government of Ireland Scholar.

Address for correspondence: Emmanuelle Schön-Quinlivan, University College Dublin, School of Politics and International Relations, Bel"eld, Dublin 4, Ireland. email: e.schon@ucc.ie

ACKNOWLEDGEMENTS

I would like to thank the Commission of"cials who agreed to be interviewed and insightfully discussed the Kinnock reforms. I am greatly indebted to my supervisor, Brigid Laffan, the peer reviewers, Michael W. Bauer as well as Aodh Quinlivan for their comments on earlier versions of this paper.

NOTES

1 Interview done on 20 July 2006.
2 Interview done on 13 July 2006.

3 Interview done on 15 March 2007.
4 Interview done on 22 March 2006.
5 For a detailed description of the ability-based management cycle, please refer to Kassim (2004a).
6 Interview done on 21 March 2007.
7 Interview done on 18 July 2006.
8 Interview done on 17 July 2006.
9 The European Court of Auditors DAS looks at the legality and regularity of the underlying transactions and at the reliability of the Community accounts. For more details, see http://ec.europa.eu/commission_barroso/kallas/positive_declaration_en.htm
10 See CIE (1999: 3.2.2) for a detailed de" nition of shared " nancial management.
11 Interview done on 22 November 2006.
12 Interview done on 19 July 2006.
13 Interview done on 19 July 2006.
14 Interview done on 18 July 2006.
15 Interview done on 21 March 2007.

REFERENCES

Bauer, M. and Knill, C. (2007) *Management Reforms in International Organizations,* Baden-Baden: Nomos.
Bauer, M.W. (2006) Deserving to be made Sir ?   Effects of the reform of the European Commission on policy outputs . Paper presented at a conference in Konstanz on Reform of International Organizations, 30 June 1 July.
Bauer, M.W. (2007) The politics of reforming the European Commission administration , in M.W. Bauer and C. Knill (eds), *Management Reforms in International Organizations,* Reihe Verwaltungsressourcen und Verwaltungsstrukturen, Baden-Baden: Nomos, pp. 54 69.
Bauer, M.W. (2008) Diffuse anxieties, deprived entrepreneurs: Commission reform and middle management , *Journal of European Public Policy* 15(5): 627 47.
Bulmer, S. and Burch, M. (1998) Organising for Europe: Whitehall, the British state and European union , *Public Administration* 76 (Winter): 601 28.
Campbell, J.L. (2001) Convergence or divergence? Globalization, neoliberalism and "scal policy in postcommunist Europe , in S. Weber (ed.), *Globalization and the European Political Economy,* New York: Columbia University Press.
Campbell, J.L. (2004) *Institutional Change and Globalization,* Princeton, NJ: Princeton University Press.
Caremier, B. (1997) L Eurocratie: une function publique à la croisée du politique et de l administratif , *Revue de la Recherche Juridique, Droit Prospectif* 68(1): 229 86.
Christensen, T. and Lægreid, P. (2001) *New Public Management: The Transformation of Ideas and Practice,* Aldershot: Ashgate.
Christiansen, T. (1997) Tensions of European governance: politicized bureaucracy and multiple accountability in the European Commission , *Journal of European Public Policy* 4(1): 73 90.
Cini, M. (1996) *The European Commission: Leadership, Organization and Culture in the EU Administration,* Manchester: Manchester University Press.
Committee of Independent Experts (CIE) (1999) *Second Report on Reform of the Commission: Analysis of Current Practice and Proposals for Tackling Mismanagement, Irregularities and Fraud,* 10 September 1999.
Cram, L. (1994) The European Commission as a multi-organization: social policy , *Policy and Politics* 21(2): 135 46.
Cram, L. (1999) The Commission , in L. Cram, D. Dinan and N. Nugent (eds), *Developments in the European Union,* Basingstoke: Macmillan.

Edwards, G. and Spence, D. (2006) *The European Commission*, 3rd edn, Harlow: Longman.

European Commission (2000a) *Reforming the Commission, A White Paper, Part I*, COM (2000) 200/"nal 2.

European Commission (2000b) *Reforming the Commission, A White Paper, Part II, Action Plan*, COM (2000) 200 "nal.

European Commission (2007) *DG Regional Policy Annual Activity Report for the Year 2006*; http://ec.europa.eu/atwork/synthesis/aar/index_en.htm

Hirsch, P.M. (1997) Sociology without social structure: neoinstitutional theory meets brave new world , *American Journal of Sociology* 102: 1702 23.

Hooghe, L. (2001) *The European Commission and the Integration of Europe: Images of Governance*, Cambridge: Cambridge University Press.

Kassim, H. (2004a) An historic achievement. Administrative reform under the Prodi Commission , in D. Dimitrakopoulos (ed.), *The Changing Commission*, Manchester: Manchester University Press, pp. 33 62.

Kassim, H. (2004b) The Kinnock reforms in perspective: why reforming the Commission is an heroic, but thankless task , *Public Policy and Administration* 19(3): 25 41.

Kassim, H. (2008) Mission impossible , but mission accomplished: the Kinnock reforms and the European Commission , *Journal of European Public Policy* 15(5): 648 68.

Levy, R. (2003) Critical success factors in public management reform: the case of the European Commission , *International Review of Administrative Sciences* 69(4): 553 66.

Levy, R. (2004) Measuring management reform: the case of the Kinnock reforms in the European Commission , *EGPA Annual Conference*, University of Ljubljana, 1 4 September 2004.

Lipsky, M. (1971) Street-level bureaucracy and the analysis of urban reform , *Urban Affairs Quarterly* 6: 391 409.

Nugent, N. (2000) At the heart of the Union , in N. Nugent (ed.), *At the Heart of the Union: Studies of the European Commission*, Basingstoke: Macmillan Press.

Page, E. (1997) *People Who Run Europe*, Oxford: Clarendon Press.

Peterson, J. and Shackleton, M. (eds) (2002) *The Institutions of the European Union*, Oxford: Oxford University Press.

Pollitt, C. and Bouckaert, G. (2004) *Public Management Reform: A Comparative Analysis*, 2nd edn, Oxford: Oxford University Press.

Pressman, J. and Wildavsky, A. (1973) *Implementation*, Berkeley, CA: University of California Press.

Ross, G. (1995) *Jacques Delors and European Integration*, Cambridge: Polity Press.

Schön-Quinlivan, E. (2006) Administrative reform in the European Commission: from rhetoric to re-legitimisation . Paper prepared for EU-CONSENT Ph.D. school, Budapest, 29 April 6 May 2006; http://www.eu-consent.net/content.asp?contentid=1250

Scott, W.R. (2001) *Institutions and Organizations*, 2nd edn, Thousand Oaks, CA: Sage.

Shore, C. (2000) *Building Europe: The Cultural Politics of European Integration*, London: Routledge.

Stevens, A. (2003) Une simple amélioration ou une modernisation radicale? La réforme de l administration de la Commission européenne , *Revue Française d Administration Publique* 105/106: 81 94.

Stevens, A. and Stevens, H. (2001) *Brussels Bureaucrats? The Administration of the European Union*, Basingstoke: Palgrave.

European Commission reform and the origins of the European Transparency Initiative

Michelle Cini

INTRODUCTION

If research on reform implementation in international organizations is extremely rare (see, however, Geri 2001), studies of the periods following major reform efforts are more so. Even the wider literature on domestic administrative reform has little to say on the subject. Where reference is made to the post-reform period, the questions addressed are likely to be concerned with the implementation and/or consolidation of the reform. But even here, as Pollitt and Bouckaert (2004: 202) claim, studies of public administration often fail to capture the micro-improvements which result from changes in context and practices that follow large-scale reform efforts. Increasingly, however, empirical evidence suggests a need to reconceptualize conventional understandings of reform. Rather than viewing reforms as one-off events, it may be more accurate to see reform as an ongoing process, as the output of what Barzelay (2001) refers to as public management *policy*.

Peters (2001: 41) provides a particularly interesting take on the puzzle of what he refers to as continuing administrative reform, an approach which is used as the point of departure for this article. However, whilst Peters draws on empirical studies of national administrative reform in Europe, this article makes its contribution by directing attention towards the international (or supranational) sphere, where a similar phenomenon of continuing reform seems also to be in evidence. The article focuses on a speci"c case, that of the European Commission, which underwent a major administrative reform from 2000 to 2004. Since 2005, the Commission has been engaged in a much less ambitious set of administrative proposals under the banner of the European Transparency Initiative (ETI). It is the ETI that provides the empirical focus of this article.

Given that there are limits to what can be gleaned from a single case study of this kind, this article enriches this exploratory study by introducing an intra-case comparison of three elements within the ETI. The aim is to provide pointers to direct future research, rather than to explain de"nitively the phenomenon of continuing reform. To that end, the article proceeds as follows: the "rst section presents the analytical framework. The second section reviews the background to the post-2005 initiative. The third section introduces the ETI and the three key elements within it, and examines how and why they were proposed and adopted between 2005 and 2007. The fourth section considers what this tells us about continuing administrative reform in the European Commission; whilst the conclusions draw out the wider implications of this research.

CONTINUING ADMINISTRATIVE REFORM

In a short article published in 2001, B. Guy Peters sought to examine the puzzle that is continuing administrative reform. Peters point of departure was that the current period in the history of administrative reform differs from earlier phases because it is characterized by ongoing change and the endless efforts of governments to improve the performance of their public sectors (Peters 2001: 42). Accounting for this general shift is dif"cult, however, because the factors driving the process are closely interwoven (see also March and Olsen 1989: 56). Peters begins the process of disentangling these factors by laying out typologies and identifying patterns and logics. In addressing the logic of continuing reform, he examines the factors that make it more or less likely to occur. To do this he differentiates between its administrative/technical and political drivers (Peters 2001: 45 52). Not surprisingly, the conclusions he draws from his analysis re"ect the distinction he makes between politics and administration. As he puts it:

> there is no one single, simple explanation for the continuation of this reforming instinct ... Rather there are a number of factors ... [which] all exert some in"uence, and in practice may be dif"cult to differentiate. However, the most commonly cited of the reasons for continuing reform are administrative, and

hinge upon reactions to the reforms that have already been implemented. That having been said, perhaps the most important reasons for the continuing changes are political, and major shifts in reform strategies associated with the continuation of reform should be understood as part of a political process, political here being broadly understood to include institutional politics.

(Peters 2001: 42)

As the primary objective of this article is much in line with that of Peters, to clarify the factors that drive the process of continuing administrative reform, Peters off-the-shelf analytical scheme could be applied directly to the case presented below (Peters 2001: 48). Peters points to a range of possible variables: to the importance of perceptions of, and in particular disappointment in, past reforms; to the perverse consequences that arise unexpectedly from earlier reform efforts; to the cyclical nature of reform, where trends in one direction are often followed by a return to earlier models; or where reforms are a reaction to the perception that earlier reforms went too far in a particular direction; to dif'culties in measuring the effects of reform; to a lack of understanding about how far reforms can be pushed; to the paradox of quality, which is that the more reform is undertaken, the lower the levels of contentment with outcomes; to ideological differences across parties of government; and to the desire of new governments to be seen to be taking action to improve public administration. Finally, Peters points to the importance of organizational politics, where government agencies push for reform as they vie for control over budgets and management (Peters 2001: 45 51). Yet Peters categorization along the lines of political and administrative/technical factors may risk the omission of other important elements that do not fall into either category, or which cut across both. By drawing variables from a wider literature on administrative reform, and by using a rather different organizing principle, it may be possible to supplement and therefore move beyond Peters earlier analysis.

Agency is important in driving administrative reform. This leads us to focus on leadership and change agency (Döhler *et al.* 2007); but also on the external advocacy of those who may not be in leadership positions (Bannick and Resodihardjo 2006: 9). It is also important to acknowledge the potential of veto players who may wish to prevent or limit reform (or a certain kind of reform) to in"uence the continuation of a reform process, using their position in the decision-making framework to that end (Tsebelis 2002).

Beyond agency there are also other factors that may be taken from elsewhere in the administrative reform literature. Institutionalist theories point to the importance of the constitutional and legislative context within which agents promote or resist reform efforts (Knill 1999; Bannick and Resodihardjo 2006: 4 7). Moreover, the literature often points to policy crises or scandals as providing windows of opportunity for administrative reform (van der Walle *et al.* 2005; Bannick and Resodihardjo 2006: 9 10). A number of studies have also highlighted the importance of the diffusion or policy transfer of new ideas about administrative reform whether from other national systems or through international intermediaries such as the Organization for Economic Co-operation and Development (OECD) (Peters 1997; Bulmer *et al.* 2007).

Bringing together the explanatory factors identi"ed by Peters and the variables found elsewhere in the administrative reform literature forms the basis of an analytical framework presented in Table 1. This involves divorcing those factors that relate to agency (which become the independent variables) from other factors of a structural, functional and ideational kind (which for the purposes of this research become intervening variables). These intervening variables are understood here as resources which provide actors with opportunities to advance or hold back a continuation of reform. The concept of an opportunity is a necessarily broad one, as it stretches both beyond that of *political* opportunity to include factors that are not primarily political; and beyond that of opportunity *structure* to subsume within it factors that are functional and ideational (as well as structural) (see Koopmans 2004 on this point). Thus the more encompassing metaphorical notion of a window of opportunity "ts better in this context than does Kitschelt s narrower de"nition of a political opportunity structure (Kitschelt 1986).

One might expect agency to be important in driving continuing reform, as the concept of change agency is widely used in the reform literature, highlighting the importance of leadership (Döhler *et al.* 2007: 7 8). This is particularly relevant where new governments come into of"ce bringing with them new commitments to change. These may rest on a particular ideological position; may be a response to (perceived) mismanagement in the past; or may simply be a way of differentiating their party programmes from those of their predecessors (Peters 2001: 49 50). Other agents, whether internal or external, are also important in activating demands and providing support for further reform; or alternatively in voicing opposition to it. Advocacy helps to create an environment conducive to reform. Where advocacy coalitions are constructed, a commitment to reform amongst its supporters rests on shared beliefs that give added cohesion to the

Table 1 Analytical framework

Agency (independent variables)	Opportunity (intervening variables)	Outcome (dependent variable)
Leadership	constitutional or legal constraints;	
External advocacy	functional deficiencies arising out of previous reforms; consequences of incomplete reform;	continuing administrative reform
Veto players	perceptions of earlier reforms; policy crises/scandals; diffusion of new administrative ideas	

lobby (Sabatier 1998). By contrast, where there is opposition to reform, veto players may seek to construct barriers to a continuation of reform, though it is not impossible for veto players to commit to reform given the right kind of political leadership (Héritier 2001: 56). Whether the focus is on support or opposition, however, an agency perspective allows consideration of the role of actors and groups who are engaged in organizational politics and who struggle in the post-reform period to maintain their autonomy or authority under changed circumstances (Peters 2001: 51 2). Externally, agency points to the encouragement or discouragement given by actors from within institutions including national governments, parties and civil services, and from civil society (Döhler *et al.* 2007). Thus Peters (2001: 49) points to a paradox of quality in the case of civil society: namely, that demands of citizens for reform increase as a direct consequence of earlier reforms. Paradoxically, awareness intensifies at the same time as the quality of public service increases.

Opportunities for action (and, conversely, constraints preventing or limiting action) take many different forms, and there is often a substantial degree of interplay and interdependence between them. Structural factors may affect the capacity of actors to translate their support for or opposition to further reform into reform outcomes. There may be constitutional limits to contend with; or less tangible quasi-constitutional implications of reform (March and Olsen 1989: 111 12). Legislative barriers can also act as an opportunity for further change. Such constraints are not always insuperable, but may depend on the capacity of agents to alter the rules of the game. This is more likely to be a medium-term than a short-term task, and, as such, may cause delay, preventing reform from continuing as it might otherwise.

Functional issues may also matter when it comes to identifying the logic of continuing reform. These factors generally relate to functional deficiencies resulting from the unintended consequences of the earlier reform efforts (Peters 2001: 46 7). Functional deficiencies may not make further reform inevitable, but they do strengthen arguments in its favour, even though March and Olsen (1989: 60) suggest that reform successes may provoke greater change than past failures. Functional issues may also arise, however, as a consequence of the unfinished business of earlier reforms.

Finally, ideational factors cover perceptions of past experiences of reform which may be important in influencing its continuation. Lessons learnt, whether by actors internal or external to the reform, shape expectations about the future. These perceptions are not necessarily grounded in any empirical evidence. They may be positive or negative (Peters 2001: 45 6) and may be triggered or intensified by a policy crisis or scandal (Döhler *et al.* 1997: 8). Alternatively, new ideas about public administration and management, emerging from epistemic communities (Haas 1992) or via a process of policy transfer (Bulmer *et al.* 2007), may also inform the reform process and contribute to the emergence of new priorities and demands for continuing reform.

It is in applying the framework above to a case or to cases of continuing reform that some initial indication of the relevance of these variables may be judged. As explained above, whilst the case study presented in this article is that of administrative reform in the European Commission, three elements within the wider ETI that followed the comprehensive reform of 2000 04 allow for an intra-case comparison, which serves to enrich this exploratory study. The three elements, which will be introduced in the next section, are (i) the introduction of a new system of "nancial transparency which allows end bene"ciaries of European Union (EU) subsidies in EU member states to be identi"ed; (ii) the regulation of EU lobbying; and (iii) the introduction of ethics rules to govern the work of EU public servants. The empirical research in this article draws on the secondary literature on the 1999 2004 administrative reform of the European Commission and on an analysis of primary sources such as Commission communications, speeches and policy statements on the post-2004 initiatives. The research also rests on a small but important number of interviews on the origins of the ETI conducted in January and February 2006 with key actors involved in the process.

ETHICS, TRANSPARENCY AND REFORM IN THE EUROPEAN COMMISSION

Administrative ethics has been of political concern in the EU since before the resignation of the Commission in March 1999. This concern re"ects not only a response to criticism from certain quarters about ethical standards in the EU institutions, but also a growing trend more generally in European public administration towards taking more seriously issues of integrity. Administrative ethics concerns the sources, content and implications of ethical misconduct within public administrations: that is, the behaviour which is judged by administrative bodies or their political leaders to be appropriate or inappropriate on the basis of ethical principles (Bossaert and Demmke 2005). For some, those ethical principles are contested, re"ecting different, perhaps even con"icting, administrative traditions. For others, administrative ethics constitutes absolutes, resting on such principles as integrity, accountability, responsibility, transparency, fairness and equity (Bovens 1998). These concepts are set up in opposition to conduct which results in the misuse of public resources.

Before the late 1990s the Commission had little interest in how it might regulate the ethics of its of"cials and Commissioners beyond the framework that already existed in the EU Treaty and the EU s Staff Regulations. The Commission s resignation in March 1999 contributed to an environment in which ethics took centre-stage, prioritizing an administrative reform process that one might have expected would focus particularly on ethical issues. Yet the substance of the Kinnock reforms was much less about ethics than it was about the ef"-ciency and effectiveness of the Commission (Interview 25 January 2006); and in the Reform White Paper of March 2000, the ethics dimension was low-key.

The most concrete manifestation of a discrete ethics dimension took the form of a proposal to establish an inter-institutional Advisory Group on Standards in Public Life, though no agreement could be found on this issue between 2000 and 2004. Otherwise it was only *after* the publication of the Reform White Paper that the Commission began to see ethics as a reform category in its own right, adding an ethics heading to its Reform web-pages (Commission 2002a). Four key areas were identi"ed at this point: disciplinary proceedings/wrongdoings; whistleblowing; professional underperformance; and con"icts of interest in/simpli"cation of the Staff Regulations. There was no explicit reference to the Advisory Group, as by this stage the proposal was already moribund. In all four of these issues, the Staff Regulations were the primary tool used to hone and improve earlier rules governing the conduct of of"cials. For Commissioners the situation was very different, however, and softer instruments formed the basis of their ethics framework. This includes codes of conduct, and declarations and register of interests and gifts.

Just as it is clear that the ethical dimension of the reform was de"ned as much after the White Paper as within it, the reform agenda itself continued to change as a consequence of certain events as the Commission s term of of"ce progressed. One of these events concerned Marta Andreassen who, shortly after taking up of"ce as the Commission s Chief Accountant, made public complaints about the Commission s archaic accounting system, which led to her suspension. The Andreassen case dragged on for a couple of years until she was "nally dismissed for breaching the Staff Regulations. The experience was a salutary one for the Commission leadership who denied throughout that she was a whistleblower. It contributed, together with earlier cases, to the introduction of rather tough rules within the revised Staff Regulations of 2004 that seemed to have more to do with preventing whistleblowing   at least the kind that involves going public   than encouraging it (Cini 2007: 153 8).

Of all the post-2000 events it was the Eurostat affair that was most damaging for the Commission. This was because the Commission leadership had to acknowledge that it had made mistakes in this case, and that even when fully reformed this would probably not save the Commission from a similar set of occurrences in the future. The case involved the establishment of unapproved bank accounts by Commission of"cials that they had used to hive off funds for unauthorized use (albeit public rather than private use, it seems). It also raised questions about the movement of staff between the Commission and bodies funded or contracted by it, and the fact that in some cases the same individuals had been both approving funding and receiving it. Moreover, the affair demonstrated the Commission s inability to identify such problems, and to deal swiftly with them once the Commission had identi"ed them (see Cini 2007: 81 107, for a more detailed account of the case). In the annual Progress Report on the Commission Reform produced in 2005, a number of new initiatives were proposed to respond to the lessons learnt from the Eurostat affair (Commission 2005c). One of these initiatives involved the setting up of a new unit in the Secretariat-General, called the *Professional Ethics* unit (*Déontologie* in French), which would act as a "lter for information on ethics-related issues, liaising with bodies such as OLAF, the EU s Anti-Fraud Of"ce, the Internal Audit Service (IAS) and the Commission s internal disciplinary body, IDOC. The unit, which had not been foreseen in the Reform White Paper, was set up with some speed in February 2005 (Interview 3 February 2006).

THE EUROPEAN TRANSPARENCY INITIATIVE

The setting up of the Professional Ethics unit came early in the new Commission s term of of"ce, as did the launch of a number of initiatives linked by a common objective: to inject greater transparency into the workings of the European institutions. However, the agenda of the new Commission which came into of"ce towards the end of 2004 re"ected Commission President José-Manuel Barroso s commitment to deregulation, and to the prioritization of a number of policies within the Lisbon Strategy (on competitiveness and employment) and the EU s global role. There was no reference to administrative reform at the start of 2005. Within the new Commission, the President entrusted Siim Kallas with responsibility for the administration portfolio, the post held by Neil Kinnock in the previous Commission. Kallas had substantial knowledge of administrative practices, as well as a vast amount of reform-related political experience, having been Prime Minister, Foreign Minister, Finance Minister and President of the Central Bank in his native Estonia. Kallas was keen to stamp his imprint on the Commission; but the question was how to do this now that the Commission had of"cially concluded the Kinnock reforms in 2004?

The ETI became the vehicle for new administrative initiatives by the Commissioner. It consisted of a package of three sets of proposals. The "rst contained proposals relating to anti-fraud and "nancial management; the second focused on various aspects of interest group activity; the third re"ected concerns about the lack of rules on ethical standards for EU of"cials.

The "rst mention of the ETI appeared in very general terms in a speech in Nottingham in the UK in March 2005. After a lengthy period of consultation, in May 2006, the Commission published a Green Paper on those aspects of the ETI that necessitated inter-institutional agreement. After a further period of consultation, the Commission was able to propose legislation. In 2007, despite the progress made in the adoption of certain elements of the ETI, many commentators remained sceptical of its value. Clearly it is in no way comparable to the Commission reforms of 2000 04 either in its scale or ambitions, and critics have argued that even its modest objectives were watered down substantially at the consultation stage. Yet it may still constitute an interesting example of the continuing reform phenomenon.

Financial transparency

The "rst part of the ETI, the rationale of which was to contribute to the EU s anti-fraud efforts, included a proposal on the availability of information about the end bene"ciaries of EU funds. While the EU s revised Financial Regulation of 2002 provided for transparency in those aspects of the Community budget managed centrally (either directly by the Commission or indirectly by agencies), there was no equivalent requirement placed on national governments. As less than 20 per cent of the Community budget was centrally controlled, this meant that it was unclear how a very large proportion of the Community budget was allocated. Aggregate data existed, as did a public accounting of how much each member state received, but there was little useful detail.

Some member states had unilaterally decided to provide this information, or some of it. As of early 2006, 11 of the then 25 EU member states had a reasonable level of openness. In some cases, this had come about as a direct consequence of the introduction of freedom of information legislation at the national level. This was what happened in the UK where, following the coming into force of the Freedom of Information Act on 1 January 2005, an application for information on the end bene" ciaries of agricultural subsidies provoked the Labour government to publish some of the relevant information. By contrast, in Finland, France, Germany, Greece, and Poland, access to this information was at this time denied.

The original idea behind the " nancial transparency component of the ETI came at the very start of Kallas s term of of" ce. During the Commissioner-elect s hearing before the European Parliament s Budgetary Control Committee (COCOBU) on 11 October 2004, Kallas was asked by Member of the European Parliament (MEP) James Ellis to consider whether he would be prepared to put the names of recipients of European funds on the Union s Europa website. Kallas was somewhat taken aback, admitting surprise that this information, readily available in Estonia which had just joined the Union, was not accessible in all EU member states (European Parliament 2004a and interview 25 January 2006). He agreed to follow up on this matter.

Although the Commission had little more than a moral authority in proposing that member states provide this information, after consulting with national governments an agreement was reached. Revisions to the EU s Financial Regulation were " nally approved on 13 December 2006 (Commission 2007), after a process of conciliation between the Parliament and the Council. These revisions included a commitment to the annual ex-post publication of the bene" ciaries of the EU s Structural Funds (as of 2008) and of the common agricultural policy (as of 2009). This was lauded by the Commission as a " rst success for the ETI (Commission 2007).

The regulation of lobbying

The second element of the ETI reviewed here concerns the lobbying of EU institutions by interest groups. Lobbying had been a focus of attention during the 2000 04 period, though this had not been a component of the Commission reform package. The Commission issued a Communication in 2002, though this focused on consultation practice rather than on lobbying. As of 2004, the existing system of lobbying regulation was a diverse one, with different systems operating across the EU institutions. In the European Parliament, there was a Code of Conduct for lobbyists and a registration system, which gave participants access to the Parliament with an annual pass. For the Commission, an earlier 1992 Communication set out a much looser framework for relations with lobbyists. Non-governmental organizations (NGOs) have long complained that the Commission favours corporate interests, and have argued that a more transparent system could allow clearer judgements to be made about the role of money and interests in the EU s decision-making process. One such option included in the Initiative was the idea of providing more information on emails received by Commissioners. However, here the issue under debate was what kind of action to take: whether it was necessary to create a system of mandatory registration for lobby groups or simply to rely on voluntary self-regulation on the basis of a common code. In the end, on 21 March 2007, the Commission took the decision to establish a public register of interest representatives working in the EU institutions. Registration was to be voluntary and web-based. In addition, a common code of conduct for lobbyists was to be introduced (Commission 2007).

The interest group regulation component of the ETI came directly from an NGO, Corporate Europe Observatory (CEO), in an open letter sent to the Commission President on 25 October 2004 (CEO 2004). CEO is a small Amsterdam-based group which, in its own words, lobbies against threats to democracy, equity, social justice and the environment posed by the economic and political power by corporations and their lobby groups (CEO 2006). CEO was instrumental in establishing the Alliance for Lobbying Transparency and Ethics Regulation (ALTER-EU), which was set up on 18 May 2005 in response to Kallas s aforementioned Nottingham speech . ALTER-EU is a coalition of approximately 140 civil society groups, academics, public affairs rms and trade unions, all of which had some interest in supporting the Commission s Initiative.

The reaction from business interests and especially from the public affairs consultancies was initially hostile. Many groups wrote to the Commission expressing their concerns, arguing that there was no need to address this issue as there was no evidence of any misconduct in their relations with the EU institutions (Interview EPACA, 26 January 2006). Most vociferous in lobbying against the Kallas proposals was a representative trade organization called the European Public Affairs Consultancies Association (EPACA). EPACA was formerly the Code of Conduct Group , a more informal set-up established after the 1992 Communication, that was instrumental in developing a code of conduct for lobbyists which, according to the EPACA Chair, was then picked up by the Parliament as their own in-house code. After deciding not to merge with the Society of European Affairs Practitioners (SEAP), the Group decided to set up their own organization (Interview EPACA, 26 January 2006) just prior to the Nottingham speech, on 28 January 2005. Along with SEAP, EPACA expressed a particular concern that the Kallas initiative might end up targeting *them* more than any other set of interests. They were especially keen to argue against a US-style system, but if some kind of regulatory system were to be introduced it should cover all groups including civil society NGOs, trade unions and law "rms. However, EPACA argued that regulation was unnecessary because of the recently revamped self-regulatory ethics code, revised in February 2005, which worked perfectly well in their opinion. They were also critical of the claim that it is somehow possible to *balance* corporate interests and civil society group concerns within the EU system (Interview EPACA, 26 January 2006).

Ethical standards of EU officials

The third element of the ETI is related most explicitly to the ethics dimension, as discussed earlier. This was to provoke a debate on the de"nition of common ethical rules and standards for public of"ce holders in the European institutions, such as those found in the Commission s Codes of Conduct for Commissioners and Of"cials, in the hope that other EU institutions would be prepared to work with the Commission on this. Moreover, there was an attempt to reawaken the proposal dating from 2000 that had sought to set up an inter-institutional Advisory Group on Standards in Public Life.

As for the general objective regarding ethics standards, little had been done on this front by early 2006 (Interview Commission SG/B/2, 3 February 2006). The Inter-Departmental Working Group discussing this issue (Commission 2005b) raised the possibility of a revision to the Code of Conduct for Commissioners. However, the College had a particular take on this at the time: The Commission considers that this would only be useful if it is part of an inter-institutional debate on an inter-institutional Advisory Group (Commission 2005a: 7). The responsibility for co-ordination was passed to the Bureau of European Policy Advisers (BEPA), the Commission s in-house think-tank, as lead service. In early February 2006, a member of the BEPA team was invited to draw up a call for tender for such a study, which was published in April 2006. The brief was to undertake a review of ethics rules and standards across Europe, including countries beyond the EU. The "ndings of the study are to be used as the basis for future action (Commission 2007).

The European Parliament was also instrumental in pushing for a new ethics agenda inside the Commission, though not speci"cally for the revisiting of the earlier proposal on the Advisory Group on Standards in Public Life. This element of the ETI took on a particular resonance during a political row in May 2005, which began with accusations over a holiday taken by Commission President Barroso on the yacht of an old friend, Spiros Latsis, a shipping magnate who had been in receipt of EU subsidies during the Commission s previous term. Although this turned out to be something of a political storm in a teacup , instigated by the UK Independence Party, the Commission President was alerted to the fact that insofar as the Commissioners Code of Conduct was concerned, he was responsible for the Code s application to *his own* conduct. This rather bizarre situation strengthened the argument for some kind of inter-institutional solution for dealing with the conduct of senior EU of"cials (and politicians). This issue was also very much on the mind of Kallas and his cabinet at the time because of the forthcoming Advocate-General s ruling on the fate (relating to her pension rights) of former Commissioner Edith Cresson, accused in 1999 of misconduct.

There is some evidence here to suggest that, in bringing together these issues linked by the unifying concept of transparency, and launching them as a named initiative in early 2005, the ETI was something new; an attempt by the Commissioner to make his own mark on the Commission in a context that was clearly shaped by the momentous reforms introduced by his predecessor. The obvious exception was in the revival of the Advisory Group proposal. It was also clear that the Initiative was greeted with a less than enthusiastic reception by the Commission President and other leading Commissioners who thought the Initiative at best of marginal interest, and at worst pernicious and potentially regulatory at a time when Barroso had launched his proposals to cut EU red tape. This does not mean that the Initiative was not new and politically driven; just that it was not owned by the Commission as a whole. It really was an agenda driven by the Commissioner and his team.

The original idea behind the setting up of an Advisory Group to deal with the ethics of senior of"cials can be found in the Second Report of the Committee of Independent Experts (CIE 1999); and it also appears as a consequence in the Reform White Paper as Action No. 1 (Commission 2000a, 2000b). The idea originated, however, in a similar initiative within the UK Parliament (Interview 25 January 2006). The reference in the White Paper led to the drafting of a Commission proposal in 2000 (Commission 2000c). However, there was no support for this initiative in the European Parliament where it was quickly shot down (Interview 25 January 2006) and buried (Clegg and van Hulten 2003: 41) by the Parliament s Legal Affairs Committee. The implication was that the Commission should not be interfering in the ethics of other EU institutions, but should look after its own organization before starting to meddle in the affairs of those scrutinizing it. Clegg and van Hulten state that German and Spanish MEPs were responsible for the rejection of this proposal, with the latter using rather emotive language to reject it, warning of a return to the days of the Weimar Republic ... expressing the fear that it would lead to civil servants controlling politicians (2003: 40). Kinnock also faced accusations that efforts to impose a committee of this kind were evidence of an Anglo-Saxon plot (Interview 3 February 2006). By 2003 Kinnock had put this element of the reform agenda on hold, and it was eventually abandoned (Hine and McMahon 2004: 27), though the draft remained on the table. It was this proposal that was picked up again in 2005.

UNPACKING CONTINUING REFORM IN THE EUROPEAN COMMISSION

Of the three agency-oriented variables identi"ed earlier (see Table 1), which have mattered most and in which of the three elements of the ETI? It is clear that the leadership of the European Commissioner cuts across all three elements. In the absence of a prioritization of a new administrative agenda in the Barroso Commission, Siim Kallas took it upon himself to push this agenda forward. It was his pet project. The only exception is on the ethical standards of officials over which President Barroso had some influence. There was, however, also a substantial degree of external advocacy, a precondition across the three elements of the ETI of the adoption of the issue by the Commissioner. In the case of the financial transparency agenda, this originally came from the European Parliament, in the form of a push by James Ellis, MEP (who first raised the issue). For lobbying regulation, the letter from the NGO Corporate Europe Observatory was particularly important, as was the subsequent pressure from ALTER-EU, the ethics alliance which it set up. In the case of the proposals promoting ethical standards amongst EU officials, advocacy — in a general sense — came from the European Parliament, even if the latter was uncertain whether it wanted an EU-wide system of control. Third, the activity of veto players was particularly visible in the case of lobbying regulation, especially from the EU public affairs consultancies who considered the proposal as an attack on their ability to conduct business freely. On financial transparency, some national governments which had previously been opposed to the provision of information on the end beneficiaries of EU grants were reluctant to accept this proposal. However, it did not take much to overcome the resistance in both these cases by compromising over the content of the reform proposed. This allowed the initiates to continue, albeit in a watered-down form. See Table 2.

Table 2 Agency and continuing reform in the European Commission

Agency	Financial transparency	Lobbying regulation	Ethical standards of officials
Change agency	Yes. The Commissioner's role is crucial	Yes. The Commissioner's role is crucial	Yes. The Commissioner's role is crucial. Some input from Barroso
Advocacy	Yes. MEP James Ellis's role was crucial	Yes. The role of NGO Corporate Europe Observatory was crucial	Some pressure to reform from the European Parliament
Veto agents	Yes. Some member state opposition, but this did not prevent an agreement	Yes. Opposition from public affairs consultancies in particular	Yes. Some resistance from other EU institutions; possible delays (further research) prior to presenting a formal proposal

What of the intervening factors conceptualized earlier as opportunities and used by actors involved in the process? Here structural factors appeared as constraints in the continuing reform process, even though none of them proved to be insuperable barriers to further reform. In all three cases the need for inter-institutional support delayed agreement, but ultimately did not prevent it. The functional factors identified were the unintended consequences of earlier reforms and the desire to complete unfinished business. The first was not relevant in any of the above cases. However, the second was important in two out of the three cases. In the financial transparency initiative, the reforms followed on from those included in the 2002 revision of the EU s Financial Regulation as part of the Commission s reform package. In the case of the ethical standards of officials, the initiative was first proposed in the 2000 Reform White Paper, but had not been implemented in the 2000 04 period.

With regard to ideational factors, there seem to be no direct effects of changing ideas, resulting from perceptions of earlier reforms, policy crises or scandals, or the injection of new administrative ideas at this time. This does not preclude, however, the relevance of longer-term and less direct ideational influences. See Table 3.

Table 3 Opportunity and continuing reform in the European Commission

Variable	Financial transparency	Lobbying regulation	Ethical standards of officials
Constitutional issues	No	No	No
Legislative constraints	Yes. There was a need to gain member state agreement	Yes. An inter-institutional agreement was necessary	Yes. An inter-institutional agreement was necessary
Unintended consequences	No	No	No
Unfinished business	Yes. Financial transparency was included in the 2002 Financial Regulation; further revisions needed to include this aspect	No	Yes
Perceptions of earlier reforms	No	No	No
Policy crises/ scandals	No	No	No
New administrative ideas	No	No	No

Indeed, it is possible to argue that the ETI, as a whole, constitutes a return to the early ambitions of the Kinnock reforms, given that the reform was originally driven by concerns about the Commission s legitimacy and its ethics (see Cini 2007: 13 15 on this). The Eurostat affair in 2003 can be understood as a wake-up call for Commission reform leaders, who may well have pushed some of the original objectives of the reform to the back of their minds. Indeed, there is even some evidence that points to the ETI as a linear extension of the Kinnock reforms. Transparency was one of the original principles in the 2000 White Paper and as we saw earlier there was an ethics dimension to those reforms, albeit one which was not fully developed. It is possible, therefore, that the ETI, in emphasizing the importance of transparency, was merely picking up one of the key principles of the Reform White Paper, and pushing forward this earlier agenda beyond what was envisaged "ve years before.

Moreover, while the earlier Commission reforms focused attention on the internal workings of the Commission (and only involved an inter-institutional dimension when this was necessary for achieving its internal reform objectives), the ETI pushed this agenda outwards, focusing on the Commission s relationship with and obligations to actors outside its organizational boundaries; namely, citizens and taxpayers, stakeholders, and its institutional neighbours. Thus, we see in the "nancial dimension of the ETI recognition of the rights of citizens to know how their taxes are being allocated and spent. In the case of lobby groups, we see an acknowledgement too that citizens have a right to know how European policy is being made, who is in"uencing, and who has access to, key decision-makers. This information is also important, in the interests of equity, for the groups themselves. Thus the ETI constitutes a concrete manifestation of the Commission s desire to disseminate outwards to the EU the principles of the reform to which it has been subject.

CONCLUSIONS

From the intra-case comparison presented in this article, it is possible to understand continuing reform as driven by reform agents and advocates who use the un"nished business of earlier reforms, alongside other windows of opportunity, as justi"cation for further reforms. Change agents at the centre are particularly important. Veto players use structural factors as constraints, but these may not pose insuperable barriers to reform where reform agents are willing and able to negotiate over the content of reform, even if this may mean a watering-down of substantive issues. Ideational factors may also serve as resources working to support continuing reform, helping reform agents to overcome potential constraints, though there is less evidence that this mattered in any direct sense in this particular case.

One must approach the generalizations presented in this article with caution, however, and remember that the purpose of this article was an exploratory one. Moreover, as the reform literature repeatedly reminds us, administrative reform is a highly contingent process. The particular context within which the reform process occurs is of crucial importance and cannot be wished away. Yet, it is interesting, all the same, to identify those factors that seem to matter in these cases, so that we might, through an accumulation of empirical knowledge, learn more about the conditions under which continuing reform might occur and why it seems more prevalent now than ever before. As noted at the start of this article, the concept of continuing reform implies an alternative conceptualization of reform. Whereas the notion of a post-reform period suggests that reform has a beginning and an end, continuing reform suggests a process. In exploring this distinction it might be helpful to move beyond our usual understanding of administrative reform   especially large-scale administrative reform   as an event, or in the words of March and Olsen (1989: 94), as an occasional foray or as a sporadic crusade . If, by contrast, public management is considered as a policy domain (Barzelay 2001), one might see administrative reform as an instrument of that policy, taking a variety of different forms (comprehensive or more modest). From this perspective, continuity in the reform process makes more sense. The task for researchers becomes one of applying the tools of public policy to reform efforts. To a degree this is what this article has attempted to begin to do. With further empirical research in this "eld, it may be possible to move beyond questions of continuity and change to unpack more systematically and over the *longue durée* why different kinds of reform strategies are selected at different junctures; and why at other times reform is more remote from the political agenda.

Biographical note: Michelle Cini is Professor of European Politics at the University of Bristol, UK.

Address for correspondence: Michelle Cini, Department of Politics, University of Bristol, 10 Priory Road, Bristol BS8 1TU, UK. email: Michelle.Cini@bristol.ac.uk

REFERENCES

Bannick, D. and Resodihardjo, S. (2006) The myths of reform , in L. Heyse, S. Resodihardjo, T. Lantink and B. Lettinga (eds), *Reform in Europe: Breaking the Barriers of Government*, Aldershot: Ashgate.

Barzelay, M. (2001) *The New Public Management. Improving Research and Policy Dialogue*, London: University of California Press.

Bossaert, D. and Demmke, C. (2005) *Main Challenges in the Field of Ethics and Integrity in the EU Member States*, Maastricht: European Institute of Public Administration.

Bovens, M. (1998) *The Quest for Responsibility: Accountability and Citizenship in Complex Organizations*, Cambridge: Cambridge University Press.

Bulmer, S., Dolowitz, D., Humphreys, P. and Padgett, S. (eds) (2007) *Policy Transfer in European Union Governance: Regulating the Utilities*, London: Routledge.

CEO (2004) European Commission must act to curb excessive corporate lobbying power . Open letter to José Manuel Barroso, President of the European Commission, 25 October.

CEO (2006) Corporate Europe Observatory , www.corporateeurope.org/

CIE (1999) *Second Report on the Reform of the Commission: Analysis of Current Practices and Proposals for Tackling Mismanagement, Irregularities and Fraud*, 10 September.

Cini, M. (2007) *From Integration to Integrity: Administrative Ethics and Reform in the European Commission*, Manchester: Manchester University Press.

Clegg, N. and van Hulten, M. (2003) *Reforming the European Parliament*, Policy Brief, Foreign Policy Centre, London, May.

Commission (2000a) *Reforming the Commission: A White Paper*, Part 1, COM (2000) 200 " nal, Brussels, 5 April.

Commission (2000b) *Reforming the Commission: A White Paper*, Part 2, COM (2000) 200 " nal, Brussels, 5 April.

Commission (2000c) *Proposal for an Agreement between the European Parliament, the Council, the Court of Justice, the Court of Auditors, the Economic and Social Committee and the Committee of the Regions establishing an Advisory Group on Standards in Public Life*, SEC(2000) 2077 " nal, Brussels.

Commission (2002a) Ethics ; www.europa.eu.int/comm./reform/2002/sheet4_en.htm

Commission (2002b) *Communication from the Commission: Towards a Reinforced Culture of Consultation and Dialogue   General Principles and Minimum Standards for Consultation of Interested Parties by the Commission*, COM(2002) 704, 11 December.

Commission (2005a) *Communication to the Commission from the President, Ms Wallstöm, Ms Hübner and Ms Fischer Boel Proposing the Launch of a European Transparency Initiative*, Memorandum to the Commission, 9 November.

Commission (2005b) *Commission Staff Working Document Report of the Inter-Departmental Working Group on a Possible European Transparency Initiative*, SEC (2005) 1300 " nal.

Commission (2005c) *Communication from the Commission to the European Parliament and the Council. Progress Report on the Commission Reform Beyond the Reform Mandate*, COM(2005) 668 "nal, Brussels, 21 December.

Commission (2006) Green Paper. European Transparency Initiative, COM(2006) 194/"nal, Brussels, 3 May.

Commission (2007) Transparency Initiative , www.ec.europa.eu/commission_barroso/kallas/transparency

Döhler, M., Fleischer, J. and Hustedt, T. (2007) Government reform as institutional politics   varieties and policy patterns for a comparative perspective , Forschungspapiere Regierungsorganization in Westeuropa , Universität Potsdam, Heft 03.

European Parliament (2004) European Parliament Resolution on Eurostat , P5_TA(2004)0372, OJ C104E/1022, 30 April.

Geri, L.R. (2001) New public management and the reform of international organizations , *International Review of Administrative Science* 67: 445 60.

Haas, P.M. (1992) Introduction: Epistemic communities and international policy coordination , *International Organization* 46(1): 1 35.

Héritier, A. (2001) Differential Europe: national administrative responses to Community policy , in M.G. Cowles, J. Caporaso and T. Risse (eds), *Transforming Europe: Europeanization and Domestic Change*, Ithaca, NY: Cornell University Press, pp. 44 59.

Hine, D. and McMahon, R. (2004) Ethics management, cultural change, and the ambiguities of European Commission reform . Working Paper, Department of Politics and International Relations, University of Oxford; http://government.politics. ox.ac.uk/Projects/Papers/Hine-McMahon_Ethics_Management.pdf

Kitschelt, H.P. (1986) Political opportunity structures and political protest: anti-nuclear movements in four democracies , *British Journal of Political Science* 16(1): 57 85.

Knill, C. (1999) Explaining cross-national variance in administrative reforms: autonomous versus instrumental bureaucracies , *Journal of Public Policy* 19(2): 113 39.

Koopmans, R. (2004) Political opportunity structure. Some splitting to balance the lumping , in L. Goodwin and J.M. Jasper (eds), *Rethinking Social Movements: Structure, Meaning and Emotion*, Lanham MD: Rowman & Little"eld, pp. 61 73.

March, J.G. and Olsen, J.P. (1989) *Rediscovering Institutions: The Organizational Basis of Politics*, New York: The Free Press.

Peters, B.G. (1997) Policy transfers between governments: the case of administrative reforms , *West European Politics* 20(4): 71 88.

Peters, B.G. (2001) From change to change: patterns of continuing administrative reform in Europe , *Public Organization Review* 1(1): 41 54.

Pollitt, C. and Bouckaert, G. (2004) *Public Management Reform. A Comparative Analysis*, 2nd edn, Oxford: Oxford University Press.

Sabatier, P.A. (1998) Policy change over a decade or more , in P.A. Sabatier and H.C. Jenkins-Smith (eds), *Policy Change and Learning: An Advocacy Coalition Approach*, Boulder, CO: Westview Press, pp. 13 39.

Tsebelis, G. (2002) *Veto Players: How Political Institutions Work*, Princeton, NJ: Princeton University Press.

van de Walle, S., Thijs, N. and Bouckaert, G. (2005) A tale of two charters , *Public Management Review* 7(3): 367 90.

Enlargement, reform and the European Commission. Weathering a perfect storm?

John Peterson

A new, enlarged, and rather different European Union (EU) has emerged. Arguably, its recent enlargement is the greatest single achievement of European integration. Lines of political division that had cut Europe through its heart for more than 50 years were swept away in 2004 07. Enlargement has been as much a policy as a political success: ten post-communist states in Central and Eastern Europe, along with Cyprus and Malta, have embraced signi"cant internal reforms and economic modernization as the price of EU membership.

The European Commission can rightly claim much of the credit. The EU s main administration led the enlargement negotiations, assessing progress and ultimately signing off on the readiness of the applicants before "nal, political decisions were made on dates of admission for the EU-12.[1] The Commission is delegated formidable powers by the EU s Treaties more generally. Uniquely among international institutions, the Commission   along with the European Parliament (EP) and Court of Justice   has the capacity and legitimacy to act relatively independently of member states assent (Christiansen 1997: 73). As such, the Commission may be the world s most powerful international administration.

Yet, the Commission must now digest enlargement, integrating most of the nearly 4,000 EU-12 of"cials set to join the Union s institutions by 2009. It must do so after the most wrenching internal changes in its history, arising from the administrative reforms piloted by Vice-President Neil Kinnock (2000 04). All administrations are limited in their capacity to absorb reform (Olsen 2003). Few adjust quickly to changes in the pool from which they acquire their personnel. Changes of this order of magnitude might be particularly traumatic for the Commission, since it is accepted wisdom that it has been in decline since the 1999 resignation of the entire College of Commissioners amidst charges of cronyism and maladministration under the Presidency of Jacques Santer.

This paper s central research question is: how have the Commission s work, role and status changed since the Santer resignation? The Kinnock reforms and enlargement were both, in and of themselves, major challenges. The convergence of the two might be viewed as a sort of perfect storm, especially for an institution in decline. Have administrative reforms weakened the Commission s capacity for policy entrepreneurship? Has the Commission contributed to its own decay by shepherding enlargement to completion?

De"nitive answers are clearly years away. This paper contents itself with placing these questions on the research agenda, and using them to confront even bigger questions about the nature of the new EU, and how future historians will decide it was changed (and how much) by enlargement. Drawing on extensive "eldwork,[2] it "nds that the early twenty-"rst century has been tumultuous for the Commission, not least because it has been the subject of many of the same processes of reinvention that other western bureaucracies have had to endure (Osborne and Gaebler 1992; Pollitt and Bouckaert 2004; Pollitt and Talbot 2004; Pollitt et al. 2007). Enlargement could be viewed as extending the era of internal reform of the Commission, while also bringing to bear new and different pressures for transformation. Put simply, the Commission has been through a period of dramatic and, in some senses, traumatic change.

Yet, the end result may be a renewed, more modern, and less self-absorbed Commission. Its role may be more modest in a post-vision era [3] of European integration, or one in which a radically enlarged Union focuses on pragmatic policy results more than new political acts of integration. Crucially, the Commission shows signs of reconciling itself to the position, speci"ed in network theory, of a strategic node in EU policy networks, even if it has far to go before it can provide the motivation, trust, or leadership needed for effective network governance.

All the while, it has become more dif"cult to generalize about the Commission. It is very much a hybrid institution divided between its College and permanent services and, increasingly, in recent years, split between these two levels. Thus, section 1 focuses on the College, while section 2 grapples with recent developments within the services. Section 3 considers the impact of the Kinnock reforms and enlargement on the administration as a whole.

Section 4 investigates the prospects for a Commission that acts less as an engine of integration than a co-ordinator of networks. A concluding section suggests that a more *intergovernmental* Commission may be emerging: less autonomous but more integrated into the EU system. However, the very meaning of inter-governmental may have changed in the transition to a new EU.

1. A COLLEGE OF STRANGERS?

The Commission has always been a hybrid: the EU s largest administration and main policy manager but also a source of political and policy direction (see Peterson 2006: 80 2). Both the Kinnock reforms and enlargement have made trickier the balancing act that the Commission must perform as both an executive and a technocracy. There is no question that the political side of the Commission the College and *cabinets* has, over time, become a con-siderably different world from that of permanent of cials in the Commission s services or Directorates-General (DGs): the Brussels equivalent of ministries. There is evidence of increasing tension between them (see section 2 below).

One source of tension is the emergence of a considerably larger College of 27 Commissioners, up from 20 under the Presidency of Romano Prodi (2000 04).[4] The President of the enlarged Commission José Manuel Barroso established that his would be a highly Presidential Commission, warning repeatedly of the dangers of Balkanization in the absence of a presi-dent that is seen by members of the Commission as the last resort arbiter and authority.[5] One of cial with experience of multiple Commission *cabinets* claimed: The President s power is increasing dramatically. It is now a clear, secular trend that the Commission is becoming more Presidential. The Nice Treaty gave the President stronger powers and Barroso is using them.[6]

The argument that a strong President had become a purely functional neces-sity was viewed as disingenuous by Barroso s political opponents. After his selec-tion in 2004, Barroso came under attack from the political left, which loathed his earlier support (as Portuguese Prime Minister) for the Iraq War and accused him of privileging a liberal Atlantic clique within the Commission (see Peterson 2006: 93). Hyperbole aside, there was little question that the share of liberals in the Barroso College was disproportionate to their representation in the EP,[7] and quite possibly in the Commission s services (see Hooghe 2001). It was not uncommon to hear of cials in the DGs accuse Barroso of:

> packing the services with neoliberals. The reactive instinct of most of us is I m just a civil servant with political masters; I have no opinion. But not these people. There is a centre-left minority group in the College, of whom (Vice-President Margot) Wallstrom is the ring-leader. But they are not winning.[8]

In any event, Barroso used the expansion of the College, as well as the percep-tion that Prodi had been a weak President, to his advantage. The fact that no formal votes were taken within the College during the rst three years of his mandate was cited by officials far more often as a sign of Barroso s dominance than his penchant for compromise.

One vestige of a more Presidential Commission was the creation of a new Impact Assessment Board, working under Barroso s direct authority. Here we find an institutional reform entirely disconnected from the Kinnock reforms but very much in the same spirit of expanding a growing market in scrutiny of what the services do. The Impact Assessment Board was given authority to block any legislative proposal if its impact assessment was deemed to be deficient or the Board concluded that the cost of new legislation outweighed its benefits.[9] The Board was considered a key foil in Barroso s drive to ensure that the EU produced better regulation , which was widely viewed in the services as cover for producing less regulation. A senior official in one of the main economic DGs commented on the Impact Assessment Board: these are all Barroso s people and they can stop anything. [10]

An obvious question was whether Barroso s strong grip on the College was justified because his was the first Commission ever in which each member state nominated one and only one Commissioner. As such, the College resembled an offshoot of the Council, such as one of its working groups, or (in the Brussels jargon) a COREPER [Committee of Permanent Representatives] 3 (see Lewis 2006). Defenders of its traditional role worried that Commissioners had lost its independence from national capitals. One Commissioner from an EU-12 state mused, they tell me that when the big member states had two Commissioners, it was less intergovernmental because there was one to defend the national interest, and another to defend the European interest. [11] This assessment chimes with empirical evidence that small member states which had always appointed only one Commissioner nominated party-inclusive members of the College (who shared party affiliations with governments) far more often than large states prior to 2004. We thus might expect governments more often to appoint one of their own in a one Commissioner per member state College (Wonka 2007). Yet, one very senior official offered a far more nuanced view:

> Having one per member state makes an enormous difference, but actually in making the College more collective and coherent. What matters above all is that 22 of 25 are new to the College, and many have found their learning curves to be steep. Lots of them are frustrated: they think too much is pre-cooked and that there s a lack of political input. Having 25 in the College means that it is hard to have debates, and so more is done in smaller groups.[12]

Any shift towards a more intergovernmental Commission also seemed tempered by the presence of few strong political personalities in the College compared to Prodi s. As one *chef du cabinet* put it: there is no (Pascal) Lamy, no (Antonio) Vitorino, no (Frits) Bolkestein, no (Mario) Monti, and no (Chris) Patten in the Barroso College. This College is much greyer than the previous one. [13]

Generally, given their lack of experience of EU membership, governments from the new member states took pains to appoint top members of their political classes or senior diplomats who had been involved with EU accession and knew the Brussels system well. Yet, besides Poland, all of the EU-12 were small states whose political classes were mostly unknown outside their home countries. Enlargement seemed to have the effect of making the College more technocratic. One head of *cabinet*, with experience at that level in several Commissions, explained that Barroso s was not a political Commission in part because an intermediate generation of technocrats dominated the "rst post-Communist political classes in the new member states. One consequence is that there is not a lot of ideological debate in this Commission. [14] Out of the ten Commissioners appointed by states that joined in 2004, three had the unusual distinction of having no party political af"liation (see Peterson 2006: 90 1). The 2006 nominees from Bulgaria, Megelena Kuneva, and Romania, Leonard Orban, both appeared to be chosen largely because of their distance from domestic party politics.[15]

A separate question was whether Barroso s was effectively a two-tier College. Most of the EU-12 Commissioners were given relatively minor portfolios. Kuneva and Orban were given portfolios   consumer protection and multilingualism, respectively   that one senior of"cial described as humiliating and not worthy of someone who has the title of European Commissioner .[16] One implication of the move to one Commissioner per member state was that the formal equality of Commissioners from, say, Germany and Cyprus, became a "ction (Peterson 2005: 516). Still, there seemed little doubt that Commissioners more closely represented their member states, both because of the College s new composition and the insecurity of EU-12 governments, in the Barroso Commission.

The College was obviously too big: a collection of strangers that was too large to have many meaningful political debates (whatever other factors limited them in number). Yet, in a sense, the College was also too small: lacking representatives of important political forces, particularly those in large member states, such as the German Christian Democrats or French Socialists. Adequate representation of the new EU, whose population was one and a half times that of the United States, was somewhere between dif"cult and impossible. The College under Barroso just about managed it, even if it also became more Presidential, liberal, technocratic, and   to use a loaded and probably outmoded term (see below)   intergovernmental.

2. THE SERVICES: HYBRID UNHINGED?

If a rift appeared between the College and services under Barroso, it certainly was not making its "rst appearance. Kassim s (2004b: 27) verdict was that tensions between the College and services (along with problems of inter-service co-ordination) under the Prodi Commission ma[d]e it very dif"cult for a member of the Commission, even a Commission President, to mobilize the institutional resources that the experience of national governments suggests are necessary to formulate and drive through a programme of reform. Similarly, students of comparative administration tend to agree that the Commission is a distinctively unpromising arena for a programme of institutional reform (see Pollitt and Bouckaert 2004: 232 7).

Nevertheless, Kinnock managed to push through a comprehensive administrative reform programme between 2004 and 2007, albeit at considerable cost to the Commission s cohesion. The rift between the College and the services did not originate with the Kinnock reforms. But the reform programme was highly divisive and resentment of it within the services was still fresh by the time of the 2004 enlargement.

Prior to enlargement, and the arrival of Barroso, the relationship between the College and services differed in multiple respects. It is worth recalling that Prodi s was an unusually impressive College in terms of expertise, which was matched to portfolios in a way never seen in any previous Commission (Peterson 2006: 87). It was also unusually ministerial, with Commissioners working in the same buildings as the DGs for which they were responsible, making the services more like national ministries: that is, places where other Commissioners were welcome only by invitation and policy debates on speci"c dossiers were mostly internal affairs. The reuniting of the College in the central Berlaymont building by Barroso appeared to reify a different kind of division: DGs that operated with considerable independence from the College. An early signal of disconnect came from Trade Commissioner, Peter Mandelson, in mid-2005:

> my guess is that power within the Commission has inexorably shifted to the services . . . the unique position of the College as envisaged in the Treaties, as a political body to give political leadership to Europe from the standpoint of the European interest, has been eroded by a pincer movement: loss of control over its own services pursuing special interests, however legitimate, on the one hand, and a loss of leadership to the Council on the other.[17]

Just over a year later, Günter Verheugen, the Enterprise Commissioner, accused the DGs of being technical and arrogant . . . Some bureaucrats think: the Commissioner is off again in "ve years. He is just a temporary lodger, while I m staying . . . [it is] a constant power struggle. [18]

The background to Verheugen s outburst was rich with intrigue. In 2004, Barroso had been pressed by the German government to make Verheugen, who had shown considerable skill as Enlargement Commissioner under Prodi, a super-Commissioner as a way to compensate Germany for the loss of its second Commissioner. Barroso resisted the pressure, and Verheugen ended up with the enterprise portfolio. One senior of"cial described Verheugen as a foreign policy specialist who is out of his depth, with a portfolio that doesn t really add up to anything .[19]

Verheugen s foreign policy expertise made him a candidate to become High Representative for the EU s common foreign and security policy when Javier

Solana stepped down.[20] Thus, he was widely suspected of Commission-bashing as a sop to endear himself to member governments,[21] a number of which turned Eurosceptical after the demise of the Constitutional Treaty in 2005, when it was rejected in French and Dutch referenda. As if all of that were not enough, Verheugen had powerful incentives to change the subject after appointing a long-time female friend   with whom he had been photographed on what appeared to be a romantic holiday   as his *chef du cabinet.*

In any event, Verheugen s comments sent a chill through the Commission. Its Secretary-General (and top permanent of"cial), Catherine Day, took pains to state that the civil service understands that we are not the bosses. It is the Commissioners that are the bosses. [22] For his part, Barroso chose to defend both Verheugen and the Commission s services, describing the latter as very competent and could stand comparison with any national administration .[23]

Interesting questions arise about how enlargement "gured in the mix. It was not immediately obvious that EU-12 Commissioners had more trouble imposing their wills on the DGs than did those from the EU-15. Commissioners have always been, by de"nition, outsiders upon their arrival in Brussels. The services have always been more powerful *vis-à-vis* their Commissioner than are most national ministers *vis-à-vis* their ministries, especially since Commissioners lack the power to hire or "re of"cials at the top of the services: the Directors-General.

On the one hand, enlargement forced a number of changes on the services almost immediately after they had absorbed the Kinnock reforms. Nearly all had to stretch their knowledge base to design or monitor policy for a considerably more diverse collection of states. Many reorganized themselves into geographical sub-units with responsibility for speci"ed groups of states or regions. It was estimated that close to 200 new units were created across the Commission in 2005 alone.

On the other hand, newly recruited of"cials from the EU-12 tended to be similar in background to their colleagues in the Commission. Most were cosmopolitan, multilingual, and had degrees from outside their country of origin. One senior of"cial in the Secretariat-General wondered whether the Commission was recruiting clones of ourselves .[24] What was truly different about of"cials from the new member states was their age   considerably younger than the Commission average   and, perhaps above all, their outlook. As one Director-General put it:

> It will take a generation for the effects of enlargement to "lter through. The quality of the top of"cials coming from the new states varies a lot . . . But the younger of"cials are a wonderful, enthusiastic, breath of fresh air. They make us realize how jaded many of us have become.[25]

Again, what is perhaps most distinctive about the new Commission is how far the two halves of the hybrid had drifted apart. In some ways, the arrival of the post-vision era made it inevitable that the College had trouble de"ning a political vision, let alone coaxing the DGs into servicing it. More generally, as a Director in the services put it, it was perhaps always predictable that:

> Enlargement pushes things down and makes the services more powerful. The Council can t negotiate. The Parliament struggles. So what is actually in the proposal is now more important than before. Even though very few Commission proposals are spontaneous, and dreamt up exclusively by us, more gets pushed down to Commissioners or to their *cabinets*. And if either of those levels are weak, as is sometimes the case in this Commission, responsibility for the actual content and impact of what we do gets pushed down to the services.

Even if this view is valid, it is counterbalanced by the tendency for the Commission to be a natural repository for the latest reformist fetishes in European public administration or policy. Consider, as one example, impact assessments (IAs): the Impact Assessment Board was very much in keeping with the "avour of the month elsewhere in Europe, particularly the UK.[26] A senior Commission of cial with *cabinet* experience voiced cynicism that seemed typical of the services: it is still easy to get slaughtered with a great IA based on the best data in the world ... by the same token, if the Council wants it, IAs don t matter. They rarely change views and are often tailored to what individuals want politically.[27]

A second caveat to the enlargement pushes things down view arises from the push for better regulation. Again, the UK could claim to be spearheading the drive for better EU regulation .[28] But better regulation was by no means an exclusively British preoccupation: "ve other member states signed up to a Six Presidency Initiative on Advancing Regulatory Reform in Europe under a 2004 Dutch EU Council Presidency. Barroso s embrace of a better regulation agenda may have made him unpopular in the Commission s services. But it kept him in the good graces of the European Council, where he appeared to command more respect than any Commission President since Jacques Delors in the 1980s. Here, we may see an indicator of a Commission that is at the same time more Presidential but perhaps also less independent, in the sense of being more integrated into decision-making at the highest political level, compared to its predecessors.

Increased complexity arises from changes with contradictory effects, as has been amply illustrated during a period of multiple and dramatic shifts within the Commission. For example, the shift towards a more intergovernmental College might also contribute to a deeper split between the College and the services. By late 2007 three years after ten states had joined the EU the recruitment of of cials from the new member states to the services was still far behind the Commission s targets: only 12 per cent of Commission of cials were EU-12 nationals and most held relatively junior posts. At the élite level of Directors-General and their Deputies, only nine of 75 of cials hailed from the new states (and all were Deputies) by mid-October 2007.[29] Meanwhile, EU-12 of cials accounted for a far higher percentage of all *cabinet* members than of "cials in the services. The disparity between the College and services in terms of basic representation of the EU-12 was hardly a source of unity in what had become, for a rich variety of reasons, a highly bifurcated administration.

3. ENLARGEMENT AND THE KINNOCK REFORMS

One lesson of research on administrative reform is that change usually occurs slowly. Several generations must often pass through an institution before the effects on its culture and behaviour become clear (Putnam *et al.* 1993; Pollitt and Bouckaert 2004). Research on EU institutional reform highlights how it typically aims to achieve multiple objectives, which are often incompatible with one another (Metcalfe 2000; Olsen 2003).

Enlargement and the Kinnock reforms were never intrinsically connected. Of course, the key changes in personnel management came into force precisely on the day (1 May 2004) when the EU expanded from 15 to 25 member states, unlike "nancial management reforms that came into effect years earlier. The relative lateness of the new Staff Regulations was mostly a consequence of a lack of progress on reforming them under Santer and lengthy consultations and negotiations after that (Stevens and Stevens 2006: 472). Nevertheless, many in the administrative and political classes of EU-12 member states viewed them as a device to prevent them from achieving parity with the EU-15 within the Commission. One senior (EU-15) of "cial in the Commission s Secretariat-General spoke for many in describing the decision to implement the new Staff Regulations at the precise moment of the 2004 enlargement as a huge political mistake .[30]

There is little question that the Commission s new system of administrative grades, which expanded their range, will slow the pace of promotion of new of "- cials compared to their immediate predecessors. New entrants, who will be disproportionately EU-12 of "cials for years to come, enter at lower grades and lower salaries than would previously have been the case for recruits to policy-level jobs (Stevens and Stevens 2006: 475). Enlargement was always going to lower the cost of the Commission, because recruits from the EU-12 would (eventually) lower the average age of Commission of "cials.[31] That aside, new entrants now faced a new promotion system that doubled the number of promotions needed to get to the same administrative grade as before, with only half as much additional pay per promotion. Meanwhile, a complicated system linked appraisal to promotion and was based on an unfathomable system of awarding points for performance. But what fuelled the perception of double standards above all was that part of the price paid for the support of Commission trade unions for the personnel reforms was generous transitional arrangements that more or less guaranteed EU-15 of "cials the same pay rises as they would have had under the old system.

One young (Hungarian) of "cial dismissed as conspiracy theory the claim that the staff reforms were designed to slow the absorption of of "cials from the new member states since the rules applied to *all* new recruits. Still, the same of"cial conceded that the theory was widely believed in EU-12 national capitals .[32] It was not dif"cult to see why, given problems associated with the new (as of 2002) European Personnel Selection Of"ce (EPSO), created as a joint recruitment organization for all EU institutions. EU-12 of"cials frequently complained about procedures that seem designed to keep people out .[33] One example was EPSO s refusal to offer the *concours*, the examination which prospective EU of"cials must pass, in any language besides French, German and English, thus (according to one of"cial) freezing out all but those already working for international organizations .[34] EPSO s problems seemed more accidental than designed as illustrated, for example, by allegations (denied by EPSO) that one *concours* in Lithuania was advertised only days before the exam was held. But they animated the intergovernmental politics of post-enlargement personnel policy.

Moreover, the conspiracy theory was given credence by the bid of the Finnish Council Presidency in late 2006 to cut around 1,700 Commission posts as part of its drive to improve productivity within EU institutions. There was no question that the cuts would have made recruiting politically acceptable numbers of EU-12 of"cials far more dif"cult. The Finnish plan was robustly opposed by Poland and other new member states (along with Italy and Spain), amidst charges that the Finns were obsessed with the job cuts.[35] Eventually, the Finnish plan was dropped and the Commission asked for 890 additional posts for 2008, all to be "lled by EU-12 nationals, with 250 reserved for entrants from Bulgaria and Romania. Even so, at least ten Commissioners expressed concern that recruitment on this scale was not enough for the Commission adequately to pursue its policy priorities in energy, climate change, and political communication, adding to perceptions of an administration under siege.[36]

We might dismiss conspiracy theories and still conclude that the Kinnock reforms were inspired by an agenda to hamstring the Commission, insofar as they eliminated what Stevens and Stevens (2006: 478) call the haphazard informality of the pioneering spirit which characterized the Commission s early years. Bauer (2008) is surely right that they turned many middle-level of"-cials from policy entrepreneurs to managers because of their onerous reporting requirements. No student of administrative reform would be surprised that even some of the most sensible reforms, such as those for "nancial management or the rotation of senior of"cials, had unintended effects. One Director-General illustrated the point:

> One effect of all the reporting we now have to do is that there is major paranoia about mistakes, especially with the European Parliament always on the prowl for ones that will make news. And we re in a situation of constant instability, with rotation of senior posts all the time. It all makes the divide between *la maison* and the College even wider.[37]

Unintended consequences aside, there is little doubt that the reforms were overdue. They ushered in far more systematic budgeting and personnel management, and better preparation and consultation (Kassim 2004a,

2004b). New provisions for appraisal and training gave credibility to the verdict of one senior of"cial that compared to other international organizations, we are so much better at giving people a chance to make a career outside their national systems. [38]

Equally, the Kinnock reforms failed to make the Commission a meritocracy. Intergovernmental politics, or the wishes of the Commission President, could still determine who ends up in which senior post. One of"cial in the *cabinet* of an EU-12 Commissioner lamented, there are constant delays in recruiting of"cials from the new member states, especially to powerful DGs like Competition and Eco"n. It is disappointing and shows a lack of trust. [39] A head of unit from one of the new member states complained, it is still harder to advance within the Commission compared to national civil services. And it doesn t depend on how bright you are. [40] Another senior of"cial put it more bluntly, The Commission really has no personnel policy. And it doesn t tell [its own] people the truth. [41]

4. THE COMMISSION AND NETWORK GOVERNANCE

Political interest in network forms of governance has grown in Europe and beyond in recent years (see Skogstad 2003; Pollitt and Bouckaert 2004; Jordan and Schout 2006). Viewed as a modern alternative to governance by hierarchy, network governance "nds public administrations engaging with private and non-governmental policy stakeholders on a non-hierarchical basis and negotiating non-legislative policy agreements. The shift to network governance has found favour in settings ranging from Bavaria s *Land* government (Suleiman 2003: 269) to the US Pentagon (see Boot 2006).[42] Research on the EU sometimes struggles to be speci"c about how the Commission would operate differently as a network organization (see Metcalfe 2000; Peterson 2008). But an usually clear injunction is:

> The Commission as a strategic node in many networks is in an unrivalled position to gather information, to compare and evaluate various attempts to build, change and reform policy networks and to learn lessons from different experience(s) that can be applied when new problems and new opportunities arise.
>
> (Metcalfe 2004: 92)

The Commission s position in EU policy networks differs enormously across sectors as diverse as (say) competition to defence policy. But three points are worth making if our purpose is to make a general judgement about how the Commission s role, work and status are changing.

First, enlargement has made the design of EU legislation   good, bad, or better   considerably more dif"cult. Policy problems in an EU-27 are now considerably more diverse and localized than before 2004. Yet, ironically, they are also more often a consequence of the rapid pace of economic change that is endemic to globalization. The EU s role in solving such problems logically involves "nding ways to add value to national-level activities, and usually acting far more quickly than it can by resorting to the relatively slow processes of legislating or building up new administrative capacities in Brussels (Jordan and Schout 2006).

Second, integrated European markets now touch on policies that are almost entirely within the remit of member states   such as pensions, health care, and employment law   in ways that both invite (at least potentially) destructive races to the bottom between EU states and expose the additional costs of doing business in Europe (compared to other large markets) that arise from its diversity. One consequence is the Barroso Commission s focus on the so-called Lisbon agenda, designed to make the EU the most dynamic economy in the world by 2010 , as well as its better regulation agenda. Both involve co-ordination of the actions of national authorities, through devices such as the so-called open method of co-ordination (Hodson and Maher 2001; Borràs and Jacobsson 2004), far more often than EU legislation. The Commission acts as a strategic node but only as a kind of coxswain, trying to persuade governments to embrace policy reforms through peer pressure, league tables, policy transfer, and so on, and often to the exclusion of its role as the initiator of EU legislation. The result is often an unusually pure form of non-hierarchical, network governance. Even if Barroso s focus on the Lisbon agenda was by no means universally popular within the services, few could deny that his emphasis on a Europe of results was driven by a pragmatic policy agenda in areas where Europe most needed reform, as opposed to one driven by concerns about the Commission s institutional dignity, which sometimes seemed to border on the obsessive under Prodi (Peterson 2006: 88 9).

Third, the Commission s role in constructing, managing, and auditing networks is usually viewed in the EU policy world as critical to their effective operation. But it is frequently seen in the research literature as beyond the Commission s wherewithal. Among the many dif"culties faced by the Commission in making the transition to EU network governance, three stand out: motivation, trust, and leadership.

Schout and Jordan (2005: 207) note the Commission s tendency to assume: one, that networks *are* an effective means of coordinating policies; and, two, that the most relevant actors *will* be suf"ciently motivated to want to join them (emphases in original). Yet, the Commission often fails to re"ect on how to motivate voluntary co-operation, assuming it will occur naturally and spontaneously. Collective action problems have become increasingly severe in an EU of 27 when policy pathologies such as carbon emissions, migration pressures, and energy dependency arise from the differences between uncoordinated national policies. The Commission still frequently presupposes that all policy stakeholders are suf"ciently motivated to embrace collective action to solve them.

Second, trust is viewed across the policy literature as *the* generic, crucial lubricant of collective action within networks (see Hindmoor 1998; Peters 1998; Klijn and Koppenjan 2000). Yet, the evidence to suggest that lack of trust is a particularly intractable obstacle to effective EU network governance is compelling. Radaelli (2007: 200) cites a lack of trust on the part of the member states in the Commission as a major problem of the better regulation agenda. One result is the tendency of the Commission to oversell its own analysis to the point where its legitimacy is undermined and the entire agenda loses credibility. Legitimacy is more generally the Achilles heel of regulatory quality initiatives (Radaelli 2007: 200) and the Commission continues to lack it, not least because (contrary to what it frequently assumes) [r]egulatory legitimacy ... is not automatically delivered by the presence of robust networks of stakeholders , which is a necessary but not suf"cient condition for it (Radaelli 2007: 201). Here, we might recall Ostrom s (1990) classic statement of what is required for effective governance: that actors in a network recognize their interdependence, that they are relatively few in number, and that they know and trust one another. To an extent that frustrates the Commission, actors in EU policy networks often do not recognize their interdependence. They are frequently and decidedly not few in number in an EU-27. Part of the price of enlargement is that, in many policy sectors, it may require years of the EU operating at 27 before actors know, let alone trust, one another.

Third, the problem of leadership in an enlarged EU may be particularly acute where the Commission must engage in network governance. Demand has clearly grown for a Commission that leads by providing effective management: speci"cally, by co-ordinating both horizontally between different EU policies   such as agriculture and environmental protection   as well as vertically between different levels of government. These tasks involve thorny co-ordination problems that have been made thornier by enlargement, given the added diversity of EU policy effects on the ground in a Union of 27 and the raw , added complexity of the intergovernmental level of EU governance. Schout and Jordan (2005: 218) are not alone (see Metcalfe 2000, 2004) in suspect[ing] that network management is a generic problem in the EU ... far more leadership is needed to diagnose weaknesses in networks and propose alternative action. The Commission is the most obvious candidate for such a role.

Being the most obvious candidate does not imply that making the transition from being legislative initiator to network manager will be easy for the Commission. The recent bifurcation of the Commission between the College and the services itself may be an obstacle. Consider that a more intergovernmental College may add most value when the EU legislates. One of"cial observes that a College of 27 gets national input early in the decision-making process when legislating. That is still very important. [43] Yet, in a climate in which legislating becomes more dif"cult, the tendency of the services over time may be to try to resort to more informal means of governing by networks, and in ways that allow for little political input from the College. The Commission may have to work with only a weak and rickety hinge between the services and the College, at least until the Reform Treaty is implemented (assuming it is rati"ed) and the College is reduced in size to two-thirds the number of its member states (possibly, say, 20 in an EU-30) in 2014.

Yet, by that time, an administratively reformed and enlarged Commission might well be more up to the tasks of supplying motivation, trust, and leadership in EU network governance than ever before. The "rst years of the twenty-"rst century have certainly been traumatic for the Commission. But there are signs that the Commission has begun to accept that it must invest in assets that do not "ow directly from its formal treaty powers, and that many of Europe s most important problems resist solutions through traditional Community legislation. These perceptions were clearly held at the top of a highly Presidential Commission under Barroso, and there were signs that they had begun to trickle down to the services, despite how bifurcated the Commission had become. To illustrate the point, it was revealing that of"cials in the services learned, as a strategy for getting the College to back whatever project they were working on, to link it to the Lisbon agenda.[44]

CONCLUSION

How and how much has the perfect storm changed the European Commission s work, role and status? One vastly experienced of"cial (and *chef du cabinet* for an EU-12 Commissioner) argued that enlargement and administrative reform had not fundamentally altered the place.[45] More generally, there was a strong sense across the EU s institutions that the Brussels system was remarkably unchanged by such a radical enlargement (see Best *et al.* 2008), if also a shared acceptance that the institutional reforms contained in the Reform Treaty were essential to the smooth functioning of the system in the longer term.

In some respects, the Commission seemed to have changed more from the powerful imprint of Barroso s Presidency than from enlargement or the Kinnock reforms *per se*. But it was dif"cult to separate these factors. For example, a majority of Commissioners from the EU-12 broadly shared Barroso s liberal, reformist agenda. Enlargement gave Barroso poetic licence to stamp his authority on the College, but the shift towards a more Presidential Commission predated Barroso and was a natural reaction to Santer s weakness. Still, Barroso established himself as a more forceful leader than Prodi, with far more control over the prioritizing of policy goals, but setting and imposing priorities was considerably aided by the Kinnock reforms.

Of course, we might be seduced into thinking, falsely, that little has changed in EU governance because the Commission, along with all EU institutions, has been subject to ambiguous and even contradictory changes. The Commission seemed empowered by Barroso s strong Presidential grip, but also weakened by the mind-numbing amount of scrutiny to which it was subject in the post-reform era. The Commission sometimes seemed a guinea pig for every fashion of new public management including what Power (1999) calls an audit explosion (see also Pollitt *et al.* 2007). In political terms, a senior of"cial with *cabinet* experience in both the Prodi and Barroso Commissions argued that the Kinnock reforms re"ected increasing distrust in the Commission under

Santer. A deliberate political decision was taken to make the Commission less attractive to good people. [46]

Ultimately, we are forced to try to synthesize the effects of forces that reinforce, contradict and entirely bypass one another if we want to pinpoint how EU governance generally   let alone the role of the Commission speci"- cally   has changed. Consider the re"ections of a senior of"cial with eight years of *cabinet* experience:

> The numerical advantage of the big member states has been lost, and in a way that is re"ected in all decision-making structures, including comitology, advisory committees, and so on. The French are now just one of 27. It makes the Commission s job a lot easier . . . If you want to be reticent in any debate, you only have a couple of minutes to be reticent. [47]

We might pro"tably conclude by considering both what this observation hits as well as what it misses. It is re"ective of how the Commission may be empowered by the recent enlargements, particularly since they almost exclusively added small states (and a lot of them) that naturally see the Commission as their defender and an honest broker.

Our last of"cial s comment also hints, at least indirectly, at a stark change at the level of College, where all Commissioners from large member states are now just one of 27 . At its highest level, the Commission s composition is now the same as all offshoots of the Council. The effect is to diminish signi"cantly its institutional uniqueness and, probably, also its independence, as well as the equality of all Commissioners. Again, no one pretends that the views or weight of the Maltese or Bulgarian Commissioner count for the same as those of their British or French counterparts. Yet this reality in itself may be re"ective of a more intergovernmental Commission.

Perhaps the real question has become: what does intergovernmental (always analytically slippery) actually *mean* in the new EU? It almost certainly means more complicated bargaining and coalition-building, which in itself might actually make the position of the Commission stronger, a point on which Barroso himself has insisted. [48] It certainly does not mean a sharp, simple, enhanced rivalry between EU member states, on the one hand, and EU institutions, on the other. It may actually mean more resort to non-legislative, soft law type agreements reached via bargaining within networks, not least because the Commission invests more in constructing and managing them, and accepts that formal legislation is often a bridge too far in an EU of 27 plus.

It might be argued that the new intergovernmentalism at least partly re"ects that Barroso himself is an intergovernmentalist at heart (see Peterson 2006: 94), who has both kept a strong grip on his College but also embraced a policy agenda that concentrates Commission activity on areas where it lacks strong powers. Again, however, other forces are at work. The EU s policy agenda shifted well before Barroso became President to areas, many of them part of the Lisbon agenda or broadly within Justice and Home Affairs, where the traditional Community method of legislating is either inappropriate or politically unimaginable.

A good barometer of how much the Commission has changed may be the 2007 study, funded by the Commission and conducted by a team of European historians, of the administration s "rst 25 years (Dumoulin and others 2007). Predictably, the resulting 626-page tome offers a self-referential, even narcissistic, recounting of the Commission s early glory days. Still, only the most hard-boiled sceptic could dismiss what the study s authors call the imagination, long-term vision, enthusiasm and tenacity of the earliest of"cials and Commissioners. A political decision was made at the birth of what is now the EU to model the Commission on a national administration, as opposed to an international secretariat like most others (see Stevens and Stevens 2006: 454). The decision was rooted in a conviction that what was being created was not just another international organization. This one was going to be different, more powerful, with a strong and powerful administration at its heart.

Even in the post-vision era, the Commission remains a uniquely powerful international administration. But it has become a very different administration from what it was in its early years: far more diverse, more professionally managed, less privileged, less united, less obsessed with its own institutional position, more open to network governance, and more intergovernmental, although in a re"ned, modern sense of that term. It will take far more research before we can settle on a de"nitive, modern de"nition. But the new intergovernmentalism seems different from the old version: more "uid, less great power dominated, with more widely distributed veto points that are likely to be overcome, if at all, through new network forms of governance. In the new version, the Commission may be less autonomous but also more integrated into the EU s institutional system. It may wield less raw power but have more and more subtle means to in"uence outcomes. Or so it might be hypothesized.

Biographical note: John Peterson is Professor of International Politics and Head of Politics and International Relations at the University of Edinburgh, UK.

Address for correspondence: John Peterson, Politics, University of Edinburgh, School of Social and Political Studies, Adam Ferguson Building, 40 George Square, Edinburgh EH8 9LL, UK. email: John.Peterson@ed.ac.uk

NOTES

1 Nugent (2004) refers to the 10 + 2 enlargement to signal that a political commitment was made (effectively in 1999) to admit 12 states, but just not all at the same time. For simplicity, we use the term EU-12 here.

2 A total of 52 non-attributable interviews were conducted in Brussels or Edinburgh between June 2004 and October 2007. Interviewees included four Commissioners, 13 members of *cabinets* (nine working in the of" ces of Commissioners from the EU-12), "ve Directors-General, 22 of" cials in the DGs (all A grade or above; "ve from EU-12 states), four Council of" cials, two former Commission of" cials, and two Members of the European Parliament. I am grateful to all who granted me interviews.

3 This choice of words was " rst suggested to me by one of the most senior of" cials in the Commission in an interview on 5 July 2006.

4 For a short time after 1 May 2004, Prodi s College numbered 30.

5 Quoted in *European Voice*, 26 October 1 November 2006, p. 2.

6 Interview, 4 July 2006.

7 Compare data on party political af" liations of members of the College with party group membership in the EP after 2004 available in Peterson (2006: 90 1) and Raunio (2006: 297). It should be noted here that Barroso s own in" uence over the nominees chosen by member governments for his College was minimal to none.

8 Interview, 21 November 2006.

9 See http://ec.europa.eu/enterprise/regulation/better_regulation/index_en.htm (accessed 20 December 2006) and http://ec.europa.eu/governance/impact/iab_en.htm (accessed 28 October 2007).

10 Interview, 21 November 2006.

11 Interview, 21 September 2006.

12 Interview, 5 July 2006. At the time of this interview, the College consisted of 25 Commissioners.

13 Interview, 4 July 2006.

14 Interview, 2 October 2007.

15 Orban, a political independent and engineer-turned-diplomat, was chosen after the original nominee, Varujan Vosganian, a Romanian Senator, stood down amidst charges of corruption and links to the domestic secret police. For her part, Kuneva was chief negotiator for Bulgarian EU accession under multiple governments after originally serving in the post-2001 government headed by Bulgaria s King Simeon II, despite having no previous political background.

16 Interview, 20 November 2006.

17 Peter Mandelson, The idea of Europe: can we make it live again? , speech to the University Association of Contemporary European Studies (UACES), Brussels, 20 July 2005; available at http://ec.europa.eu/commission_barroso/mandelson/speeches_articles/sppm045_en.htm (accessed 14 December 2006).

18 Quoted in *Financial Times*, 19 October 2006, p. 6 and *European Voice*, 12 18 October 2006, p. 2.

19 Interview, 21 November 2006.

20 Solana was chosen to be the EU s " rst Minister of Foreign Affairs (MFA) when the post was created by the Constitutional Treaty agreed in 2004. However, its rati" cation failure led EU member governments to revert to the title High Representative (with the same, expanded powers as designated in the Constitutional Treaty for the MFA) in the 2007 Reform Treaty. It was unclear whether Solana would remain in post long enough to take on the new role when (and if) the Reform Treaty was rati" ed.

21 The strategy   if that is what it was   appeared to work as Verheugen was reportedly praised by EU " nance ministers soon after attacking the Commission s services. See *Financial Times*, 19 October 2006, p. 6.

22 Quoted in *European Voice*, 19 25 October 2006, p. 12.

23 Quoted in *European Voice*, 26 October 1 November 2006, p. 2.

24 Interview, 5 July 2006.

25 Interview, 22 November 2006.
26 A Google search for impact assessment on 13 December 2006 was revealing, with no fewer than 18 of the top 20 sites listed being UK-based and linked to a diverse array of institutions including the Cabinet Of"ce, Scottish Executive, National Health Service, and various British universities.
27 Interview, 20 November 2006.
28 This claim was trumpeted on the UK Foreign and Commonwealth Of"ce s EU policy website. See http://www.fco.gov.uk/servlet/Front?pagename=OpenMarket/Xce-lerate/ShowPage&c=Page&cid=1140684822337 (accessed 13 December 2006). One of the last policy initiatives of Tony Blair s premiership sought to quantify the costs for British business of the administrative burden of complying with government regulations, and to cut it by 25 per cent by 2010.
29 The Commission publishes data on recruitment of EU-12 of"cials in its *Bulletin Statistique* and at: http://ec.europa.eu/civil_service/docs/bs_dg_nat_en.pdf (accessed 26 June 2007). Of"cials involved in recruitment, particularly in the of"ce of Vice-President for Administration, Siim Kallas, stress that the Commission has a long-term target of recruitment of EU-12 of"cials with a deadline of 2009. However, there was no question (by late 2007) that it would have to accelerate the pace of recruitment considerably to reach its target, and this despite pressure sometimes intense   from EU-12 national capitals to recruit more of their nationals (see Peterson and Birdsall 2008).
30 Interview, 2 October 2007.
31 It should be noted that the Kinnock reforms included provisions for early retirement that lowered the average age of Commission of"cials by about two years (from 44 to 42) even before enlargement.
32 Interview, 13 September 2006.
33 Interview, 11 September 2006.
34 Interview, 13 September 2006.
35 See *European Voice*, Finns obsessed with job cuts , 23 November 2006, available at http://www.europeanvoice.com/archive/article.asp?id=26752 (accessed 14 December 2006). The Finnish proposal was removed from the draft budget by the EP, and not reinstated by the Council. As a quid pro quo, the Commission, however, agreed to produce a screening , identifying its human resources needs until 2013, and also looking at how ef"ciently it used staff. This proposal was sent to the Parliament in March 2007, and the Commission still awaited their formal reaction in late October.
36 See Simon Taylor, Worries over lack of Commission staff , *European Voice*, 1 7 March 2007, p. 4.
37 Interview, 22 November 2006.
38 Interview, 4 July 2006.
39 Inteview, 13 September 2006.
40 Interview, 11 September 2006.
41 Interview, 22 November 2006.
42 Boot s (2006: 601) prognosis towards the end of a 624-page tome on the history of war is that: unless the US government can streamline its Industrial Age bureaucracy and become a networked organization, it may "nd that even purchasing the latest and best technology will not offer suf"cient protection against the country s woes.
43 Interview, 2 October 2007.
44 For example, after the stalling of the Doha Development Round of world trade talks, DG Trade announced its intention to negotiate ambitious bilateral trade agreements with South Korea, India and other Asian countries, with a top of"cial urging that such deals should be seen as part of the Lisbon Agenda, aimed at fostering European competitiveness . Quoted in *European Voice*, 30 November 6 December 2006, p. 1.

45 Interview, 4 July 2006.
46 Interview, 2 October 2007.
47 Interview, 20 November 2006.
48 Barroso makes this point speci"cally in an interview based on his reading of "ve major academic works on European integration (a full transcript is available at: http://www.eu-consent.net/library/BARROSO-transcript.pdf; accessed 28 October 2007).

REFERENCES

Bauer, M.W. (2008) Diffuse anxieties, deprived entrepreneurs: Commission reform and middle management , *Journal of European Public Policy* 15(5): 691 707.

Best, E., Christiansen, T. and Settembri, P. (eds) (2008) *The Institutions of the Enlarged European Union: Change and Continuity*, Cheltenham and Northampton, MA: Edward Elgar, forthcoming.

Boot, M. (2006) *War Made New: Technology, Warfare and the Course of History, 1500 to Today*, New York and London: Gotham Books.

Borràs, S. and Jacobsson, K. (2004) The open method of co-ordination and new governance patterns in the EU , *Journal of European Public Policy* 11(2): 185 208.

Christiansen, T. (1997) Tensions of European governance: politicized bureaucracy and multiple accountability in the European Commission , *Journal of European Public Policy* 4(1): 73 90.

Dumoulin, M. and others (2007) *The European Commission, 1958 72: History and Memories*, Luxembourg: European Communities.

Hindmoor, A. (1998) The importance of being trusted: transaction costs and policy network theory , *Public Administration* 76(1): 25 43.

Hodson, D. and Maher, I. (2001) The open method as a new mode of governance , *Journal of Common Market Studies* 39(4): 719 46.

Hooghe, L. (2001) *The European Commission and the Integration of Europe. Images of Governance*, Cambridge and New York: Cambridge University Press.

Jordan, A. and Schout, A. (2006) *The coordination of the European Union: Exploring the Capacities of Networked Governance*, Oxford and New York: Oxford University Press.

Kassim, H. (2004a) An historic accomplishment: the Prodi Commission and administrative reform , in D.G. Dimitrakopoulos (ed.), *The Changing European Commission*, Manchester and New York: Manchester University Press.

Kassim, H. (2004b) The Kinnock reforms in perspective: why reforming the commission is an heroic, but thankless, task , *Public Policy and Administration* 19(3): 25 41.

Klijn, E.H. and Koppenjan, J.F.M. (2000) Public management and policy networks: foundations of a network approach to governance , *Public Management* 2(2): 135 58.

Lewis, J. (2006) National interests: Coreper , in J. Peterson and M. Shackleton (eds), *The Institutions of the European Union*, Oxford and New York: Oxford University Press.

Metcalfe, L. (2000) Reforming the Commission: will organizational ef"ciency produce effective governance? , *Journal of Common Market Studies* 38(5): 817 41.

Metcalfe, L. (2004) European policy management: future challenges and the role of the Commission , *Public Policy and Administration* 19(3): 77 94.

Nugent, N. (2004) *European Union Enlargement*, New York and Basingstoke: Palgrave.

Olsen, J.P. (2003) Reforming European institutions of governance , in J.H.H. Weiler, I. Begg and J. Peterson (eds), *Integration in an Expanding European Union: Reassessing the Fundamentals*, Oxford: Blackwell.

Osborne, D. and Gaebler, T. (1992) *Reinventing Government: How the Entrepreneurial Spirit is Transforming the Public Sector*, Reading, MA: Addison-Wesley.

Ostrom, E. (1990) *Governing the Commons: The Evolution of Institutions for Collective Action*, Cambridge: Cambridge University Press.

Peters, B.G. (1998) Managing horizontal government: the politics of co-ordination , *Public Administration* 76(2): 295 311.

Peterson, J. (2005) Where does the Commission stand today? , in D.G. Spence (ed.), *The European Commission*, London: John Harper.

Peterson, J. (2006) The College of Commissioners , in J. Peterson and M. Shackleton (eds), *The Institutions of the European Union*, 2nd edn, Oxford and New York: Oxford University Press.

Peterson, J. (2008) Policy networks , in A. Wiener and T. Diez (eds), *European Integration Theory*, 2nd edn, Oxford and New York: Oxford University Press.

Peterson, J. and Birdsall, A. (2008) The European Commission: enlargement as re-invention? , in. E. Best, T. Christiansen and P. Settembri (eds), *The Governance of the Wider Europe: EU Enlargement and Institutional Change*, Aldershot and Northampton, MA: Edward Elgar.

Pollitt, C. and Bouckaert, G. (2004) *Public Management Reform: A Comparative Analysis*, 2nd edn, Princeton, NJ: Princeton University Press.

Pollitt, C. and Talbot, C. (eds) (2004) *Unbundled Government: A Critical Analysis of the Global Trend to Agencies, Quangos and Contractualization*, London and New York: Routledge.

Pollitt, C., van Thiel, S. and Homburg, V. (eds) (2007) *New Public Management in Europe: Adaptation and Alternatives*, Basingstoke and New York: Palgrave.

Power, M. (1999) *The Audit Society: Rituals of Veri cation*, Oxford and New York: Clarendon Press.

Putnam, R.D., Leonardi, R. and Nanetti, R.Y. (1993) *Making Democracy Work: Civic Traditions in Modern Italy*, Princeton, NJ: Princeton University Press.

Radaelli, C.M. (2007) Whither better regulation for the Lisbon agenda? , *Journal of European Public Policy* 14(2): 190 207.

Raunio, T. (2006) Political interests: the European Parliament s party groups , in J. Peterson and M. Shackleton (eds), *The Institutions of the European Union*, 2nd edn, Oxford and New York: Oxford University Press.

Schout, A. and Jordan, A. (2005) Coordinated European governance: self-organizing or self-steering? , *Public Administration* 83(1): 201 20.

Skogstad, G. (2003) Legitimacy and/or policy effectiveness?: network governance and GMO regulation in the European Union , *Journal of European Public Policy* 10(3): 321 38.

Stevens, H. and Stevens, A. (2006) The internal reform of the Commission , in D.G. Spence (ed.), *The European Commission*, London: John Harper.

Suleiman, E. (2003) *Dismantling Democratic States*, Princeton, NJ: Princeton University Press.

Wonka, A. (2007) Technocratic and independent? The appointment of European Commissioners and its policy implications , *Journal of European Public Policy* 14(2): 169 89.

Research agenda section

Edited by Berthold Rittberger

THE CONVENTION ON THE FUTURE OF EUROPE AND THE DEVELOPMENT OF INTEGRATION THEORY: A LASTING IMPRINT?

Christine Reh

INTRODUCTION: THE DEVELOPMENT OF INTEGRATION THEORY AND EU REFORM

On 13 December 2007, Europe s 27 Heads of State and Government signed the Lisbon Treaty , thereby putting a preliminary end to a reform debate which began six years earlier with the Laeken Declaration on the Future of Europe. In the history of the European Union (EU), similar steps of constitutional change have not only transformed the course of supranational integration, but have given rise to new conceptual and theoretical developments. Indeed, explaining both the evolution and the nature of the beast (Risse-Kappen 1996) was at the heart of the two classic strands of integration theory, responding to the political developments of the 1950s and 1960s: neo-functionalism (Haas 1958; Lindberg and Scheingold 1970) and intergovernmentalism (Hoffmann 1966).[1] Similarly, the single most in"uential and comprehensive integration theory   Moravcsik s liberal intergovernmentalism (LI)   was designed to explain how the grand bargains of treaty reform have driven and de"ned Europe s history and constitutional shape from Messina to Maastricht and beyond (Moravcsik 1998; Moravcsik and Nicola"dis 1999).

During the past decades, constitutional change has become a self-perpetuating and semi-permanent (de Witte 2002) feature of European integration, with the EU undergoing seven Intergovernmental Conferences (IGCs) since the mid-1980s. Against this backdrop, it is surprising that   except for Moravcsik s contributions   the political salience of treaty reform was not matched with similar academic attention to, let alone theorizing of, constitutional change in the EU. Political scientists focused on analysing the outcome and impact of individual IGCs, rather than on making use of these reform rounds to test or to further develop integration theories. Whereas the Maastricht IGC on political union triggered a renewed interest in Europe s normative foundations, the conceptual and theoretical discussion of the Union s constitutional evolution was thus largely left to legal scholars. This situation was to change fundamentally when the Convention on the Future of Europe (CFE) was set up in February 2002 as a new mode of EU reform   not only raising public attention and absorbing political resources, but quickly reaching centre-stage in the academic debate.

The mushrooming contributions on the Convention can be divided into three broad strands. First, scholars beyond the con"nes of legal theory and Europe s federalist fringe began to debate the substance of a European Constitution (Dobson and Føllesdal 2004; Eriksen et al. 2004), to explore European constitutionalism conceptually (Bellamy 2001; Wiener 2003), and to explain the process of constitutionalizing the EU (Christiansen and Reh, forthcoming; Rittberger and Schimmelfennig 2007). Second, a plethora of descriptive-analytical studies have looked at the Convention as an actor, at different actors in the Convention, and at the outcome of the Convention (see among others Norman 2003; Milton et al. 2005; Shaw et al. 2003). Third, political scientists and theorists have systematically analysed the Convention as a novel forum for collective decision-making in Europe. Given its limited scope, this article zooms in on the latter body of scholarship, and discusses the theory-guided analysis of decision-making in the Convention and the subsequent IGC, as well as the link between the Convention process and democratic theory.

In the following, I argue that research on the Convention both con"rms and advances the predominant post-ontological (Caporaso 1996: 30) trend in integration theory. Rather than tackle grand questions about the nature of Europe or the direction of supranational integration, scholars continue to build on meso-level approaches from international relations (IR) and comparative politics (CP), as well as on democratic theory. More speci"cally, recent scholarship has used the Convention as an empirical starting point to further develop integration theory in three directions. First, Europeanists have analysed the Convention to criticize, re"ne and reappraise Moravcsik s LI by importing approaches and methods from CP, in particular the (quantitative) analysis of preference formation. Second, the CFE has been studied as a negotiation arena, serving as fertile testing ground for theories of arguing and bargaining as developed in IR. Finally, the Convention process has triggered an unprecedented intake of normative thought, introducing standards of comparative constitutional design, and further embedding a Habermasian (or deliberative) turn in integration theory.

1. PREFERENCE FORMATION AND THE FUTURE OF EUROPE: REVISITING LIBERAL INTERGOVERNMENTALISM

The most comprehensive theoretical response to EU treaty reform in the last two decades has been Moravcsik s LI, explaining European integration in three steps: (1) domestic preference formation based on economic interdependence; (2) inter-state bargaining conducted as a two-level game; and (3) the delegation of powers to international institutions ensuring credible commitments. With the Convention generating an unprecedented wealth of primary data on EU reform, it comes as little surprise that numerous scholars have revisited LI in its wake   to apply, re"ne and challenge Moravcsik s framework. The following discusses how research on the CFE has triggered a wider theoretical, methodological and empirical engagement with LI s "rst explanatory step: the formation of national preferences on EU reform. This is a very welcome endeavour, as both IR and CP have seen much theorization about the relevance of governmental and institutional preferences, yet little systematic investigation into how preferences are formed, and how they can be measured. Indeed, [i]n most research papers, preferences are actually assumed (Tsebelis 2005: 378).

Numerous scholars from different ends of the theoretical spectrum have used the CFE to "ll this gap. First, the DOSEI group   an international consortium of political scientists working on domestic structures and European integration   discusses the methodological challenges of measuring preferences in a special issue of *European Union Politics* (2005), and analyses domestic preference formation in the Convention and the 2003/04 IGC in an edited volume (König and Hug 2006b). Second, a special issue of *Comparative European Politics* (2004) sets out to inquire how governments identify what they want in view of the EU s future (Dimitrakopoulos and Kassim 2004: 241). Confronting LI with an ideational and institutionalist critique of both preference formation and domestic mobilization, the framework is subsequently tested in qualitative case studies of six EU member states. Third, an issue of the same journal complements the analysis of the domestic level with detailed accounts of how supranational institutions   the Commission, the Court of Justice, the European Parliament   have established their preferences on EU reform (Dimitrakopoulos and Kassim 2005; Granger 2005; Hix 2005). Arguing that LI is unable to grasp the complexity of domestic preference formation, the qualitative comparisons challenge a number of Moravcsik s assumptions (see in particular Closa 2004a; Dimitrakopoulos and Kassim 2004; Jabko 2004). They conclude, "rst, that preference formation is less contested than LI assumes; second, that in spite of domestic economic pressures governments have considerable autonomy *vis-à-vis* their constituencies; third, that variables such as political culture, domestic institutions and opportunity structures, as well as time, impact on preference formation; and, fourth, that neither LI s assertion regarding the exogeneity of national preferences nor its insistence on the separation between preference formation and interstate bargaining ultimately holds (Dimitrakopoulos and Kassim 2004: 255). The third argument in particular directly contradicts DOSEI s claim that neither institutional nor economic variables but public opinion shapes domestic preferences (König and Hug 2006a: 275).

Yet, irrespective of these conclusions, DOSEI is likely to leave a more lasting mark on integration theory and to export some of its insights into political science more generally. First, the special issue of *European Union Politics* approaches an under-investigated yet crucial methodological challenge: how to actually measure actors preferences, and how to account for distortions through strategic action when doing so. Four methods have been suggested to meet this challenge (Tsebelis 2005): expert interviews, opinion polls, quantitative document analysis, and voting records; the DOSEI group critically assesses the "rst three. Testing a model that is replicable across languages and negotiation contexts, Benoit *et al.* (2005) apply computerized word-scoring to compare the positions of Convention delegates with those of their national parties;[2] König *et al.* (2005) explore the potential of different models to account for positions that rational actors hide for strategic reasons; and Dorussen *et al.* (2005) review the reliability of expert surveys which have been at the heart of preference measurements in CP. More generally, the special issue is a rare example of a large-scale research consortium re"ecting publicly on its methodological challenges   a laudable exercise, likely to have a more lasting impact than the project s substantive conclusions.

Second, two of the "ndings generated by DOSEI s comparative case studies stimulate re"ection on the domestic international nexus in EU reform and international negotiation more generally. On the one hand, König and Hug (2006a: 277) conclude that the Convention process, despite its much acclaimed openness and transparency, has not in"uenced public opinion on the matter an important (if unsurprising) "nding in view of the literature reviewed in section 3 below. On the other hand, they argue that public opinion rather than institutional or economic variables explains the cohesiveness of national positions in an IGC. The latter "nding challenges a core liberal intergovernmentalist argument, namely that domestic preferences are economically de"ned, but backs another, namely that governments use domestic public opinion as a bargaining chip in two-level games (see also section 2 below).

Finally, it would be worthwhile to further investigate a theoretical objection raised against LI in the 2004 special issue of *Comparative European Politics*. Here, Dimitrakopoulos and Kassim argue that Moravcsik uses the language of principal-agent theory without taking up its assumptions about agency control   namely, that an agent s preferences, once delegated, will diverge from the principal s, and that the agent is likely to drift or shirk (Miller 2005: 205). Only by considerably underplaying the extent to which the state may act with relative autonomy (Dimitrakopoulos and Kassim 2004: 248) can Moravcsik establish his theory s relationship between domestic society (the principal) and national governments (the agent). Considering the prominence of delegation theory in European studies (Franchino 2007; Pollack 2003), this question of theoretical consistency is well worth pursuing.

The discussed works generate valuable insights, but they share a fundamental pitfall: they do not distinguish systematically between preferences as the ordered and weighted set of values placed on future substantive outcomes (Moravcsik 1998: 24) and the concrete positions taken by governments in the Convention and in the IGC   although the distinction is implicit in several contributions (Jabko 2004). Thus, we learn more about the empirical co-ordination of negotiation positions (Kassim 2004) than about preference formation itself, with contributors partly sharing the problem they set out to solve.

2. NEGOTIATION IN THE CONVENTION: ARGUING AND BARGAINING, CONSENSUS AND COMPROMISE

The above contributions re" ne the " rst of Moravcsik s three-step explanation of European integration: the measurement of preferences and related methodological challenges. The body of literature reviewed in the ensuing paragraphs is dedicated to LI s step two: the negotiation over preferences at the international level. Two sets of studies fall into this category, one drawing on rational choice institutionalism, the other on argumentation theory. The CFE s transparent decision process and the wealth of accessible primary documents (including minutes of the plenaries) offer unique opportunities for both.

A " rst group of scholars, af" liated with the above-discussed DOSEI project, use their data on domestic reform preferences to explain bargaining in the Convention and the subsequent IGC (Hug and Schulz 2007; König and Finke 2007; König and Slapin 2006; Lenz *et al.* 2007). In doing so, they make a two-fold contribution. On the one hand, König and Slapin corroborate the institutionalist critique of intergovernmentalism by explaining the Convention s results through the (informal) decision rule of consensus, and by de" ning power as an actor s proximity to the status quo. On the other hand, they attempt to explain how international organizations are reformed and to demonstrate that negotiations in an existing international organization might differ from those setting up a new institution (Hug and König 2007: 109). The argument that domestic veto-players   " rst and foremost parliaments and voters   crucially impact on reform decisions logically builds on the above-discussed " nding that public opinion rather than economic or institutional variables account for domestic preferences, and re"nes our understanding of two-level games.

A second group of scholars uses the Convention to assess and re"ne the debate about arguing and bargaining in IR (see among others Deitelhoff and Müller 2005; Elster 2000; Risse 2000). The ensuing research makes an important contribution to integration theory, where the latest fault line arguably runs between rational choice institutionalism and social constructivism (Pollack 2001). Indeed, when constructivism hit IR (and, somewhat later, European studies) as a meta-theory, its proponents called for the development of middle-range approaches (Ruggie 1998), while opponents bemoaned the lack of testable hypotheses (Moravcsik 1999). Theories of argumentation and persuasion can provide both (Checkel 2004), and through their systematic application to the Convention put constructivist European studies on "rmer ground. Several scholars have taken up the opportunity and asked three questions about the Convention as a discursive space : (1) Were negotiations in the CFE dominated by bargaining (where agreement is sought through concessions, trade-offs and compensations, yet leaves preferences unaffected) or arguing (where agreement is reached through persuasion) (Magnette 2003, 2005; Magnette and Nicola"dis 2004)? (2) Has the CFE s institutional design favoured the occurrence and effectiveness of a particular interaction mode (Göler and Marhold 2003; Kleine and Risse 2005; Panke 2006)? (3) How can we conceptualize the agreement reached in the Convention (Bellamy and Schönlau 2004)?

In his case study of how the Convention negotiated the simpli"cation of Europe s treaties, Magnette (2003, 2005) points beyond the action-theoretical dichotomy of arguing and bargaining in IR and develops a set of conceptual tools to analyse con"ict resolution more broadly. Drawing on the work of Perelman and Olbrechts-Tyteca (1969), he identi"es three strategies and tracks their application: (1) the diplomatic approach that either prevents or defers actual con"ict (used in the Convention to deal with institutional reform); (2) the logical approach based on formal reasoning and on shared rules, norms and laws (applied by the Convention to negotiate simpli"cation and the EU s legal personality); and (3) practical reasoning designed to solve problems by drawing on concrete examples rather than on abstract principles (the Convention s preferred strategy and applied when negotiating subsidiarity, the distribution of competences or the role of national parliaments). Approaching con"ict resolution from a rationalist perspective, Tsebelis and Proksch (2007) identify leadership strategies that facilitated agreement in the CFE, and that can be fruitfully used to analyse decision-making and agenda-setting more generally: agenda control through time limits to curb the number of amendments, iterated agenda-setting to modify amendments, and the introduction of consensus rather than voting to arrive at concrete results.

Panke (2006) sets out to assess (and challenge) the widely shared, yet undertheorized argument that the CFE s institutional design renders it more favourable to arguing and deliberation than an IGC. The majority of scholars take this assumption as their starting point and then look for empirical evidence in the

Convention (see among others Göler and Marhold 2003; Kleine and Risse 2005); Panke, by contrast, proceeds deductively and demonstrates that institutional (or polity) variables cannot theoretically explain the variation in interaction and outcome between Maastricht, Amsterdam and Nice, and the Convention. Her systemic account of interaction is a powerful framework to analyse international negotiation and socialization, and a rare example of EU research that could (and, in this case, should) trickle up to IR theory. On a meta-theoretical level, it convincingly bridges the rationalist constructivist divide, and explains persuasion by two factors beyond the individual actor: (1) the free "ow of ideas, and (2) shared standards of evaluation. Second, it systematically assesses established constructivist variables   most prominently norm density and transparency   to demonstrate counter-intuitively that an IGC s institutional design is on the whole more favourable to arguing and ideational change than the Convention s.

Magnette and Nicola'dis reach a similar conclusion: in spite of its original design and composition   the European Convention did not systematically differ from previous rounds of treaty reform in the EU, except in areas marked by a high level of formalism that could be " tted under the rubric of simpli"cation (2004: 399). Both Panke and Magnette and Nicola'dis explain the occurrence and success of arguing through issue properties (or policy variables): persuasion is most likely where issues are regulatory and peripheral, or legal-constitutional. By challenging established institutionalist variables, the two studies open up promising new routes to researching interaction modes and their effectiveness in international negotiations, and caution against political and theoretical hopes for effective institutional engineering.

Bellamy and Schönlau (2004) set out to conceptualize the type of agreement reached by the Convention. While Magnette and Nicola'dis show how a compromise that merely conceals preference divergence   such as the Convention s agreement on institutional reform   is unravelled in the IGC to follow, Bellamy and Schönlau turn to the nature of the compromise itself. Drawing on Bellamy s previous work on liberalism and pluralism (1999), the authors challenge another core assumption in the IR debate, namely that arguing leads to consensus (or far-reaching outcomes), and bargaining results in compromise (or lowest common denominators). Instead, they differentiate between three types of compromise: (1) direct or distributive compromise reached through bargaining; (2) integrative compromise reached through deliberation; and (3) procedural compromise based on the fairness of the decision process. Here again, the Convention only serves as empirical trigger for a wider theoretical contribution: linked to recent IR scholarship on the role of incomplete agreements (Steffek 2005), Bellamy and Schönlau s argument could "ll a conceptual void in European studies, where scholars repeatedly invoke a culture of compromise or consensus re"ex , without conceptualizing these terms or theorizing their effectiveness.

In sum, drawing on insights from argumentation theory and political philosophy   the above contributions develop middle-range theories to analyse international negotiation, transcending the action-theoretical dichotomies of arguing and bargaining; introduce new tools to analyse con"ict resolution; and link up to recent scholarship in IR that moves the analytical focus from modes of interaction to types of agreement. Similar to the rational institutionalists who explain bargaining outcomes in the Convention and the subsequent IGC, these scholars only use EU reform as their starting point to make a much wider contribution to European studies   assigning negotiation theory and analysis its long overdue place, and equipping us with new conceptual and theoretical tools to explain both constitutional and everyday decision-making in Europe.

3. THE CONVENTION AND THE NORMATIVE TURN: CONSTITUTION-BUILDING AS A CATALYST FOR DEMOCRACY?

The literature discussed in this section adopts a decidedly normative approach to the CFE as an exercise in and catalyst for democracy-building in Europe. As such, these studies further the deliberative turn in integration theory highlighting the contribution of argumentative interaction for the coherence of a polity, its social acceptance and its normative acceptability (Neyer 2006: 779). Led by Erik O. Eriksen, John E. Fossum and August'n J. Menéndez of ARENA, this group strives to establish normative standards of how Europe *should* be constitutionalized. Two arguments unite these   decidedly Habermasian   scholars. First, they argue that the inclusive, transparent and representative Convention method comes closer to the ideal of deliberative democracy than an IGC. More akin to a constitutional assembly than to a diplomatic forum, and favouring a deliberative decision style, the Convention is considered more legitimate to draft Europe s Constitution than an IGC (Closa 2004b; Fossum and Menéndez 2005; Maurer 2006; Risse and Kleine 2007).[3] Second, they claim that inclusiveness, openness and deliberation are likely to make the Convention s *output* more democratic, while the Convention *process* will further democracy-building. Fossum and Menéndez (2005: 409) claim that the democratic writing of a Constitution for Europe, when it takes place, will constitute a major contribution to mending the democratic de"cit of the European Union while others invoke Habermas s concept of constitutional patriotism (Closa 2005; Fossum 2004). The latter argument was developed more than ten years ago by Habermas himself, in response to the claim that a European Constitution is impossible without a pre-political identity (Grimm 1995). Instead, Habermas argues that a constitutional process creates the very conditions that are considered missing, with deliberative constitutional politics and democratic practice having a catalysing effect (Habermas 1995: 307). Habermas reiterates this point in Europe s latest constitutional debate (Habermas 2004), echoed by deliberative scholars who claim that [citizens] will have to articulate and activate discourses and arguments on values when positioning themselves in relation to the Constitution and the values it cherishes. Even those that may reject the Constitution will be compelled to counter-argue an alternative set of values (probably, national constitutional ones) as superior and/or preferable

(Closa 2005: 431). In a similar vein, proponents of deliberative constitutional politics (Closa and Fossum 2005) link the EU s nature to the type of consti-tution-making required: the EU as a norms or rights-based Community springs from and necessitates deliberative, post-national constitution-making (Closa 2005: 416ff.).[4]

Whereas the above studies doubtlessly make an important contribution to normative European studies, and demonstrate how deliberative democratic theory can be fruitfully employed in empirical research, three aspects warrant clari"cation and further exploration. Concerning the group s "rst argument that the Convention is more deliberative than an IGC one would have hoped for a more critical engagement with those studies that question the con-duciveness of transparency for deliberation (Chambers 2004; Naurin 2007). Second, scholars have used the CFE s para-parliamentary (Maurer 2006: 121) nature to support a deliberative reading of the Convention. Yet, one wonders why parliamentarians all accustomed to voting as the main form of con"ict resolution should be necessarily more prone to deliberate than an IGC s diplomats. Third, the Convention s exact function in Europe s consti-tutional history is under-speci"ed: was it set up to *build* a Constitution or to *change* one? Surely, the normative challenges and conditions would vary with the answer we give. Finally, deliberative scholars allege rather than theorize the path leading from deliberation in the Convention over democratic consti-tutional choice to a more democratic EU. In this context, Skach s study of com-parative constitutional design is illuminating (2005). Drawing on Dahl s concept of polyarchy (1973), she develops a typology of constitution-making, depending on whether the public plays a role in drafting and debating the nascent Constitution, and acts as ultimate veto-player. In stark contrast to the above-discussed view that an inclusive and contested hence polyarchic constitutional process could bolster democracy in Europe, her empirical inves-tigation of constitution-building in Brazil, South Africa, Spain, Germany and the US shows little evidence that polyarchic constitution-making processes improve the chances of establishing polyarchy. Similarly there is no evidence that closed, hegemonic processes produce non-democratic polities (Skach 2005: 167). Following her line of argumentation, Europe s democracy, legiti-macy and effectiveness would be best served by adopting a basic European law through hegemonic constitutionalization.

CONCLUSIONS

The Convention did not turn out to be one of the most important real-scale political realities of our time (Tsebelis 2005: 377). Instead, the Lisbon Treaty suggests moderate constitutional change, much more in line with pre-vious rounds of treaty reform than a European Philadelphia . At the same time, the above *tour d horizon* has shown that the Convention process only served as the empirical starting point for a much wider process of theory development along three lines: (1) description and analysis; (2) explanation or understanding; and (3) critique and normative intervention (Diez and Wiener 2004). While largely bracketing the plethora of descriptive-analytical studies of the CFE, this article discussed conceptual and explanatory as well as normative research on the Convention, demonstrated the contributions wider implications for theorizing the Union and its decision processes, and argued that some of the contributions are likely to leave a lasting imprint beyond the con" nes of integration theory.

In studying the Convention, Europeanists have followed the predominant theoretical trend of the last two decades, namely to import established approaches from CP, IR and democratic theory, rather than to theorize about the Union s nature and the integration process as their *explanandum*. However, beyond continuing (and re" ning) this trend, a number of the discussed contributions have generated insights that should be re-imported into wider debates in political science. This is certainly true for the methodological answers to the challenges of preference measurement; for the novel conceptual tools to study con"ict resolution and types of agreement in international negotiation; for the systemic approach to interaction and the introduction of policy variables to the debate about arguing and bargaining; and for the renewed interest in deliberative democracy and comparative constitutional design. Ultimately, the CFE will give rise to yet another reform of the EU s treaties rather than to a European Constitution. However, beyond this real-world contribution, the Convention was an institutional experiment that generated an unprecedented wealth of primary material on EU reform and served as a fruitful laboratory to test, re" ne and potentially export European integration theory.

Biographical note: Christine Reh is Lecturer in the Department of Political Science, School of Public Policy, University College London, UK.

Address for correspondence: Christine Reh, Department of Political Science, School of Public Policy, University College London, 29/30 Tavistock Square, London WC1H 9QU, UK. email: c.reh@ucl.ac.uk

ACKNOWLEDGEMENTS

The author would like to thank Harry Bauer, Berthold Rittberger and an anonymous referee for their helpful comments on an earlier version of this article.

NOTES

1 European integration theory is here de" ned as the systematic re"ection on the process of intensifying political cooperation in Europe and the development of common political institutions, as well as on its outcomes (Diez and Wiener 2004: 3).

2 See Laver *et al.* (2003) for an earlier development of word-scores, as well as Tsebelis (2005) for a well-founded criticism of the study s failure to distinguish between concepts and words , and of the potential distortion of results.

3 By contrast, a number of scholars have stressed the dominant role played by the Convention s Presidium and President Giscard d Estaing in particular (see among others Kleine 2007; Tsebelis and Proksch 2007).

4 However, the nexus between the polity type and the desirable process of constitution-building remains unclear: does a particular constitutional process necessarily create a particular type of Union, or does a particular type of Union pose particular normative challenges to the process through which it is created or changed?

REFERENCES

Bellamy, R. (1999) *Liberalism and Pluralism: Towards a Politics of Compromise*, London and New York: Routledge.

Bellamy, R. (2001) The right to have rights : citizenship practice and the political constitution of the European Union , in R. Bellamy and A. Warleigh (eds), *Citizenship and Governance in the European Union*, London: Continuum, pp. 41 70.

Bellamy, R. and Schönlau, J. (2004) The good, the bad and the ugly: the need for constitutional compromise and the drafting of the European Constitution , in L. Dobson and A. Føllesdal (eds), *Political Theory and the European Constitution*, London and New York: Routledge, pp. 56 74.

Benoit, K., Laver, M., Arnold, C., Pennings, P. and Hosli, M.O. (2005) Measuring national delegate positions at the Convention on the Future of Europe using computerized word scoring , *European Union Politics* 6(3): 291 313.

Caporaso, J.A. (1996) The European Union and forms of state: Westphalian, regulatory or post-modern? , *Journal of Common Market Studies* 34(1): 29 52.

Chambers, S. (2004) Behind closed doors: publicity, secrecy, and the quality of deliberation , *The Journal of Political Philosophy* 12(4): 389 410.

Checkel, J.T. (2004) Social constructivisms in global and European politics: a review essay , *Review of International Studies* 30(2): 229 44.

Christiansen, T. and Reh, C. (forthcoming) *Constitutionalizing the European Union*, Basingstoke: Palgrave Macmillan.

Closa, C. (2004a) The formation of domestic preferences on the EU Constitution in Spain , *Comparative European Politics* 2(3): 320 38.

Closa, C. (2004b) The Convention method and the transformation of constitutional politics , in E.O. Eriksen, J.E. Fossum and A.J. Menéndez (eds), *Developing a Constitution for Europe*, London and New York: Routledge, pp. 183 206.

Closa, C. (2005) Deliberative constitutional politics and the turn towards a norms-based legitimacy of the EU Constitution , *European Law Journal* 11(4): 411 31.

Closa, C. and Fossum, J.E. (2005) Deliberative constitutional politics , *European Law Journal* 11(4): 379.

Dahl, R.A. (1973) *Polyarchy: Participation and Opposition*, New Haven, CT: Yale University Press.

De Witte, B. (2002) The closest thing to a constitutional conversation in Europe: the semi-permanent treaty revision process , in P. Beaumont, C. Lyons and N. Walker (eds), *Convergence and Divergence in European Public Law*, Oxford: Hart, pp. 39 57.

Deitelhoff, N. and Müller, H. (2005) Theoretical paradise empirically lost? Arguing with Habermas , *Review of International Studies* 31(1): 167 79.

Diez, T. and Wiener, A. (2004) Introducing the mosaic of integration theory , in A. Wiener and T. Diez (eds), *European Integration Theory*, Oxford: Oxford University Press, pp. 1 21.

Dimitrakopoulos, D. and Kassim, H. (2004) Deciding the future of the European Union: preference formation and treaty reform , *Comparative European Politics* 2(3): 241 60.

Dimitrakopoulos, D. and Kassim, H. (2005) Inside the European Commission: preference formation and the Convention on the Future of Europe , *Comparative European Politics* 3(2): 180 203.

Dobson, L. and Føllesdal, A. (eds) (2004) *Political Theory and the European Constitution*, London and New York: Routledge.

Dorussen, H., Lenz, H. and Blavoukos, S. (2005) Assessing the reliability and validity of expert interviews , *European Union Politics* 6(3): 315 37.

Elster, J. (2000) Arguing and bargaining in two constituent assemblies , *University of Pennsylvania Journal of Constitutional Law* 2: 345 403.

Eriksen, E.O., Fossum, J.E. and Menéndez, A.J. (eds) (2004) *Developing a Constitution for Europe*, London and New York: Routledge.

Fossum, J.E. (2004) Still a Union of deep diversity? The Convention and the Constitution for Europe , in E.O. Eriksen, J.E. Fossum and A.J. Menéndez (eds), *Developing a Constitution for Europe*, London and New York: Routledge, pp. 226 47.

Fossum, J.E. and Menéndez, A.J. (2005) The Constitution s gift? A deliberative democratic analysis of constitution making in the European Union , *European Law Journal* 11(4): 380 410.

Franchino, F. (2007) *The Powers of the Union: Delegation in the EU*, Cambridge: Cambridge University Press.

Göler, D. and Marhold, H. (2003) Die Konventsmethode , *Integration* 26(4): 317 30.

Granger, M.-P. (2005) The future of Europe: judicial interference and preferences , *Comparative European Politics* 3(2): 155 79.

Grimm, D. (1995) Does Europe need a Constitution? , *European Law Journal* 1(3): 282 302.

Haas, E.B. (1958) *The Uniting of Europe: Political, Social and Economic Forces, 1950 1957*, Stanford: Stanford University Press.

Habermas, J. (1995) Remarks on Dieter Grimm s Does Europe need a Constitution? , *European Law Journal* 1(3): 303 7.

Habermas, J. (2004) Why Europe needs a Constitution , in E.O. Eriksen, J.E. Fossum and A.J. Menéndez (eds), *Developing a Constitution for Europe*, London and New York: Routledge, pp. 19 34.

Hix, S. (2005) Neither a preference-outlier nor a unitary actor: institutional reform preferences of the European Parliament , *Comparative European Politics* 3(2): 131 54.

Hoffmann, S. (1966) Obstinate or obsolete: the fate of the nation state and the core of Western Europe , *Daedalus* 95(3): 862 915.

Hug, S. and König, T. (2007) Domestic structures and constitution-building in an international organization: introduction , *The Review of International Organizations* 2(2): 105 13.

Hug, S. and Schulz, T. (2007) Referendums in the EU s constitution-building process , *The Review of International Organizations* 2(2): 153 76.

Jabko, N. (2004) The importance of being nice: an institutionalist analysis of the French preferences on the future of Europe , *Comparative European Politics* 2(3): 282 301.

Kassim, H. (2004) The United Kingdom and the future of Europe: winning the battle, losing the war , *Comparative European Politics* 2(3): 261 81.

Kleine, M. (2007) Leadership in the European Convention , *Journal of European Public Policy* 14(8): 1227 48.

Kleine, M. and Risse, T. (2005) Arguing and persuasion in the European Convention , *Contribution to the State of the Art Report FP6 NEWGOV*, available at www. fu-berlin.de/atasp

König, T. and Finke, D. (2007) Reforming the equilibrium? Veto players and policy change in the European constitution-building process , *The Review of International Organizations* 2(2): 153 76.

König, T. and Hug, S. (2006a) Conclusion , in T. König and S. Hug (eds), *Policy-making Processes and the European Constitution: A Comparative Study of Member States and Accession Countries*, London and New York: Routledge, pp. 260 78.

König, T. and Hug, S. (eds) (2006b) *Policy-making Processes and the European Constitution: A Comparative Study of Member States and Accession Countries*, London and New York: Routledge.

König, T. and Slapin, J.B. (2006) From unanimity to consensus: an analysis of the negotiations at the EU s constitutional convention , *World Politics* 58: 413 45.

König, T., Finke, D. and Daimer, S. (2005) Ignoring the non-ignorables? Missingness and missing positions , *European Union Politics* 6(3): 269 90.

Laver, M., Benoit, K. and Garry, J. (2003) Extracting policy positions from political texts using words as data , *American Political Science Review* 97(2): 311 31.

Lenz, H., Dorussen, H. and Ward, H. (2007) Public commitment strategies in inter-governmental negotiations on the EU constitutional treaty , *The Review of International Organizations* 2(2): 131 52.

Lindberg, L.N. and Scheingold, S.A. (1970) *Europe s Would-Be Polity: Patterns of Change in the European Community*, Englewoods Cliff, NJ: Prentice Hall.

Magnette, P. (2003) Why and how arguing in a constitutional convention? , *Federal Trust Online Papers* 34, available at www.fedtrust.co.uk/uploads/constitution/34_03.pdf

Magnette, P. (2005) In the name of simpli"cation: coping with constitutional con"icts in the Convention on the Future of Europe , *European Law Journal* 11(4): 432 51.

Magnette, P. and Nicola"dis, N. (2004) The European Convention: bargaining in the shadow of rhetoric , *West European Politics* 27(3): 381 404.

Maurer, A. (2006) Deliberation and compromise in the shadow of bargaining: the Convention method as a test for EU system development , in S. Puntscher Riekmann and W. Wessels (eds), *The Making of a European Constitution: Dynamics and Limits of the Convention Experience*, Wiesbaden: Verlag für Sozialwissenschaften, pp. 120 55.

Miller, G.J. (2005) The political evolution of principal agent models , *Annual Review of Political Science* 8: 203 25.

Milton, G. and Keller-Noëllet, J. with Bartol-Saurel, A. (2005) *The European Constitution: Its Origins, Negotiation and Meaning*, London: John Harper Publishing.

Moravcsik, A. (1998) *The Choice for Europe*, Ithaca, NY: Cornell University Press.

Moravcsik, A. (1999) Is something rotten in the state of Denmark? Constructivism and European integration , *Journal of European Public Policy* 6(4): 669 81.

Moravcsik, A. and Nicola"dis, K. (1999) Explaining the Treaty of Amsterdam: interests, in"uence, institutions , *Journal of Common Market Studies* 37(1): 59 86.

Naurin, D. (2007) Backstage behavior: lobbyists in public and private settings in Sweden and the European Union , *Comparative Politics* 39(2): 209 27.

Neyer, J. (2006) The deliberative turn in integration theory , *Journal of European Public Policy* 13(5): 779 91.

Norman, P. (2003) *The Accidental Constitution: The Story of the European Convention*, Brussels: Eurocomment.

Panke, D. (2006) More arguing than bargaining? The institutional designs of the European Convention and Intergovernmental Conferences compared , *Journal of European Integration* 28(4): 357 79.

Perelman, C. and Olbrechts-Tyteca, L. (1969) *The New Rhetoric: A Treatise on Argumentation*, Notre Dame: Notre Dame University Press.

Pollack, M.A. (2001) International relations theory and European integration , *Journal of Common Market Studies* 39(2): 221 44.

Pollack, M.A. (2003) *The Engines of European Integration: Delegation, Agency, and Agenda-Setting in the EU*, Oxford: Oxford University Press.

Risse, T. (2000) 'Let s argue! Communicative action in world politics', *International Organization* 54(1): 1 39.

Risse-Kappen, T. (1996) 'Exploring the nature of the beast: international relations theory and comparative policy analysis meet the European Union', *Journal of Common Market Studies* 34(1): 53 80.

Risse, T. and Kleine, M. (2007) 'Assessing the legitimacy of the EU s treaty revision methods', *Journal of Common Market Studies* 45(1): 69 80.

Rittberger, B. and Schimmelfennig, F. (eds) (2007) *The Constitutionalization of the European Union*, London and New York: Routledge.

Ruggie, J.G. (1998) 'What makes the world hang together? Neo-utilitarianism and the social constructivist challenge', *International Organization* 52(4): 855 85.

Shaw, J., Magnette, P., Hoffmann, L. and Vergés, A. (eds) (2003) *The Convention on the Future of Europe: Working Towards an EU Constitution*, London: The Federal Trust.

Skach, C. (2005) 'We, the peoples? Constitutionalizing the European Union', *Journal of Common Market Studies* 43(1): 149 70.

Steffek, J. (2005) 'Incomplete agreements and the limits of persuasion in international politics', *Journal of International Relations and Development* 8(3): 229 56.

Tsebelis, G. (2005) 'Assessing the contribution of the DOSEI project', *European Union Politics* 6(3): 377 90.

Tsebelis, G. and Proksch, S.-O. (2007) 'The art of political manipulation in the European Convention', *Journal of Common Market Studies* 45(1): 157 86.

Wiener, A. (2003) 'Editorial: Evolving norms of constitutionalism', *European Law Journal* 9(1): 1 13.

Index

Page numbers in **bold** refer to figures. Page numbers in *italics* refer to tables.

For Product Safety Concerns and Information please contact our EU
representative GPSR@taylorandfrancis.com
Taylor & Francis Verlag GmbH, Kaufingerstraße 24, 80331 München, Germany